MOSTLY FRENCH is a stunningly beautiful cookbook developed and photographed at La Pitchoune, Julia Child's home in Provence.

Inspired by the olive trees and hills of lavender, thyme, and wild asparagus, author and cooking instructor Makenna Held shares 150 recipes that pay homage to the serenity of Southern France. Through dishes such as Roast Chickens with Lemon and Sumac, Caprese with Peaches and Strawberry, and Lavender Salted Caramels, among dozens of others that lean into France and ease, she channels the best of French cooking: simple ingredients, technique, and balanced flavors.

Mostly French is also Makenna's story of living in the slower pace of the French countryside. She lives with the spirit of Julia Child and honors her legacy, while forging her own path as a cook and teacher. In the narrative woven throughout, Makenna writes as much about developing as a person as she does about developing delicious recipes.

Like its author, *Mostly French* is at once classic and subversive. Here are French staples—Roasted Cherry Tomato "Jam," Your Dream Vinaigrette, and sauces like an easy Hollandaise—put to use next to roasts and meal-sized salads and omelettes. Throughout, readers will find shortcuts and tips designed for an American kitchen. And, perhaps best of all, *Mostly French* devotes an extensive section to cheese and charcuterie boards for the golden hour of l'apero, wherever you are.

This cookbook will delight anyone with its modern approach to everyday cooking.

Mostly French

Mostly French

— ∗ —

Recipes from a Kitchen in Provence

MAKENNA HELD

PHOTOGRAPHY BY EMMA LEE

SIMON ELEMENT

NEW YORK   AMSTERDAM/ANTWERP   LONDON   TORONTO   SYDNEY   NEW DELHI

For Beth and LouAnn
May you cook with aplomb
among the stars.

TABLE OF CONTENTS

MY OTHER HOUSE
IS IN FRANCE

Tucked just off a quiet, meandering road between the perfumed hills of Grasse and the neon blue waters of the Côte d'Azur lies a small hillside domaine known as Bramafam. Roughly translated from Provençal to English, Bramafam means "to bray or cry from hunger." The name is ironic. It was at Bramafam that Julia Child and Simone Beck tested much of *Mastering the Art of French Cooking*, volume 1, and wrote and then tested volume 2. And it was at Bramafam where Julia constructed a modest vacation retreat, La Pitchoune.

La Pitchoune means "little one," and indeed, the house was modest for someone of Julia's stature and fame. With its small bedrooms and only two small bathrooms, one toilet in the hall, it surely wasn't an entertaining paradise by today's standards. Yet, it was Julia and Paul's space to cavort and mingle with friends from myriad parts of their life and culture. Some were invited from afar, while others just happened to be in the area and were asked if they could just stop by for a bite. An invitation to La Pitchoune came over the phone or by mail and required detailed directions about mile markers and postboxes, and could include a fuzzy photocopied, but deeply annotated, map designed by Paul himself.

From the mid-1960s until the end of their tenure at La Pitchoune, she and Paul welcomed to the house some of the most iconic writers and thinkers about food in modern history, such as M. F. K. Fisher, Richard Olney, Judith Jones, and James Beard. People outside of the food world, from Paul's community, visited, too: dignitaries, American diplomats, artists—a slew of illustrious folks.

Bramafam is a food lovers' heaven, an unparalleled destination for anyone who likes to cook, or just to eat. Historically, Bramafam took its name from the thick, clay-ridden soil and steep terraces that make raising cattle and traditional produce nearly impossible. The only exceptions? Ancient olive trees that remind me of the biblical ones that grow in Gethsemane, gnarled and teeming with centuries of history whispered into their roots and limbs. They grow effortlessly from the stiff ground, the branches laden with blossoms in spring, developing fruit in summer that tumbles ripe and black onto the ground in fall. Those who shake and rake these olives, who cart them in woven harvest baskets and laundry bins to a local press, are richly rewarded with liquid gold.

This land, the Domaine de Bramafam, some thirty acres now owned by four families, has not wanted for visitors, delectable food, and good company since the 1950s when Simone Beck and her husband, Jean, began spending most of their time there.

Simone Beck isn't who comes to mind when you think of the person who "revolutionized accessibility to French cooking in America," which is what Julia said about herself. Simone Beck isn't a household name. And

yet she was instrumental in bringing the foundational classics, *Mastering the Art of French Cooking*, volumes 1 and 2, to generations with Julia, although it was Julia who became famous for shifting the American approach to cooking forever. (There was a third collaborator, Louisette Bertholle, but she left the trio right after the first volume was published.)

During the multidecade collaboration of writing these cookbooks, there was an imposed closeness between Simone and Julia, because they had to spend so much time together to write such immense tomes. Before La Pitchoune was built, they worked together in Simone's three-story, yet quite narrow, traditional *mas*, or farmhouse, and it was getting *un peu just*, which is a polite way of saying things are "more than a bit snug." When applied to the fit of a dress it means "Not for you, perhaps try a bigger size or a different garment, *s'il vous plaît?*" When it comes to a shared old house, situated on a property in the South of France? It means "Time for some more space, please come visit again, but stay over thataway. *S'il vous plaît, et merci.*"

So, Simone Beck, admittedly also a bit jealous of Julia's greater fame, hatched a plan. The Childs would build another house just 100 meters away, close enough to continue the collaboration effectively, yet far enough to cultivate some privacy for everyone.

With the success of *Mastering* volume 1 and its sequel on the way, the Childs welcomed the offer to build La Pitchoune. The South of France enthralled them: its languid pace, the terraced hills, cool evening air that required a light sweater. Julia fell in love with the Marché Forville in Cannes, a covered outdoor food extravaganza. I am enthralled with it, too. I love to wander in this market to gather supplies for my mushroom carpaccio, to source ingredients imported from Italy just that morning, or to buy fresh mozzarella for a wood-fired pizza to make in our outdoor kitchen's clay oven. It is here where I'll pick out ripe cranberry beans for my take on a traditional pistou soup (see page 157). Where I can find fresh-from-the-sea *oursin*, the small and prickly sea urchins with delicate interiors that make ridiculously perfect sauces in the wintertime.

Marché Forville is a market of sorts but not in the traditional, Provençal outdoor, once-a-week pop-up sort of way. Rather it is a stable venue, permanent in its purpose, bursting with shoppers from sunup to lunchtime six days a week, with more than a hundred stands (little more than tables, honestly), dragged in daily from hidden storage that I have yet to find. From end to end, fruit and vegetables are piled high on those teetering tables. Your fruitmonger might ask when you want to eat your melon *Ce soir ou demain?*, and he'll pick the perfect one for you. Nearby, you can find dishes that have been prepared within just a few miles, including fish soup with a spicy rouille (a cousin of aioli); fried-on-demand frogs legs doused in parsley butter sauce; escargot, heated right there on the spot; warm juniper-speckled choucroute served with a choice of a dozen sausages; detox soups and juices made by a fast-talking Antillaise woman; yards of olives, ranging from irresistible chartreuse varieties paired with preserved oranges to little, brown, wrinkly, and oil-cured plump beauties, and every possible color of olive tapenade. By 1:00 p.m., the stands are gone. A cleaning crew has arrived. And the building is suddenly meticulously clean and completely empty.

As Julia rocketed to stardom with her PBS hit, *The French Chef*, she meticulously built La Pitchoune to be a modest and easily maintained cottage on the Becks' property. Julia never technically owned the home or the land. But in 1965, she moved in. She retreated to the cottage for as much as half the year, and gathered a rotating guest list of friends and fellow food lovers. These included the aforementioned M. F. K. Fisher, Richard Olney, and James Beard, the last of whom attended a weight-loss clinic nearby in the town of Grasse (mostly known for its perfume). I often sit on the terrace of La Pitchoune and imagine the conversations from times past. How that specific quartet cooked together, who ruled which roost. (Ironically, spell-check keeps wanting to change this to *roast*. My guess is that both are apropos.)

Did Simone come over often? What was the vibe like? They most certainly quarreled over details such as: Should hollandaise have water or not? Is it still a boeuf bourguignon if the wine isn't from Burgundy? To double-whip your soufflé, yay or nay? Is French food really the "hautest" of cuisines? (Simone would fervently fight for yes, but Julia, after all her travels, might argue *not quite*.) I imagine Simone clucking to M. F. K. Fisher that perhaps James Beard might be better off leaving that pastry on the table, since after all he was attending the weight-loss center. I imagine the banter was catty and lighthearted. If a bit brusque at times.

Admittedly, much hasn't changed.

On November 13, 2015, just a few months after my thirtieth birthday, I woke up on a snowy morning in Colorado. I had just moved there to start a new life as a ski instructor, leaving behind a lucrative business as a consultant and the tiresome life of looking at a computer screen for twelve-plus hours a day. Money, it turned out, hadn't solved the existential angst of my late twenties, nor had it fixed my marriage (which was in shambles). I tucked into a cup of pour-over coffee and opened Facebook on my laptop to see a *New York Times* article headlined "The House That Julia Built" topping my feed. The article had been posted by a Smith College alumna on our college's online forum.

I clicked through it—and the eleven-photo slideshow. The images took my breath away: an autumnal leaf-littered terrace with a mustard-colored metal coffee table; ivy-creeped windows with tiny heart cutouts in the shutters; mint-condition terra-cotta tiles, styled eclectically with Provençal toiles and tablecloths; and the pegboard kitchen, with original Dymo-printed labels squeezed into life by the grande dame Julia herself. There was a link to the listing and a short narrative about the history of the property. I was immediately transfixed.

I bought the house.

It hadn't exactly been my year. My partner lost their job in the military (as a lifer, the dismissal was a wounding surprise). I lost my beloved Oma, my grandmother, and one of my best friends in all the world; she went from fine-ish to no longer with us in about two months. Adding to the loss was the death of the single soul bringing joy to me at the time: my eleven-month-old puppy, Mabel. She mysteriously fell ill during Oma's memorial service and then died two days later. It was a gutting year.

Cooking comforted me. In my tiny Colorado mountain cabin kitchen, I made feasts as the wind whipped through.

Although I had never visited the South of France, I was entranced by its magic from afar. I, too, had the mystical allure of Provence etched deep into my soul. I had never traveled much past Paris, no farther south than Mâcon, in the middle of France. Nevertheless, during French classes throughout middle and high school and finally college, I found myself mesmerized by the South of France. I was transported by the way in which the region's food was depicted in books and travel magazines. I wanted to eat bouillabaisse in Marseille, and *socca* (a local chickpea pancake) in Nice. The charm of French country living, and the seemingly endless possibilities for people who love food, struck me. I had grown up reading books by Peter Mayle, poring over images of the rocky coastline, envisioning walking the same streets as Virginia Woolf in Cassis.

I had a keen sense of "yes, this is what I am meant to do". But I had yet to understand how or in what capacity that could *ever* be possible.

Until I saw that dappled light, iconic pegboard, and shimmering swimming pool in the *New York Times* photos.

The photos on my computer showed me a clear dream: a small, convivial cooking school. Kathie Alex, the then-current homeowner of La Peetch, had founded it as an immigrant from the United States to France; she had opened Cooking with Friends and ran it for years. So why couldn't I?

I envisioned a place where I would welcome strangers from around the world, and where they would find kindred spirits and a home at the cottage for a week of wine, cooking, and affable conversation on the sun-soaked terrace. We would discuss the best oil for sautés. Taste olive oil from the property. Sample wines from around the region.

I had read the article at 5:30 a.m. that morning, and by 8:00 a.m. I screwed my courage to the sticking place. I sent a blind copy email to about a dozen people who either worked in food and wine directly or invested in culinary projects. My subject line was "Wouldn't it be cool to own Julia Child's house in France?"

By 11:00 a.m., I had a business plan and a name—the Courageous Cooking School, a slight hat tip to Julia's "have the courage of your convictions" ethos. I sent the two-page document to people who had cautiously responded to my email.

But, a day later when I went to the listing's link (hidden deep in the article, requiring a bit of sleuthing to track down, and more than three redirects), the listing itself had evaporated. In my gut, I knew that someone else had purchased it. But how could it have happened that fast?

Panicked, I called the real estate agent. An offer had been accepted a few days before the *Times* piece was even published.

Dejected, I piled my dogs into the car, set the dial to NPR, and drove down the mountain to have lunch with my family. I had barely made it out of the driveway when a news bulletin took over the broadcast. Paris was in an active shooter situation, with multiple actors and multiple locations. Including the Bataclan theater. My face blanched.

Paris was a sort of home to me—not one that I really had any right to, I just loved it. I had a tendency to purchase last-minute, discounted tickets and just go. My heart ached. I emailed my Parisian friends and longed for the city. And then about an hour into my dread, it hit me. . . . I bet the house would go back on the market. An upbeat epiphany for me on a dark day.

And just as I expected, by Monday, just three days later, the house was back on the market. I made the call to the real estate agent, Peter Illovsky, and I gave Peter the rundown of my plan and told him my life story (more or less): I was a Smith College graduate, just like Julia Child, and I wanted to keep La Pitchoune as a cooking school.

"Madame," he said, "I already have one other very, very enthusiastic buyer. And she is ready to purchase in cash. And she's already been in touch with Kathie Alex directly." Once again my hope was dashed. I felt my shoulders slump. Peter continued. "But, Madame, Kathie Alex isn't doing well and only wants me to handle this sale, please tell me you haven't emailed her yet?"

I hadn't even thought to contact Kathie.

"Madame, let's set up a call with Kathie. I think she will like what you want to do with the space. You'll need to act fast, and just don't email her, okay?" I thanked Peter, hung up. And held my breath for twenty-four hours.

Peter emailed me with an appointment. Kathie was hoping to sell in the next three weeks. He asked if I was available to have a phone call with his office, some lawyers, and bankers at 2:00 p.m. Paris time on Thursday, I said yes. Despite that meaning it would be 6:00 a.m. on Thanksgiving in Colorado.

As an apple-cider-basted turkey roasted away, and a banker prattled on about interest rates (much lower than I had thought they would be, and significantly better than any mortgage I had held in the United States), I caught out of the corner of my eye a pillow that taunted *My Other House Is in France*.

My jaw dropped.

Tears immediately filled my eyes. That pillow? It had been the last gift Oma had given to my Francophile father.

I took it as a sign.

A week later, I dumped my life savings and the estimated capital gains on my house (that I would subsequently sell to help fund La Pitchoune) into the pot with funds from two people who had responded to my initial email blast.

Every once in a while, I get an email from someone who said they almost bought La Pitchoune. I always smile, because I know the truth. The real estate agent received very few inquiries. Fewer than a dozen, in fact.

All of us "almost" do things. But the capacity actually *to do it* comes from the follow-through, taking things from *almost* to completion. And sometimes the doing is where the magic happens. This ethos bleeds into my cooking approach as well. Until we've *made the thing*, it doesn't exist. The magic is in the doing. The exploration. The creating something from nothing.

The philosophy of Courageous Cooking is this: Anyone, yes anyone, can cook well. It just requires one to trust their gut. Practice. Use recipes as a guide and not as a manifesto. Engage your senses. Avoid helicopter parenting your meals. Even risotto should be stirred less than you might think. Taste more and obsess less over perfection. I removed the word *perfect* as much as possible in this book because perfection is a myth. There is no such thing as a perfect anything. There are ideal, less ideal, and gorgeous approaches. But I think perfect trips people up. It drives them to focus on the end result and not on the process, not on the present. Paying attention to the process so that you develop your intuition as you go is very much the philosophy of Courageous Cooking—and of this book.

As I write this, I've been in France for the better part of a decade, nearly a quarter of my life, and the

Courageous Cooking School has been right there with my family and me. We were the subject of a television show that aired on Max, Hulu, and Magnolia Network. We weathered COVID. We've opened a restaurant in our home of Grasse. We built a pedagogy for our cooking school, the Courageous Cooking Method, which we've now taught to over five thousand people. I wept openly over this manuscript during hard times, and laughed uproariously during the good times. What all of this has taught me, more than anything, was just how important gathering with people is. And how much I rely on the intermingling of humans in one place in order to feed my soul.

La Pitchoune is technically no longer my home as I've moved twice since arriving. First, into the nearby medieval village of Valbonne, with its raucous central square, bustling gaggle of restaurants, a 120-year-old *boulangerie*, *fromagerie*, and *poissonnerie*, and a specific store for everything else you could ever want to eat or cook with. It is a community place that welcomes visitors as if they live here, too. As if they are family, not simply guests.

And then to Grasse. Its twisted streets used to feel labyrinthian, in a way that boggled my mind, and I was always lost even just steps into the village. And now? I can easily navigate the hillside hodgepodge of one-way streets and dead ends like a local. It was here where we found a sense of deep belonging, in restaurants run by cranky multilinguals that are open from lunch all the way through to dinner, a rarity in Provence. It was in Grasse that we discovered an old olive oil mill to call our own, where we built a true home that belongs to me, not one shared with the ghosts of famous people gone by. Lou Pitchou is its name, which ironically also means "the little one," and is a near direct translation of La Pitchoune, but in Provençal dialect. But there is very *little that is little* about Lou Pitchou, with its two-foot-thick walls and four-story height.

It is built squarely on top of a few freshwater springs, with foundation issues aplenty. It's a little commune of sorts. My parents and in-laws spend weeks at a time here. We've had friends live with us for years, and those who come for just a week. The house is tucked deep in a valley that sprawls from the old village into the surrounding towns, and we have a few acres that now hold dozens of ducks, chickens, a few sheep, two pink peppercorn trees, nearly thirty fig trees, and every type of citrus tree I could find. I brought the citrus trees down three flights of steps to their terraces, and planted them along with an acre or so of heirloom vegetables and flowers that we bring to La Pitchoune and our restaurant.

It's a marvelous place, and I feel very much at peace here. I imagine that is how Julia must have felt at La Peetch, as well.

Although my family and I don't live at La Peetch anymore, it still very much feels like home, at least spiritually. It held me through my divorce, and through falling in love with my best friend (that's a story to tell over a cocktail, and is paired with the Pink-Swirled Margaritas on page 110). My husband, Chris, and I hosted our wedding at La Pitchoune and taught each of our guests how to make French omelets in Julia's kitchen. I endured the first forty-two hours of labor in what was once Paul Child's wine cellar, and brought my newborn home from the hospital to La Peetch when she was two days old. She has been harvesting olives with our neighbors since she could stand on her own. La Pitchoune has provided my family and me, and all our visitors, with boundless joy and exquisite company. Along the way, so far, it has seen sweet melons plucked right from the garden and wrapped with salted, raw ham at the magical *l'apéro* hour; countless glasses of rosé; probably hundreds of coq au vin iterations; and more than two thousand nights on our wisteria-shaded patio.

May it feel like home to you, too. Even from afar.

Now take off your shoes, don some house slippers and an apron, and let's get cooking.

Mostly French

A "MOSTLY" FRENCH APPROACH TO COOKING

The first time I lived in France was a raucous eight weeks during the summer between my sophomore and junior years in high school when I was an exchange student. My host mother, Véronique, was an exquisite cook, and she ruined me for enjoying French food that wasn't like hers. My best memories of France involve her cooking and a duck à l'orange from a jar. It was jarring (pun intended) that it wasn't terrible and, wait, duck in a jar? I was sixteen and had never eaten duck, let alone from a jar.

That summer I fell in love with French home cooking. The dichotomy of deliciously homemade and "easy"—a stark contrast to the ornate French restaurant cooking I knew from the States—captivated me. I had been under the impression that everything that came out of a French kitchen was fussy and involved a chef barking orders to his underlings. Véronique's cooking gave me a new way to approach cooking for good. She loved that I would sit in the kitchen and just watch her to glean what I could from her every move. Her children preferred watching reruns of *Dawson's Creek*, dubbed in French, so my passion for her cuisine made me a curiosity and we developed a fondness for each other.

Those summer afternoons watching and learning taught me the lessons that have most influenced my approach to cooking, especially French home cooking. I observed—studied, really—Véronique's innate, intuitive cooking style. I internalized her constant tasting, her having homemade stocks and broths on hand, simple sauces at the ready. Ultimately, those early observations, or lessons, combined with trial and error in my own kitchen, some culinary school polish, and observing students at the Courageous Cooking School, have convinced me that the path to both delicious cooking—and falling in love with cooking—begins with settling in, relaxing, and developing instinct as much as skill.

THE MYTH OF THE PERFECT DISH (AKA YOU'RE NOT BROKEN, OR IT DOESN'T MATTER)

This is a cookbook, chockablock full of more than one hundred vigorously tested recipes that I developed over years of playing around in the kitchen. Admittedly, this is a little strange for someone who doesn't use recipes to teach cooking. That's because I want the people who come to the Courageous Cooking School to realize that so much of cooking happens outside the columns of a recipe—in the margins, really. In other words, most choices that one makes while cooking are arbitrary, dictated by the individual's palate and their take on food.

But to cook—and hopefully fall in love with—new recipes in your own kitchen does, of course, call for some guidance, or recipes written down. I don't think there is such a thing as a perfect recipe, however, meaning one that is followed precisely and yields the same results every time. What I think might make a dish terrific doesn't mean it will be perfect to you. That's because our tastes, our palates, differ. We are cooking in different kitchens, with difficult equipment, likely in different regions. With ingredients that come from varying sources, farms, locations, and shipping distances. That said, please know that these recipes were all tested and cross-tested in France and in the United States by a small cadre of people in different parts of both countries. The recipes will always yield a delicious dish, and you can rely on the cooking times and measurements, of course. But the results will not be *identical*. And that's my real point. There will always be some variation in how a recipe turns out, even in your own kitchen, and intuitive cooking is about getting comfortable—appreciating!—those slight differences from day to day, season to season, kitchen to kitchen.

What's more, I believe that a good recipe can be tweaked to *your* tastes and ingredients on hand. The exact number of tablespoons of olive oil in most recipes doesn't really matter; the exception *might be* in an emulsion, and even then, some eggs and garlic will hold an emulsion differently due to the presence (or lack thereof) of the ambiphillic (meaning they like fat and liquids equally) molecules required—the quantity of which can vary from item to item, depending on a number of factors.

You might make a recipe one time, and think that it's sent from heaven itself. And the next time it falls flat.

You are not broken.

The recipe is not broken.

There are things out of our control when it comes to building a dish, that even if we're familiar with what we're doing, still won't work exactly right.

Let this not deter you. Let this be an opportunity for intuition and troubleshooting and, more than anything, trusting yourself. This is an opportunity to connect to the possibilities.

Our visitors at the Courageous Cooking School often arrive with a unifying sentiment: "I simply never have a dish turn out right." I always want to scoop them into a big hug and whisper, "Trust yourself. Have fun. Develop your taste, figure out what you like, work on a couple core techniques, and the rest will follow."

I wrote this cookbook to help you do just that. To encourage you to relax, to ease you into the habit of tasting as you go along, and to play. Because cooking is in fact playful. I think recipes are guiding and helpful, but they are not the only key to good food. (Baking is a different story. I am not a baker, really, and while there are some baking-adjacent recipes here, they are pretty straightforward, and I've included them because I think they are also good recipes for developing intuition.)

THE RULE OF THREE

I've been cooking with and without recipes for my whole life. Sometimes you really need to know specifically what to do—just how much of an ingredient to use and the right order of steps for using those ingredients. Other times, cooking more loosely and eschewing the recipe in

favor of following your own taste and instinct is ridiculously liberating and fun—and gets the best results.

And so in this book, I do both: I provide recipes in the expected way, but I also encourage you to riff, riff, riff based on your preferences and moods and depending on what is fresh where you live or available in your own cabinet. As you become a more seasoned and comfortable cook (it won't take long), I hope that you will come to use this book as a series of guidelines, not as hard and fast rules you must follow.

I trust you and your palate as much as you trust mine. If something in a recipe sounds off-putting or uninteresting to you, there are substitutions worth considering.

I know I just said there are no hard and fast rules, but I have one overarching belief when cooking: Use. All. Your. Senses. Every. Single. One.

But how do you actually do that?

1. TASTE, TASTE, TASTE

Don't just taste the final dish, and then season it. Taste as you go along. I taste every few minutes when I am cooking so I can make small adjustments. I am tasting for balance of seasonings, like salt and spices, especially strong spices. I am checking for the right balance of acid, such as vinegar or lemon juice, and fats, such as olive oil and butter. And I am assessing for texture. I give you cues to help guarantee that your dishes won't be mushy or tough in all the wrong places.

I remind you to taste regularly, but you can never taste enough.

2. TRUST YOURSELF (AND ME), BUT TASTE TO VERIFY

If you want to add an ingredient that I haven't included to a recipe, have at it!

For example: You might like preserved lemon but don't know how it will taste in your marinade. So, you could take a tiny bit of marinade and put in a small dish or on a spoon and add a bit of preserved lemon to see how it all works together. Does it bring you joy and make tiny fireworks explode in your mouth? Add it to the recipe.

Does it fall flat? Worry not! You just discovered new information you can use for adjusting dishes to your liking in the future and you haven't ruined what you are making in the present.

3. DON'T HELICOPTER PARENT YOUR FOOD

New and seasoned cooks alike have a tendency to stare at our dishes as we cook them, to hover over them like helicopter parents. As a result, we stifle. We angst. We panic. That old adage, a watched pot never boils, isn't really about the impossibility of changing the chemistry of boiling water, but rather, it's about how we spend too much time overmanaging the cooking process.

Cooking requires letting go, leaving it be. And trusting our senses other than touch. So throughout this book, I will give you cues about what to smell for, timing cues (which often means no touching), and also sound cues.

Sound and smell are your best friends in the kitchen. Your nose will tell you it's time to turn down the heat. The sound of popping oil means it's too hot. So, listen and smell. And taste.

In addition to the above Rule of Three, there are three additional keys to good cooking that I've picked up, most from Véronique's kitchen, some from my mother's, some from culinary school, and some from watching other chefs. Whether cooking from the hip or by recipe the following essentials will make your food more delicious with very little effort.

HOMEMADE STOCKS AND BROTHS: The store-bought versions are fine. They are speedy and convenient. But homemade really makes food sing.

SAUCES: In French cuisine sauces exist to enhance

a dish. They aren't intended to stand on their own, nor are they meant to steal the show from the main ingredients.

There are two key types of sauces: reductions and emulsions.

Reductions are traditionally made by either making a roux (which is one part butter to one part flour) and then adding liquid, and cooking briefly until reduced and thickened. However, I prefer mostly flour-free reductions, which require taking a liquid—such as stock or crushed tomatoes—and adding aromatic elements like alliums and herbs to create a concentrated flavor. This results in jus, or gravy-like sauces, or other sauces like tomato sauce. Some reductions like Beurre Blanc (page 58) include a reduction of wine *and an emulsion* of butter into said wine.

Emulsions can be simple, and prepared without heat or made more complex with heat. Emulsions like aioli, vinaigrettes, or mayonnaise come together with some elbow grease and an emulsifier (like lecithin in mustard or egg yolks). They can be made into smooth, luscious sauces simply with a whisk. More complex reductions like Hollandaise (page 54) require both heat and whisking to result in their transformation of ingredients into a silky smooth sauce.

ESSENTIALS: A small collection of basic recipes can be made quickly in the moment of cooking or ahead of time so that you always have them at the ready (greasing the wheels for the recipe) and that pack a big flavor punch—like Garlic Chips (page 62) and Universal Herbed Oil (page 63). I've gathered these all together starting on page 51.

MY MOSTLY FRENCH PANTRY

Below is a list of ingredients that I keep on hand because I use them all the time. Some keep well in the pantry, some require weekly shopping. I would never urge anyone to go out and purchase everything below in one fell swoop. Rather, build your supplies as you go, as you come to know the recipes in this book and which ones speak to you the most. That way, you will have what you need, it will be fresh, and you won't end up with a stockpile of stuff that will go to waste or deteriorate in your pantry before you get to use it. Some of these recommendations are also meant to help *shift how you cook* in your own kitchen. Staples are often viewed as things that live in your pantry all the time, but I have included somethings that aren't shelf stable. The goal of all these ingredients? Big and bold flavor enhancers *and* the basics you need.

ANCHOVIES: These little fish, usually sold filleted and packed in oil, are valued for the salty umami flavor they bring to dishes. By the time they are cooked with other ingredients (garlic is a common partner), they do not taste fishy. There are a couple of recipes (Anchovy and Arugula Toasts, page 104, and Warm Salade Niçoise, page 178) where I use the fillets straight-up. They will tell you if you are an anchovy lover or not.

BLACK GARLIC: Of East Asian origin, black garlic is the common garlic bulb, aged for a few months under special conditions to result in cloves that are black, sticky, and more mellow than their more common relative of simply . . . garlic. It is a gorgeous addition to sauces because it brings a sweet depth of flavor.

BOUQUET GARNI (SEE ALSO FRESH HERBS): A bouquet garni is a fancy term for tying some fresh herbs together into a bundle to toss into a pot to flavor sauces, braises, soups, and really anything else that will benefit from a medley of herbs. A traditional bouquet garni includes thyme, bay leaf, parsley, and rosemary, although I like to mix up the combination based on what is most fresh and will complement whatever I am making. The nice thing about a bouquet garni is that you don't have to measure out herbs or remove leaves from stems, and when they have done their job flavoring whatever you are making, you just fish it out of the pot.

To make a bouquet garni, take whatever leafy herbs you're using and, with the leaves still attached to the stems, make a tight bundle. Tie it with butcher or cooking twine. It's that simple. It doesn't need to be pretty. Its sole purpose is just to make it easy to fish out at the end of cooking. Want to make it easier? Tie the bundle to your pot handles with a longer string so you can find it at the end of cooking with no muss.

BUTTER: Even though I live in olive-centric Provence, butter is still an important ingredient in my personal approach to French-centric cooking. Use the best butter you can find, which often means buying butter imported from Europe and made from grass-fed cows. This butter is often *lightly* cultured to give it a slight tang. In the US, milk is refrigerated really quickly, and in France, they give it more time at ambient temperatures, creating a slight fermentation. Fermentation equals a bit more acidity and flour, which are frankly delightful.

In the United States, people mostly use unsalted butter so they can control the amount of salt (and therefore seasoning) in the recipe. But in France, salted butter is the main choice for a few reasons. First of all, salt is a preservative. Most French refrigerators are small, and many cooks (including myself) shop almost daily and leave staples such as butter out at room temperature. So, salted butter keeps longer under these conditions. If you like unsalted butter, just remember to add a pinch or two of salt to the recipe to compensate. And taste to see if it needs more.

CAPERS AND CAPERBERRIES: *Capers* are the brine-preserved flower buds of a shrub that grows profusely in the Mediterranean, including Provence. The buds add a delightful brininess to food and bring a unique bit of flower fragrance. Small capers are labeled *nonpareil*. The largest ones are called *caperberries*. They keep for ages in the fridge. Replace the brine in the jar with some water and a splash of vinegar so the capers are covered. Drain and rinse them before using.

CHILES: When I call for chiles in a recipe, I am refer-ring to the dried ones. However, like salt, there are many different kinds of chiles, with a huge range of heat levels. One of my favorites (in fact, I consider it a secret ingredient at the Courageous Cooking School) is Urfa biber, ground and fermented chile flakes from a region in Turkey. These dark-red (nearly black) flakes have a fruity note to them and are warm without being incendiary.

FISH SAUCE: This is admittedly not *exactly* a French ingredient, but it has made its way to France by way of colonialism (France colonized Cambodia and Vietnam and brought fish sauce back home). And I use it a lot. You can always skip it in the recipes, but the umami it provides is second to none. Additionally, much of my cooking life is influenced by the time I spent in Phnom Penh. When I was a rising senior at Smith College, I dropped out of school for a semester and moved to Cambodia to work as a teacher. I lived next door to a French-speaking family who had survived the Khmer Rouge regime. Their apartment was located off a small alley, and they cooked exquisite French and Cambodian food. They welcomed me into their daily life, and I learned to use fish sauce in French stews and I cooked coconut milk–based fish dishes with hints of butter (a nod to French cooking). Their food was a bit of a mélange of French and Cambodian, and utterly delicious. Fish sauce has been a go-to staple ever since.

FRESH HERBS: This is a bit of an outlier, because fresh herbs aren't really pantry staples, but I believe they *should be*. Anytime you can have fresh herbs on hand? You should. Each week, I buy one bunch of every herb that appears in the market, so I have up to four or five herbs in total. This is an easy endeavor in France as they sell every herb imaginable in bunches, with some but not much seasonality. But you can do the same thing at a North American supermarket. Some weeks this means cilantro, dill, parsley, and tarragon. Some weeks thyme enters the chat. I also grow herbs in window boxes outside of my kitchen. If you can keep at least three to four bundles of herbs on hand, you will always be within arm's reach of leveling up your cooking.

MUSTARD: When I call for mustard, I'm referring to brown-yellow French mustard, either the smooth classic Dijon style or seeded (also called *whole grain*). My favorite? Mustard de Meaux from Pommery. It's been around since the 1600s. Some people refer to it as life-changing, and you can practically eat it by the spoon-ful. But as long as you're using a spicy, true mustard (not the ballpark kind!) your recipes won't be left wanting.

OILS: In Provence, olive oil is abundant and the main choice for cooking most things. Fruity, green-gold (or sometimes even grass-green), and bursting with flavor, it adds depth and character to cooking. I encourage you to have two olive oils: a less expensive one that you use for cooking because once heated, it will lose some of its flavor, and then another bottle that might be a little more flavorful (or an early harvest), perhaps from a small producer that will be more expensive, but will also give your food a wonderful, earthy flavor, a French *je ne sais quoi*. When you're looking for olive oil, make sure it is extra virgin and cold-pressed.

Neutral oils, such as vegetable, sunflower, grapeseed, and canola, are flavorless and have high smoking points, so I use these when sautéing foods that need oil heated to a high temperature for proper searing and browning. Olive oil is not the best choice for this job because it may smoke before it is hot enough, and oil that has gone beyond its smoking point can taste acrid.

When a recipe calls for a glug of oil, it is about two teaspoons. When I give this cue to my students, I call it everything from a *sloosh* to a *flooble* to a *ploop*. The French say *filet*, which roughly translates to "a drizzle." But a French drizzle is a heavy thing, whereas an American drizzle is a tentative touch and suggests you're pouring next to nothing as a finish.

This matters because the same ingredients can vary wildly. Your mushrooms might be more porous than mine and absorb more oil, making your pan dry. You might like your salad more heavily dressed and tangier than someone else. So, if I call for three tablespoons of oil, and it is too oily for your liking, the recipe has failed you. So a *glug* is the technical term I am using for "some quantity of oil that you will decide for yourself," contemplating what makes sense for the dish based on your ingredients and taste.

PEPPERCORNS: There is a lot of pepper in this cookbook. If you don't already have a pepper grinder, I suggest purchasing one. Freshly ground pepper adds a layer of flavor and character, that pre-ground pepper lacks, to a dish. It really doesn't do much of anything. Using freshly ground pepper is one of my nonnegotiables.

A few recipes call for pink (*baie rose*) peppercorns. They are a very French ingredient with a similar spice profile to common black peppercorns, but with floral notes that make me think they have been running through the rose fields in Grasse. Baies Roses also have the magic quality of softening easily in soups and stews. Because pink peppercorns are easy to come by in France (they literally grow in our backyard), I use them interchangeably with black peppercorns. You can find them online and in better supermarkets in the US, but you can also substitute cracked pink peppercorns in soup. Just soften them first in liquid or simply use cracked black pepper. You'll still get the pepper flavor, but will miss out on the crunch of cooked pink peppercorns.

PRESERVED LEMONS: A staple of Mediterranean cuisine, these are lemons that have been salted and aged until their skins are very tender, nearly translucent. When I make preserved lemons, I like to preserve a couple other citrus fruits, too, and use them interchangeably with lemons to vary the flavor. While you can sometimes find preserved lemons at specialty markets, they are super easy to make at home, and I give my recipe on page 57.

DRIED HERBS AND SPICES: I use potent, very fresh dried herbs and spices. I was once the person who hoarded every spice I've ever purchased, and I let them sit in baggies in my pantry for years. I learned this from my mother who loves spices, but hates wasting things.

I am reformed now. I try to buy what I will need for about six to twelve months and then replenish my stock when I run low. If you're using something that's been around for a while, that's fine. Simply use a little more of the spice if you think it's less potent.

I use single-origin spices. Some of my favorites come from Curio, Burlap and Barrel, and Diaspora Co.

A LOVE LETTER TO SALT

When I was fifteen, I visited France for the first time. It was in the countryside where I first encountered a salt that wasn't marked *iodized* or *kosher*.

My first taste of non-iodized, naturally collected salt was the famous *fleur du sel* from the Camargue region in the southern part of France. I was an exchange student, and I was with my host parents and my parents, who had traveled with me to France before my sojourn. We all ate lunch together under a veranda in my host parent's garden. My host mother presented us with a round cardboard box with a rough cork stopper, encouraging us to salt our food, not with a shaker but with our fingers. Only later did I realize what a gift this was: Fleur de sel is hand-collected by a *saunier*, from the tippy

tops of dehydrated salt mounds. It's often deemed the world's best salt.

I spent that summer chasing salt. I visited Île de Ré and tasted five kinds from the same mounds that push up from the sea. I went to different restaurants and dipped tiny salt spoons into miniature pottery urns to taste their offerings. I ground salt to myriad coarseness, and was wowed by how the different size surface areas of the granules changed the flavor and distinct saltiness of each grind. In my salt pilgrimage, I learned that France alone produces hundreds of salts, in all kinds of colors.

I love salt. I collect it: Smoked with alder or oak. Flavored with smatterings of herbs and citrus. Salt with big granules, with small crystals, or even

LaVarenne
ECOLE DE CUISINE
34, rue Saint-Dominique
PARIS VII   705.10.16

Le Grand Diplôme d'Etudes Culinaires

a été attribué à

Simone "Simca" Beck

qui a suivi avec assiduité le cycle d'études de l'Ecole de Cuisine La Varenne et a satisfait

aux différentes épreuves du diplôme

practically powdered. Salt that's gray or white. Diamond Crystal kosher salt. I love how the texture of salt crystals delivers a bit of crunch and lends interest to the food.

I recognize that salt-chasing is a ridiculous hobby. A salt collection is hardly necessary in any kitchen, and it's certainly not needed for this book. Because salt is, in essence, still just . . . salt. As long as it's non-iodized salt, which can add a bit of unwanted metallic flavor to food, you're in business! . Plan to have three types of salt on hand:

KOSHER OR FINE GRAIN SEA SALT: You really do need a kosher or fine grain sea salt to cook, so if you are going to purchase only one type, this is it.

This will be your main salt for salting pasta waters, making brines and rubs, seasoning soups and braises, and so on. Kosher salt also works as a finishing salt, meaning it is sprinkled right on the finished dish.

TWO TEXTURED FINISHING SALTS, ONE PLAIN AND ONE SMOKED: My current favorite finishing salts are plain and smoked Maldon. I love the pyra-midal shapes that barely dissolve when they come into contact with food. It means you get crunchy, salty joy in every bite. Smoked Maldon is my not-so-secret weapon, and I use it on *almost everything* as a finishing salt.

They are excellent quality and, just as important, they are ethically sourced, meaning they farm responsibly and treat their workers well.

They can sometimes cost more than the grocery store brands. But they are also fresher and therefore will last longer.

VANILLA, WHOLE BEAN OR POWDER: If you're going to use vanilla in your cooking (not just your baking) you cannot always use vanilla extract. For some things you need whole bean. There are two ways to get whole bean: entire whole beans or as vanilla powder. I prefer vanilla powder to whole bean most of the time because whole bean requires cutting open a sticky bean and scraping its interior. I feel like there's a lot of waste in such an expensive product. *Do not* buy the white vanilla powder as that is just filler powder flavored with vanilla. For two recipes in this book you *absolutely need powder or whole bean*—Not-Too-Sweet Whipped Cream (page 59) and Savory Vanilla Dressing (page 277). Why? It's called the Marangoni effect: the alcohol in the extract reduces surface tension. And in both dishes surface tension is the whole point. Whipped cream is nothing but surface tension, and in the dressing, the eggs don't perform well with the addition of extract. Vanilla powder is a bit spendy, but it's a *game changer*. Promise.

WINE: Cooking with wine makes French food distinctive. The alcohol in wine amplifies the other ingredients' flavors. Of course, wine is made throughout France, and in Provence, we are particularly fond of our local rosé. You've probably heard the advice to choose a wine for cooking that you would be happy to drink. That may be so, but with a caveat: watch out for heavily oaked wines, which could mean that a Cabernet or Chardonnay that you love to sip may be too strong for cooking. For red wines, lower-cost blends or a Pinot Noir are usually good choices. Sauvignon blanc or an Italian pinot grigio works well when a white wine is called for. A few recipes call for rosé. Frankly, I literally just *use whatever I have left over lying around*.

Try to avoid the so-called cooking wine from the supermarket shelves. It's likely been heavily salted or made poorly, and it breaks the rule of cook with what you'd drink.

MY BATTERIE DE CUISINE

A *batterie de cuisine* is simply French for kitchen stuff: pots and pans, utensils, essentials, and then those gadgets that make life easier, or that are just simply fun to have.

When it comes to my batterie de cuisine, I focus on what I need to cook efficiently. And I don't have anything that is used for just one purpose. (My mother-in-law once asked if I had a nut chopper. To which I replied that I did not know that a nut chopper was a thing. That falls very much in the category for me of a garlic press, another device I eschew because it does only one thing.)

My list here includes the cooking tools I used to create the book, and I've kept it as simple and as classic as possible.

BLENDER: For most of the recipes in this book that require blending, you need a workhorse. You want a blender that can crush the living heck outta a smoothie and whir it into oblivion without the motor dying. If you use a blender to purée a hot soup, be sure to have some way for the steam to escape. Some blenders have removable middle tops, some don't. A way to navigate this is to leave the lid barely ajar when blending. If you don't have some space for steam, you risk splattering hot soup all over the kitchen (and you) when you take the lid off.

I admit that I do love my Vitamix. But I am not saying you need one. I know, it's a freaking expensive blender. I lost my first one in my divorce. (Along with my first KitchenAid mixer in Cobalt Blue. Yes, two kitchen appliances gone. And much of my dignity for a good while!)

DUTCH OVEN: This is a staple, and thankfully there are dozens of companies that make them. I like Staub, a

French company that makes lids with little nubbins on the underside in a fabulous array of colors. They cause steam to coalesce into water droplets, which means that moisture "bastes" the dish as it cooks. Dutch ovens without the nubbins work well, too. Whatever you buy, just make sure that the interior is enameled and easy to clean.

KNIVES: My batterie is quite chockablock full with knives. I am such a collector that when I was pregnant, I went *to Corsica to visit a knife shop on a hillside that required a hike.* If I could have only a few knives, ones I actually needed, I would choose these three:

CHEF'S KNIFE: A good chef's knife doesn't have to be expensive. You want a knife that feels good in your hand, has a blade about 8-inches long, and holds a nice edge. There are many that do this job. My current favorite at a price point that doesn't make you gasp is the Made In Chef Knife. Global knives (a brand the late Anthony Bourdain swore by) aren't my personal favorite, but they are tried and true.

PARING KNIFE: I always like to have a smaller knife on hand for prepping smaller ingredients. I like a bird's beak paring knife, but any small knife that is less than four inches in length will do here. I use them rarely, but I do like to have them on hand for prepping smaller things like radishes, garlic cloves (if I am properly mincing them), and cherry tomatoes.

SERRATED KNIFE: One big serrated knife is a crucial thing in a kitchen. I use it primarily for cutting bread, and a serrated knife is *especially useful* when making Crostini (page 60).

KITCHEN SCISSORS: This is one of those things we all need in our kitchens, but too few of us own. I love Joyce Chen scissors. They look like something from elementary school, but they are incredibly sharp and work wonders. They are strong enough to spatchcock a turkey.

SAUCEPANS: For most recipes in this book, use a medium 7- to 8-inch saucepan. I recommend this size because it makes it easier to whip air into sauces like hollandaise.

SKILLETS: I love a good skillet, and my favorites are either nonstick or carbon steel. I find cast-iron skillets too heavy and hard to manipulate. Carbon steel provides incredible heat dispersion, resulting in a very even cooking temperature across the whole pan, and at one-third or so the weight of cast-iron.

SILICONE SPATULAS: It's ideal to have a few different sizes with varying flexibility. I use these all the time for scraping down bowls, for folding egg whites, for scraping the last bit of sauce from a pan. But I don't use them to move food in a pan! When teaching cooking classes, I refer the obsession with silicone spatulas and moving food constantly while sautéing as "schmooping," which *slows down cooking* but also create hot spots in your pans simultaneously (neither of which is a good thing). So while silicone spatulas are a necessity, use them sparingly!

THERMOMETER: I have tested these recipes with an instant-read thermometer. In my own cooking, I don't use them, but they are key to confident cooking, especially if you're newer to what doneness looks and feels like. One of the challenges with writing a cookbook is that it's hard for the author to make sure that she and the reader are always on the same page. My oven is different from your oven, and my meat or squash might need to cook longer than yours. A thermometer provides consistency. The cooking time for a spatchcocked turkey (see page 274), for example, cannot be solved by weight alone or even a perfectly calibrated oven. It needs an instant-read thermometer. Follow FDA-approved temperature guidelines to assure that your meat is cooked safely.

WHISKS: You may want a couple different sizes, a narrower one to fit in a saucepan for a sauce, and a larger balloon whisk to beat air into heavy cream or egg whites. I prefer metal, but a silicone-coated one is useful if you have a lot of nonstick pans. I also use my whisks for mixing batters and smoothing out cream soups.

ZESTER/FINE GRATER: My favorite brand is Microplane, but any one will do. Just be sure to look for a handheld model with many, many tiny holes. I use it to zest citrus, of course, but also for grating garlic and Parmesan cheese, fresh ginger, shallots, and onion. Since I use the Microplane for garlic, I do not keep a garlic press around. I'm not big on single-use items, like a garlic press. I prefer multiple use, like Microplane zesters.

Here are a few pieces of kitchen equipment that are definitely nice to have but not necessary if you have the things above.

IMMERSION BLENDER: Most blenders can turn hot soup into a smooth, emulsified beauty. But! A good immersion blender makes quick work of blending hot soup, right in the pot. It will also emulsify a vinaigrette in just seconds, and without all the usual hand whisking.

MANDOLINE: Listen, I am the queen of being nervous about sharp things. (I still don't use it when I'm giving a cooking demonstration.) But if you are alone in the kitchen, with limited distractions, learning to use a mandoline correctly is a game changer for slicing potatoes, cucumbers, zucchini, and other ingredients *thinly and quickly*.

STAND MIXER: A stand mixer is not completely necessary to make the recipes in this book, but it is an appliance I am always grateful to have. I didn't realize how much I missed mine until I didn't have it for making things like cookie and pie dough, for whipping cream, for creaming butter and sugar and eggs for cakes.

LES TECHNIQUES

It doesn't take much to build some kitchen skills—and, like equipment, you don't really need a lot. I do, however, think there are few skills that are good to have not just because they will make you a more efficient cook, but also because mastering these few techniques will also make you a more *confident* cook.

KNIFE SKILLS: Now that you have a chef's knife, let's talk about how to use it. Chopping, mincing, chiffonading, and julienning quickly and effectively are skills that will make cooking at home more efficient. Less chopping brings me joy.

CHIFFONADE: This is my favorite cut when it comes to leafy, tender herbs, such as basil, cilantro, parsley, mint, and sage, because it cuts them without bruising. This means more flavor in each bite, as the volatile oils stay in the herbs until you bite into them. You can also chiffonade other leafy greens like kale, chard, radicchio, and larger lettuces, anything leafy and tender.

No matter the green or herb you're using, it's the same relatively simple technique. Remove the leaves from their stems, and discard any woody/tough bits. Pile a few leaves on top of each other, and roll them tightly, but gently, so that they don't bruise. Using a very sharp knife, slice carefully and perpendicularly to the roll to achieve beautiful, long strips.

CITRUS PREP: In French cooking, supremely perfect citrus segments, without any pith, membranes, or peel, are called *suprêmes*. (They have the same name, *supremes*, in American cooking, just without the French *e* with a circumflex.) These tender and juicy bits are wonderful in salads, entrees that use citrus, and fruit salads. Once you have a naked citrus, you can remove the segments by slicing the fruit away from the membranes or cut it into rounds. Here's how to peel

the citrus to remove the peel and pith, saving as much of the fruit as possible.

To make rounds: Place the peeled citrus on its side and cut it crosswise into rounds about ¼-inch thick.

To make supremes: Don't. (I'm mostly kidding, but it's often not necessary.) If you're feeling like you want some fancy citrus action, once you have your naked round fruit, cut each segment free from the membrane. Place the citrus on its side, and you'll see the edges of the fruit segments. Carefully cut between the membrane and the segment on one side, then the other, guiding the knife into the center of the citrus. This will free the segments and give you gorgeous little jewels of citrus.

GARLIC PREP: I essentially use garlic in three ways. Two of these, grating and slicing, I use all the time, but one (mincing), I hardly use at all.

I rarely mince garlic, even the "correct" way, where the clove is handled the same way as an onion, cut lengthwise and then sliced horizontally. It is just too fussy for me, even if it does make a beautiful mince. Rather, I prefer to grate the garlic clove on a Microplane, where it preps the clove into a fine paste in no time. I also like to slice garlic lengthwise into long slices for Garlic Chips (page 62).

MISE EN PLACE: *Mise en place* means "everything in its place" in French, or more simply the preparation of ingredients before you dive into the construction of the dish. For most of the recipes in this book, I will give a list of the equipment and setup you will need to make each dish

the citrus with your chef knife to get it ready for both techniques:

Find the top end of the citrus, and slice off the tippy top, about ¼ inch of the way in. This should give you a beautiful round of citrus with a flat top. Flip it over and repeat with the stem end of the fruit so it has a flat bottom, too. With the citrus standing on end, use your knife to cut from the top to the bottom, working around

workstation than the one I've suggested, feel free to write in this book and jot down notes for what you need to make the recipe your own. The book is meant to be loved and learned from.

ONIONS AND SHALLOTS, PREP: Deftly slicing and mincing an onion or shallot is remarkably easy and fast once you get the hang of it. The really great thing about onions and shallots? They have *layers*. That means they are very easy to mince and slice.

SLICING: You can slice either *horizontally* or vertically. Slicing horizontally will result in more cell walls broken, which means more allicin in your eyeballs, resulting in more tears. Horizontal slicing also results in a longer cook time, because less surface area is exposed. I'm not a big horizontal slicer; I prefer vertical for faster cooking, less allicin in my eyes (fewer tears!), and more flavor in the final dish. But if you want texture from your onions, horizontal is the way to go.

No matter the method, you need to cut off the sprouting end and remove the first two or so skin and leather layers before diving in. The brown skin is easy to recognize; the leather layer is the pre-onion layer and has a mediocre texture, so should be discarded (or put into your stock).

Horizontal Slices: Leaving the root intact (resist the urge to cut it!), cut off the tip of the sprouting end, giving yourself a nice flat surface. Peel. Slice horizontally until you almost reach the end; keep the nubbin left over for your stock.

Vertical Slices: Cut off the tip of your sprouting end *and* your root end (this is the only time I recommend cutting the root end). Place the onion on one of the flat,

easily. I cannot begin to tell you how many times I have forgotten a paper towel–lined plate when panfrying and I am scrambling for a new roll as my chickpeas burn to a crisp.

At cooking school, the concept of mise en place is driven into your head. Unrelentingly. Every Single Thing Needs to Be in Place before you begin the big cook for the meal. If you have a different preference for getting started on a recipe, for setting up your

MOVING TO FRANCE AND LEARNING TO BE "MOSTLY" FRENCH

Although my daughter was born in France, I'll never be truly French. I just don't fit in completely as a French person. Rather, I feel like I am *mostly* French. At the same time, I no longer fit in where I was born, either.

Becoming even French-esque has been a challenge. The hustle and go of my own hypercapitalist, "just do it" culture hasn't fallen away easily. My friends often call to invite me to dinner, to which I reply *C'est pas possible ce soir* ("It's not possible tonight"). Whatever the reason, they balk at the very notion that I don't have time for a languid dinner, whether because of my daughter's early bedtime or I have work to do. I haven't mastered the art of the miniscule refrigerator, nor have I learned how to shop at a market twice or even thrice (or more) a week to find the freshest of fresh ingredients from local purveyors. I'm more of a "once a week, drive everywhere, get it done and not have to do it again" type. But slowly, softly I have started to fall into the notion that *il n'y a pas le feu au lac*, or "there is no fire at the lake," a saying that means chill out, and that nothing is pressing.

I often joke with my French friends that there may be no fire at the lake, but I am not living my life *at the freaking lake*. To which they respond, Well, why not? I am not 100 percent certain any longer. My only answer: no matter how much I root here, I will likely always be a little "get up and go" American. Because where we come from always follows us. This isn't necessarily a *bad thing*, it's just a thing.

So perhaps I'll never be French, but I will also never be completely American again, either. What I do value, though, works in both places: and that's the notion that we can all use a little time in the kitchen to connect with our food, feed our friends, and enjoy just a touch of joie de vivre, even amid our busy lives.

freshly cut sides and cut in half lengthwise. Peel both halves. Slice vertically into whatever thickness you'd like.

MINCING: Leaving the root intact (resist the urge to cut it!), cut off the tip of the sprouting end, giving yourself a nice flat surface. Then slice the onion/shallot lengthwise in half from sprouting end to root end. Peel. Without cutting through the root end, slice vertical slices through both halves (see photo page 35). Then, slice the onion crosswise (aka perpendicular to your vertical cuts). The smaller your slices, the smaller your mince!

SPATCHCOCKING POULTRY: Roasted chicken is a mainstay in France. Rotisseries are, by far, the most common business in France after pharmacies. Or at least it *seems that way*. But there is a universal downside to French rotisserie chicken: the white meat is always overdone. So, I forgo rotisserie chickens for homemade spatchcocked ones. The result (with turkey, too) is succulent meat, and more even cooking. You can do spatchcock in two ways. You can either remove the backbone entirely or just cut down one side of the backbone and leave it in place. To do this, find the tail of the bird, and cut from one side of the tail, as close to the backbone as possible, all the way up and through to the neck. Stop here, or repeat on the other side. I save the backbone for stocks.

TIME AND TEMPERATURES: My oven is not your oven. My stove, definitely not your stove. So when I say medium-high heat, I can't guarantee your stove will react similarly. This also means that cooking times might vary, an over or under here and there. This is not a big deal. Focus on visual, sound, and smell cues over that of strict, time-bound structures. That's the best way to know how your dish is cooking and when it's done.

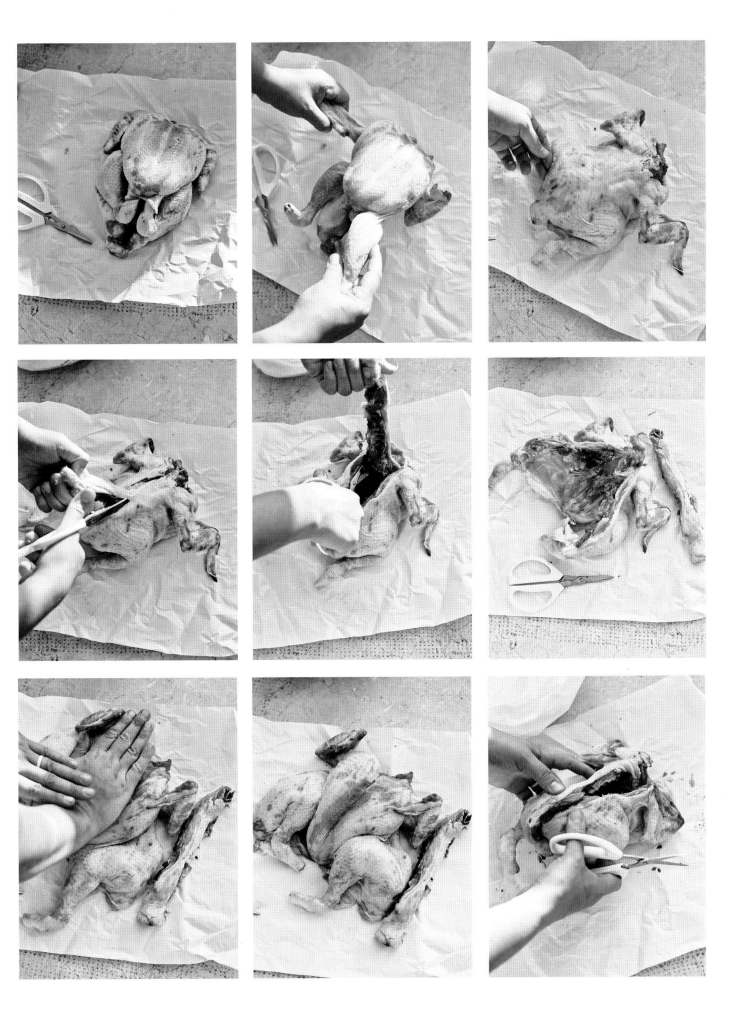

ON SEASONALITY

The South of France, and specifically the French Riviera, doesn't have distinct seasons. Produce is abundant just about all the time. So, living truly in rhythm with the seasons, as fickle as they may be, is pretty easy here.

But even before I moved to France, I endeavored to buy locally as much as possible. This habit began my junior year at Smith College. I was fed up with dining hall food and living in a house with a communal kitchen and a modest but functional array of equipment. I invested $225 of my summer income in a CSA, or community-supported agriculture share. Each week I had access to ten to fifteen pounds of produce. There was a lot in those wonderful hauls that I had never seen before—garlic scapes (the tender green shoots from the center of garlic cloves), kohlrabi (I didn't know its name for over a year), a rainbow's worth of heirloom tomatoes, romanesco (with its perfect fractals, it looks like a cauliflower on a spiritual quest to find enlightenment).

When I graduated, I moved home to Colorado with a friend from college. As a housewarming gift, our fathers brought us their trappings: her dad brought us thirty pounds of elk meat; mine gifted us the same quantity of king salmon. We stuffed our tiny freezer, leaving us room for nothing else. To even consider having a pint of ice cream on hand, we had to make elk fajitas and a king salmon roasted in the oven. We spent that summer shopping at farmers' markets and cooking our parents' spoils.

When I moved to New York City for graduate school, I joined another CSA and spent each fall trudging nearly three-fourths of a mile with so much produce stashed in reusable bags that I didn't really need a gym membership. All those years in a four-season world taught me to connect with the seasons deeply and pay attention to the nuance of how spring melts into summer, and fall into winter. One produce shift at a time.

I am very much *not* in that world anymore. The Riviera has just two fickle seasons. There's a hot, humid summer, from mid-June through the end of August, sometimes sweeping into the end of September or even October. And the rest of the year is what I call "good luck weather." You can have a week of rain in October, or two weeks of above seventy degrees Fahrenheit around Christmas. It can be cloudy and dreary for three months, snow in March, and then hit us hard in May with ninety-degree days, only switching to forty degrees and rainy a week later.

The only certainty is summer. Everything else is a gamble.

Rather than organizing this book into four seasonal sections, I decided to streamline it to reflect our "seasons" in the Riviera, and I settled on warmer and cooler, even though it really is warm here for twelve months.

Most everyone can find ingredients—even very good ones—out of season. The modern grocery store is a miraculous logistical feat. But I note in the recipes some of the intentions behind when they are best served. So I consider the warmer months a time when it's too hot to have butter in the sun or out on a table after dusk, because it will melt. It's a time when heft is not particularly desirable in food, and lighter fare is appreciated (but not required). It's too warm for Braised Chicken in White Wine with Bacon-Radish Gremolata (page 168) during the day, but it might be superb for an evening meal once the sun is down.

The cooler time of year stretches from sweater/sweatshirt weather, rainy days, and "worry not, your butter can stay out at room temperature without a fuss" weather to "oh my god it snowed in late March." The recipes in this section are for warmth, gathering, and snuggles on the couch. Or, simply put, I like these recipes for when the temperature is anything in the mid-sixties Fahrenheit and below.

CHAPTER 2
STOCKS, BROTHS, AND JUS

When a recipe calls for stock or broth, I always stick to homemade. This habit comes from living and learning to cook in France. France simply *doesn't sell broth* in the grocery store. Yes, they sell bouillon, (which is concentrated, dried, and cubed or gelled broth starter with *a lot* of salt) but canned/boxed broths? Nary a one in sight.

For the recipes in this book, you can *of course* use store-bought in a pinch. It's just not as flavorful as the homemade version, and can often taste mostly of salt with a breath of chicken/beef flavor; it's not a bad base, though, for the Almost-from-Scratch Stock on page 45. That said, once you make homemade stock, you won't likely go back.

Making stock doesn't need to be an exact science. It's really just about letting aromatics (vegetables, herbs, spices, and alliums) and bones simmer for hours so they infuse their flavors into the water and, most important, release collagen and gelatin, which give the liquid a rich, unctuous, body. Homemade stock is my not-so-secret ingredient in my cooking. Often I will make a very simple dish, but when my guests take the first bite, they ask, "What did you do to make this so delicious?" And I point to the pot of stock on my stove.

When it comes to making a stock, I am not fussy. I have a *mostly* all-in approach. Whether the vegetables and bones are fresh from the market or saved in the freezer, I use them all.

Sometimes I'll make a pot of stock from a day's trimmings, allow it to simmer overnight, and use it the next day. Other times, I make stock specifically to freeze and have on hand for future use. If I don't have enough bones, I will just buy them from the butcher and you can, too.

If you have the freezer space, I recommend keeping several large plastic grocery bags going for stock ingredients. I split them, generally, into red meats, poultry, fish, and vegetable trimmings. I keep them separate so I can control the flavor profiles of my stocks. I save the trimmings and offcuts of vegetables when I am preparing them and stash those into their own bags, too. When I am ready to start a stock, I nab a freezer bag and dump the whole thing in, add whatever fresh I have around, and cover with water.

Many French kitchens maintain "mother stocks." This is a base stock that you use every time you make a new stock. You simply take your new ingredients, add your mother stock, cover with fresh water, and ultimately create an infinite base that's enriched over time. To do this, simply always hold about 1 cup of stock in your freezer, add it to your next stock with fresh ingredients and liquid, and repeat the process once the new batch has simmered.

If this level of involvement isn't for you, don't worry. The recipes that follow work fine with "baby" stocks, doctored versions of store-bought, and store-bought varieties.

Broths are the tender-hearted cousin of stocks. They are more delicate, have less color, and therefore less flavor than stocks, which are rich from their very long simmer.

Broths are more mild and less brown than stocks, and this is handy when you want your final dish, such as the Herbed Butternut Squash Soup (page 220) to be bright yellow, rather than a bit brown. Broths are also useful for things that require a more delicate flavor profile, which is admittedly not my personal approach in this book, or in my real life. But I won't shame you for liking and using broths.

Stock is a choose-your-own adventure, once you've mastered the basics. With the following recipes as a general guide, you can be adventurous and customize stock to the flavor profiles you like best and with whatever you have on hand. You're trying to create a *mix of flavor* that is pretty indistinguishable as this or that. It's what makes the final dish it is used in so tantalizing.

Here is a rough blueprint of ingredients to get you started if you're ready to play a bit:

MEAT AND POULTRY: First, pick what kind of stock you'd like to make. My favorites are chicken (or mixed fowl), beef/lamb, pork, or a combination of both meat and poultry.

LIQUID: If you have any leftover meat or poultry stock, add it to the pot. Otherwise, add enough cold water to barely cover the ingredients.

VEGETABLES: You can use trimmings of vegetables (saved in the fridge or freezer), or use fresh ones. Just about anything and everything goes, except for produce that will discolor the stock (purple cabbage and beets are no-gos, for example).

Onion skins are magic! They bring a gorgeous depth of color to your stock. The garlic skins aren't really flavorful but there's no detriment to including them—just cut the head in half to expose the cloves and toss it in whole.

My only caveat of this devil-may-care approach is that I am prudent with the *kinds and quantities of vegetables* I use. All in, no rules: alliums and root vegetables (other than potatoes). Prudence required: brassicas and starchy vegetables (like potatoes). I rarely add tomatoes, as they cloud the stock.

SPICES: For the purpose of mostly French cooking, we're layering the flavors, ingredients, and techniques of France with new flavors. Typically when you are cooking certain cuisines, such as Indian or Chinese, you might want stock flavored with the signature spices of that cuisine. But I like to throw out the rulebook and play with flavors. An anise-rich stock that is more akin to, say, a pho broth from Vietnamese cuisine makes a beautiful braising liquid, even for a classic French bourguignon.

Choose two to three whole spices, 2 to 4 table-spoons total, at minimum. Black (or even pink, if you have them) peppercorns, anise seeds, mustard seeds, cinnamon leaves, bay leaves, cardamom seeds (watch out for these, they are strong). An inch or two of fresh ginger can add another layer of spicy and aromatic heat. Play with flavors and see what comes through. If you're nervous, start with less, let it simmer for an hour or two, taste the stock, and add more spices through the simmering process.

HERBS: Fresh or dried, at least a handful of fresh herbs or up to 4 tablespoons of dried herbs. I love to throw in a stalk or two of lemongrass (the bottom bulb end of the stalk only) if I have it around.

- *Stockpot*
- *Small bowl with cold water*
- *Fine mesh sieve*
- *Large bowl or pot*

2 pounds bones (see page 41), collected from other meals and frozen, or purchased

2 yellow onions, unpeeled, cut into quarters

4 carrots, cut into 2-inch chunks

6 celery stalks, cut into 2-inch chunks

Head of garlic, unpeeled, cut in half crosswise

12 to 20 black peppercorns (I don't really measure, I just shake my peppercorns into the pot!)

1 bouquet garni (page 25) (Or 3 tablespoons of dried herbs of choice: thyme, rosemary, savory, basil, oregano all work here. I wouldn't use more than 2 tablespoons of each kind when you're making your blend; variety is the spice of life after all.)

About 3 quarts liquid, to cover: Water or a leftover broth/stock you happen to have on hand, or a mix of both. Remember we are attempting to create an infinite stock loop.

Rich Stock

MAKES ABOUT 1½ QUARTS

1. Put the bones, onions, carrots, celery, garlic, peppercorns, and bouquet garni in a large stockpot. Add enough cold water to completely cover the ingredients, about 3 quarts total liquid. Cold water is crucial. If you start with hot, the stock will be cloudy, as the "impurities" in the bones won't rise to the top, and they will stay emulsified in the liquid. There is no harm in that, it's simply not as nice to look at.

2. Bring to a full boil over high heat. As the water comes to a boil, skim off the scum or other bubbly detritus that rises to the top with a spoon. Dip the spoon into the bowl with the cold water between skims. This will take the scum off quickly and clean the spoon for the next skim.

3. Once the water has boiled, reduce the heat to very low. Let simmer for 3 or 4 hours, or even longer if you wish, which will concentrate the flavors even more. My preference is to cook for 12 hours during the day, adding water throughout anytime the ingredients begin to peek above the surface.

4. At the end of your cook time, strain the stock: Place a fine mesh sieve over a big bowl or pot. Pour the stock through the sieve, pressing down on the solids to release all the liquid and flavor into the stock. The stock can then be cooled, covered, and refrigerated for up to 3 days or frozen for months.

Note: Planning on freezing and short on freezer space? After straining, return the stock to a saucepan, and simmer until between 1 pint and 1 quart of liquid remains. (The choice is yours, and depends on your storage space.)

- *Sheet pan*
- *Stockpot*
- *Fine mesh sieve*
- *Bowl or pot*

2 yellow onions, unpeeled, cut into quarters

4 carrots, cut into 2-inch chunks

6 celery stalks, cut into 2-inch chunks

1 head garlic, unpeeled, cut in half crosswise

12 to 20 black peppercorns (or fewer if you don't love pepper as much as I do)

1 bouquet garni (see page 25), no need to tie since the stock will be strained

2 quarts canned beef or chicken broth

Almost-from-Scratch Stock

When you don't have the time for Rich Stock you can make this excellent substitute relatively quickly. Simply simmer canned broth with roasted veggies. Roasting caramelizes the vegetables for extra flavor and gives the finished stock a much deeper flavor than canned stock alone. While I prefer homemade stock, this isn't a bad way to enrich store-bought broths. **MAKES ABOUT ½ QUART**

1. Preheat the oven to 500°F. Place the onions, carrots, and celery on a sheet pan. Roast until well browned, but not charred, about 15 minutes. Transfer to a stockpot.

2. Add the garlic, peppercorns, and bouquet garni to the pot, and add enough broth to completely cover the ingredients. (If you don't have enough broth, use water to make up the difference.) Bring to a full boil over high heat. Reduce the heat to medium and cook at a solid simmer (not quite a boil) until richly colored and deeply flavored, about 45 minutes.

3. After cooking, strain (see page 43, step 4).

4. The stock can then be cooled, covered, and refrigerated for up to 3 days or frozen for months.

MISE EN PLACE
- Stockpot
- Small bowl with cold water
- Sieve or colander
- Large bowl or another pot

3 pounds bone-in chicken parts, such as legs, wings, or necks

2 white or yellow onions, cut into quarters

2 carrots, cut into 2-inch chunks

6 to 8 celery stalks, cut into 2-inch chunks

1 whole garlic head, unpeeled, cut in half crosswise

4 dried bay leaves

10 sprigs fresh rosemary, oregano, or thyme (or a mix), or
1 tablespoon dried herbs

12 black peppercorns

Chicken Broth

While stocks rely on bones and a longer cook time, broths include the meat as well. (After the broth is finished, the cooked chicken *without* bones is a favorite with my pets. Check with your veterinarian first of course, but the great thing is that the chicken is well-cooked, delicious, and salt free!) Chicken broth is versatile and easy to make. Choose chicken parts with a good bone-to-meat ratio, such as chicken legs, which are also economical. The more meat to bone, the more of the chicken flavor you'll impart on the final product. MAKES ABOUT 2 QUARTS

1. Put the chicken, onions, carrots, celery, garlic, bay leaves, herbs, and peppercorns into a stockpot. Add enough cold water (about 3 quarts) to completely cover the ingredients. Bring to a boil over high heat. As it comes to a boil, skim the scum or other bubbly detritus that rises to the top with a spoon every few minutes. Use the cold water to clean the spoon between skims.

2. Once boiling, reduce the heat to low. Let simmer for at least 3 hours and up to 5 hours. The longer it simmers, the more color and flavor it will have. If you are in a rush, you can stop after 2 hours.

3. Strain the broth through a wire sieve or colander into a large bowl. Allow the chicken to cool enough to remove the meat from the bones. Save the meat to top salads or for the Chicken and Root Vegetable Dilly Potpie (page 249).

4. The broth can be cooled, covered, and refrigerated for up to 5 days or frozen for months.

4 onions, any color, cut in quarters (red isn't my favorite, as it colors the stock a bit dark)

8 carrots, cut into 3-inch pieces or so

8 celery stalks, cut into 2- to 3-inch pieces

2 heads garlic, cut in half crosswise

Olive oil

15 black peppercorns

1 bouquet garni (see page 25), no need to tie since the stock will be strained, or 4 tablespoons dried herbs (1 tablespoon each of oregano, thyme, rosemary, and sage is a nice mixture)

3 to 4 quarts water

Vegetable Broth

Vegetable broths don't have the same flavor symphony of meat-based broths, but they are still marvelous when you want a lighter touch, or more balanced flavor profile especially in soups. These broths can be made with roasted vegetables or with raw vegetables over the course of a long simmer. One example of a vegetable-based broth that is super fun and useful, because it adds umami, is Parmesan broth (see Pistou [Not Pesto] Soup, page 157).

I also love artichoke broth, created from the trimmings from the Oven-Roasted Artichokes on page 215. You can use the leaves from your dinner party, and the tough ones that people don't eat. (They get boiled down, so it's safe.) Artichoke broth is a quick flavor enhancer and gives a je ne sais quoi to dishes. Don't overboil the broth (only about 45 minutes is required to get it to infuse), because that can make it bitter.

Ultimately, don't be afraid to play, especially with leftovers. There's almost no downside. Extracting more flavor from something you were planning on throwing in the garbage feels like the utmost alchemy.

MAKES ABOUT 2 TO 3 QUARTS

1. Preheat the oven to 500°F.

2. Place all the vegetables on a sheet pan, add a glug of olive oil, and toss. Roast in the oven for 15 to 20 minutes, until you get a hearty golden brown over all the vegetables.

3. Remove from the oven, and place the browned vegetables into a stockpot. Add any vegetable scraps you have lying around, up to the same quantity of vegetables you have.

4. Add the aromatics—peppercorns and bouquet garni or dried herbs. Cover with water, and make sure all is fully submerged. I like there to be about 2 to 3 inches of water over the top as it will simmer down and reduce.

5. Bring to a boil, then reduce to a simmer. Simmer for a minimum of 4 hours to overnight.

6. Strain (see page 43, step 4) and store in the refrigerator for 4 to 5 days, or freeze for months.

2 tablespoons vegetable or canola oil

1 onion, diced

2 carrots, diced

2 pounds bone-in poultry parts, such as wings, legs, or necks

2 tablespoons white wine or red

1½ quarts Rich Stock (page 43), made with poultry bones

Leftover jus, any quantity (optional)

Pan drippings from any roast meat or poultry (optional)

Jus

Jus corsé, also called "strong *jus*," is a concentrated reduction of a stock that has been enriched with additional poultry pieces and vegetables, *richly brown in color*, and reduced down to a thick, intensely flavored and flourless sauce.

Some French chefs would call this a *jus*, some a glaze. Chicken jus freezes well (just scrape out what you need with a sturdy spoon if you aren't defrosting the entire batch) and will improve when you deplete your stock and use the leftovers to enrich another batch.

The purpose of a chicken glaze is to act as a sauce for any sort of poultry dish. I recommend using it with spatchcocked chicken (see page 36) and Spatchcocked Turkey with Rich Herb Jus (page 274).

MAKES ABOUT 1 CUP

1. Heat the oil in a large saucepan over high heat until it is very hot and shimmering. If you are using animal fat, heat it until it is very hot but not smoking.

2. Add the onion and carrots, and cook down for about 6 minutes, until the onion begins to sweat. Add the chicken pieces and cook, turning occasionally, until it is nicely browned all over, about 6 minutes. Add the wine and stir with a wooden spatula to scrape up any browned bits. Add enough stock to completely cover the chicken. Stir in any leftover jus and pan drippings, if using.

3. Bring to a full boil, skimming any scum that rises to the top. Reduce the heat to medium-low and cook at a strong simmer until the meat is very tender, about 1 hour. Strain the broth through a wire sieve or colander into a large bowl. Skim any fat from the surface with a spoon. Clean the pot—any remaining bits can burn onto the sides. Let the meat cool enough to remove the meat from the bones, and use the meat to top salads or for the Chicken and Root Vegetable Dilly Potpie (page 249).

4. Return the stock to the cleaned pot, and bring to a boil over high heat. Boil until the liquid is syrupy and reduced enough to coat a wooden spoon, about 1 hour, depending on the heat of your stove and the size of the pot. Keep an eye on it so it doesn't scorch. You will only get a cup or so. (The glaze can be cooled, covered, and refrigerated for up to 10 days or frozen for months.)

CHAPTER 3

SAUCES AND ESSENTIALS

Traditional French cooking—which Julia Child, arguably our most famous importer of the art, embraced—uses five mother sauces for taking dishes from basic to exemplary. According to centuries of tradition, these are hollandaise, béchamel, velouté, espagnole, and tomato. Some would argue that vinaigrette should be a mother sauce, but it is often left out. Rather than simply list the five classics, I have pared it down to two categories that I use again and again (and a third I cook with sparingly). I have personalized them by adding more contemporary flavors like preserved lemon.

EMULSIONS: These are sauces that are fat forward, and have something in them that are amphiphilic—a fancy science term that refers to an ingredient that allows two opposite substances to be melded together (usually by whisking). For example: bringing together oil and vinegar and mustard (your amphiphilic ingredient) to make a vinaigrette.

Egg yolks or mustard, or both, are often, but not always, used to help the emulsion happen. Always remember a key rule: Mix the emulsifier (your amphiphilic ingredient) with its similar friends first. Then add the different ingredient. For example, if the emulsion occurs with egg, incorporate the fats first, because egg is considered a fat. Then add the acids. If the emulsifier is acidic, like say in mustard, mix the acids and the mustard together first, then add the oils. Remembering this is key to successful, low-stress emulsions.

CONCENTRATED REDUCTIONS: These are concentrated over low heat through infusions, then evaporated over low or high heat to create a concentrated final product. The results are a thick, flavorful sauce. Jus (page 49) is a great example of a reduction. Even tomato-based sauces are considered reductions because they require long simmers to infuse and reduce at the same time. Beurre blanc is both a concentrated reduction *and* an emulsion (the concentrated acid of wine or vinegar acts as the emulsifier).

ROUX-BASED SAUCES: This is the third category. A roux is equal parts butter and flour cooked together to make a paste. When liquid is whisked in and the mixture is heated, the roux expands to soak up the liquid first, then thickens into a sauce. Three common roux-based sauces are béchamel (where milk is the liquid), velouté (where stock is the liquid), and Mornay (béchamel plus cheese). They can be useful in dishes like the Chicken and Root Vegetable Dilly Potpie on page 249.

2 large eggs yolks, at room temperature

1 tablespoon Dijon mustard

1 cup neutral oil, such as grapeseed, canola, or avocado

Juice of 1 lemon, as needed

Fine sea salt

Vinegar (I prefer a white wine or cider due to their color and flavor, but there's nothing stopping you from using another type in lieu of those two; optional)

Freshly ground white or black pepper

Mayonnaise

This is the perfect place to understand emulsions and what they look like as they come together. There are several things, some scientific, to consider when making mayonnaise.

- The oil: A neutral-flavored oil (such as grapeseed, canola, or avocado) is needed. Olive oil becomes strongly flavored when beaten, so don't use more than a quarter of it in your oil mix.
- Whipping technique: A blender is fast but whipping by hand is often more foolproof; whipped-by-hand mayonnaise will almost never break, whereas heat and overprocessing from a blender can denature the proteins that help with emulsification, thus breaking the sauce.
- Temperature: Have all of the ingredients at room temperature before you start, and use the freshest eggs for the most stable emulsion.

MAKES ABOUT 1½ CUPS

1. Whisk together the yolks and mustard well in a medium bowl. Give them a good whisk so they get to know each other. They are both emulsifiers, and we want them to be friendly with each other first.

2. Whisk in the oil, about a tablespoon at a time. Continue until all the oil is incorporated and the mixture is very thick and lightly translucent. It should be thick enough you could write your initials in the mixture. If you're not there yet, add more oil.

3. Now it's time to add acid to the mixture. This will denature the proteins at the right time and soften that sucker into a silken dream. (If your bowl is unstable, as you will have both hands in action and won't be able to hold it in place, create a brake of sorts. Take a kitchen towel and make a crumply circle with it to create a nest where you can place the bowl.) Whisk in the lemon juice, about a tablespoon at a time. Taste after each addition, and watch the mixture. It will start to turn creamy, more opaque, and soften in texture. Season with salt. If you want a bit more acidity, but with less bitterness, add the vinegar. Finish with freshly ground pepper. I like white because it won't leave specks in your perfect mayonnaise, but of course, black is fine, too.

4. The mayonnaise can be refrigerated in an airtight container for about 5 days.

MISE EN PLACE

- *Mortar and pestle*

4 garlic cloves

1 teaspoon salt, plus more to taste

½ cup olive oil, divided

1 lemon

Aïoli

This is a traditional aïoli recipe from Provence, and it's one of my favorites. Garlic isn't a staple of French cuisine, but it *is* a staple of Mediterranean cuisine. You can replace mayonnaise with this, use it to dip fries, or spread it on toast before any other topping. It is *distinctly* garlicky, and not at all greasy. It's a bit of alchemy as it's a very straightforward ingredient base and requires a fair amount of elbow grease to make happen. MAKES ABOUT ⅓ CUP

1. Pound the garlic cloves with the mortar and pestle until they are mashed, add 1 teaspoon salt, and pound again until a uniform paste forms.

2. Drizzle in 1 teaspoon of the olive oil, and pound the oil into the garlic. Once the oil has joined the garlic, drizzle in a bit more. Repeat. The less oil you add at a time, the better. Once you have about ⅓ of a cup of oil emulsified into the garlic, add juice from half of the lemon. Mix with a spoon or the pestle. Taste.

3. If it's very garlicky still, you can drizzle in a bit more oil, about 1 teaspoon at a time, until you've used the entire ½ cup. Add a bit more lemon juice to taste. Serve immediately.

½ cup white wine vinegar or champagne vinegar, or a combination of the two

5 dried bay leaves

2 large egg yolks

1 cup (2 sticks) cold salted butter, cut into tablespoons

Pinch of crushed red chile, preferably smoked

Juice of ½ lemon (optional)

Fine sea salt

Hollandaise

While this sauce is firmly in the lexicon of French technique, its name is a bit odd. While called hollandaise, meaning "from Holland," it doesn't actually appear to be of Dutch origin. The original was probably called sauce Isigny, from the butter-centric Isigny region of France. Its murky origins notwithstanding, hollandaise is easy to master, and lusciously thick, and outrageously delicious on vegetables and seafood. There is never enough hollandaise. MAKES ABOUT 1 CUP

1. Bring the vinegar and bay leaves to a boil in a small saucepan over high heat. Boil until reduced to about 2 tablespoons, 5 to 10 minutes. Discard the bay leaves. Set aside.

2. In the other saucepan set over low heat, whisk the yolks and 1 teaspoon water together until the mixture foams up and then the foam subsides, about 30 seconds. Be sure that the foam subsides. Adjust the heat as needed so the saucepan is never so hot that it burns you, occasionally checking the heat by touching the pan with the side of your hand. If it gets too hot, remove the pan from the heat for a while still whisking.

3. After the foam has subsided and the yolks are thick enough that, as you whisk, they hold their shape a bit (don't overheat or they will curdle!), start adding the cold butter two to three pieces at a time. Each time you add some butter, the mixture will cool a bit, helping to avoid curdling. You do not need to whisk constantly, but you do need to monitor the heat. If in doubt, take the pot off the heat for 30 seconds, and let the butter soften (this technique of softening the butter so it isn't quite liquid is called mounting). Whisk, and return to the heat. Keep whisking in the butter a piece or two at a time, doing the heat-and-whisk tango. Adding the butter to the yolks will take 5 to 10 minutes total.

4. Whisk in the reduced vinegar mixture and a pinch of chile. Taste. Adjust the flavor, if needed, with a touch of lemon juice, if using, and season with salt.

5. Move to a warm area of the stove, but not over a flame, to keep warm. My recipe makes a thick hollandaise that will hold for up to 10 minutes.

Note: To make a béarnaise: Boil 2 shallots, minced, with the vinegar mixture, and add 2 tablespoons minced fresh tarragon to the finished sauce.

Fine sea salt and freshly ground black pepper

1 teaspoon Dijon mustard, whole grain or smooth

3 tablespoons lemon or any tart citrus juice or vinegar—the world is your acidic oyster

½ cup olive oil

Your Dream Vinaigrette

One of the most frequent questions my students ask is how do I make the perfect vinaigrette? My recipe is a guideline for a basic vinaigrette that can be stored at room temperature to dress any salad. You can use smooth or grainy mustard; I love the texture of the tiny seeds in the latter.

Once you find your personal ratio of acid to fat, play around with variations. Some of my favorite flavors are grated shallot or garlic, ground cumin, or ground turmeric. You can make a different dressing every day by altering a few tablespoons of the basic vinaigrette with the seasoning of your choice. MAKES ¾ CUP

1. Add a pinch of salt and some pepper to a small bowl. Add the mustard and juice. Whisk together until well combined.

2. Gradually whisk in the oil, allowing the acidic/aromatic mixture to emulsify with the oil. Taste it. You should love it as is. If it's too acidic, whisk in a bit more oil. If it's too oily, whisk in more acid.

3. Transfer to a jar. (The dressing can be stored at room temperature for 2 or more weeks, though you will probably use it up before then.)

A LOVELY, SIMPLE GREEN SALAD

MAKES 1 SERVING

1. Now that you have your dream vinaigrette, you can construct a simple side salad: I love love love baby greens (known as mesclun in Provence) for this purpose. They are Technicolor dreamboats, and most supermarkets sell packages that don't require prewashing.

2. Place 1 to 2 handful of greens per person into a bowl, and drizzle over about 1 teaspoon of vinaigrette per handful. Toss with your hands, or tongs (hands are much better at evenly distributing the vinaigrette). Sprinkle the top with a flaky salt (I prefer smoked for this), and serve as a side.

Fine sea salt

6 to 8 Meyer lemons or mixed citrus, such as Eureka (standard) lemons, limes, and/or oranges, plus 2 or 3 more, for juice, if needed

5 dried bay leaves

20 pink peppercorns, or 10 black

1 tablespoon crushed coriander seed (crush with a mortar and pestle; can also use in combination with cumin seeds, nigella, fenugreek seeds, cinnamon sticks, allspice, mustard seeds, fennel seeds, or celery seeds)

Fresh lemon juice, if needed (optional)

Preserved Citrus

Preserved lemons are common in the cuisines of the Mediterranean communities of North Africa and have migrated to the French Riviera over the years. I had never tasted one until I moved here and discovered them at the farmers' market, where they are sold at all the fermented food stands. The availability of a Moroccan ingredient in my local town square shows how cooking here is both *very* French, yet *not* French. I started cooking with them immediately and eventually learned that they are easy to make at home.

Most versions are simply lemons and salt, and I prefer to expand the possibilities *just* a bit more by using mixed citrus and aromatics to bump up the flavor. Citrus with thin skins and pith work best, so skip thick-skinned grapefruit. Use them according to the recipe directions because sometimes you use the entire fruit, and others, just the rind.

MAKES ABOUT 1 QUART

1.   In a very clean, dry jar, sprinkle in 1 tablespoon salt. Cut each fruit almost into quarters vertically from stem top to blossom bottom, being sure that the quarters are left attached at the end. Do not cut the fruit into separate pieces.

2.   One at a time, stand a lemon on a plate. Open the quarters a little so you can sprinkle about 1 tablespoon of salt into the crevices. Pack the fruit in the jar and sprinkle it with about 2 teaspoons salt. Repeat with all the fruit, layering in the salt, bay leaf, peppercorns, and coriander as you go. Top with any remaining flavorings. Using your hands or a large wooden spoon, press down on the fruit to release some juices. Let stand for at least 15 minutes to allow the fruit to release more juices.

3.   Check the jar. It should have ample juice to cover all the fruit with citrus juice. If not, add freshly squeezed lemon juice to cover.

4.   Place the jar in a cool, dry place (such as your pantry) and shake it every few days. After a week or two, the citrus will have shifted its appearance and be almost a shadow of its former self, with a relatively translucent pith. This is how you know fermentation has occurred.

5.   Now that fermentation is far enough along, store the jar in the refrigerator and use the citrus with abandon. They only get better with time and keep pretty darn close to indefinitely in the fridge. Toss them if they start to mold. (But, they shouldn't!)

Olive oil

1 shallot, minced very finely

2 cups dry white wine (this will get reduced for a winey flavor)

1 tablespoon white wine vinegar or champagne vinegar

1 cup (2 sticks) cold salted butter, cut into ½-inch cubes

1 tablespoon heavy cream (optional)

Fine sea salt

Freshly ground white or black pepper

Beurre Blanc

This is my favorite of the French sauces. You have to make it just before serving—it can't wait around, so time it to finishing whatever you are serving it with. (If it gets a little room temperature, don't worry—the main dish will heat it up.) It is easier than hollandaise because you skip warming the egg yolks. And it's adaptable, a canvas for variations, such as chopped fresh thyme, sumac, Urfa biber chile flakes, basically any savory flavoring. You'll see it with preserved lemon for scallops on page 262 and with dill for roasted chicken legs on page 246. **MAKES ABOUT 1 CUP**

1. Heat a small glug of oil in a small saucepan over medium-low heat. Add the shallots and cook, stirring occasionally, until they are softened but not browned, about 2 minutes. (If the shallots brown, the sauce will lose its buttery pale color.)

2. Add the wine and vinegar and bring to a boil over high heat. Reduce to medium-high and cook at a strong simmer until the liquid is reduced to about 1 tablespoon, about 30 minutes. Check the liquid level often toward the end of the reducing time. Remove from the heat. (The wine base can stand at room temperature for an hour or two, or even overnight, if you want beurre blanc for your breakfast eggs.)

3. When you're ready to serve the sauce, gently warm the wine mixture in the pan over medium-low heat. It should be warm, but not hot. Reduce the heat to very low. Add three to four butter cubes and whisk until about three-fourths of the butter has softened into a smooth sauce. The butter should emulsify into silken enchantment within 1 minute. If it is taking longer, the heat is too low, so increase it slightly. But remember that if the heat is too high, the sauce will melt instead of soften, and it will break.

4. Continue to whisk in the butter, three to four pieces at a time, until the ingredients have emulsified into a luscious dreamboat. For extra stabilization to hold slightly longer, whisk in the cream, if using. Season with salt and pepper. Serve immediately, or store in a warm part of the stove, not over a flame, for a few minutes.

2 cups heavy cream

2 tablespoons confectioners' sugar

½ teaspoon vanilla powder or the interior of 1 whole vanilla bean

Not-Too-Sweet Whipped Cream

Whipped cream is *technically* a sauce and an emulsion. It's and emulsion of air and the fat in the cream. In France it is known as *chantilly*, but it is different from plain whipped cream. Chantilly (pronounced shan-tee) is sweetened and flavored with vanilla. I like my whipped cream to be somewhat less sweet so it doesn't overpower the dessert. You can whip a smaller batch with 1 cup of heavy cream and a hand mixer. But, for my money, it is more efficient to whip a big batch in a heavy-duty mixer, especially over holidays when things are hectic and it seems you need whipped cream at every turn. You can easily substitute the vanilla for another spice like cinnamon, cardamom, allspice, or nutmeg.

MAKES ABOUT 4 CUPS

Place a large bowl in the freezer or fridge for 5 to 10 minutes until well chilled. Pour in the cream, confectioners' sugar, and vanilla. Using an electric hand mixer on high speed, beat the cream to your desired consistency. (Sometimes you want a soft consistency to cloak a dessert, but other times you might want the cream stiffer to hold its shape. The cold bowl will decrease the whipping time, and it holds more loft into the cream.) The whipped cream can be covered and refrigerated for up to 2 days. If it separates, whisk it again to bring it back together before serving.

Crusty bread, baguette, or *bâtard* (loaf)

Olive oil

Flaky sea salt

Crostini

I don't buy crostini because making them at home is so easy, and you can flavor them, too, just as you'd find in the store. Use either a thin baguette or a thick *bâtard*—of course, the size of the loaf will determine the size of the crostini. It is also a great way to use up day-old bread and herbs that are on their way out to infuse the oil used to brush the crostini.

MAKES 18 TO 24 CROSTINI

1. Preheat the oven to 425°F. Cut the bread crosswise on an angle (you get larger slices this way) into slices about ¼-inch thick. They should be thin, but not so thin that you can see through them. If you feel they are too big (they should look like an oversize cracker), cut them crosswise for the size you like. (I like them 3 to 5 inches long.)

2. Scatter the bread pieces on the sheet pans. They can be crowded, but shouldn't be overlapping. Drizzle with olive oil, 2 or 3 tablespoons per sheet pan. Season with salt. Shake the pans to distribute the coatings a bit. (It doesn't have to be coated evenly, I swear.) (See below for flavored crostini.)

3. Bake until the bread is golden brown and crispy, about 10 minutes. Check occasionally to see how they are browning. (I often forget, and burn them.) They may take a few minutes more or less, so don't forget to check them!

FRESH HERB CROSTINI: Toss in about ¼ cup finely chopped herbs into the oil. I use whatever herbs are on their way out in my fridge. Some of my favorite combinations are rosemary and thyme, tarragon and chives, and cilantro and oregano.

DRIED HERB CROSTINI: Add about 2 teaspoons of any dried herbs—herbes de Provence is a crowd-pleaser—to the oil.

PARMESAN AND GARLIC CROSTINI: Make a paste of about ¼ cup of freshly grated Parmesan cheese and 3 grated garlic cloves (or more to taste). Spread the mixture over the bread, and bake until golden.

FLAVOR BOMB CROSTINI: For next-level crostini, make the Parmesan and garlic mixture above and mash 4 anchovy fillets packed in oil into the mixture.

Vegetable or canola oil, for frying

16 large garlic cloves, peeled, sliced thinly crosswise on a slight bias (you can do fewer, but then you don't have snacks)

Fine sea salt

Garlic Chips

I love to have these on hand as a topping and snack. When I was in culinary school, my teachers were adamant about how garlic "ruins" everything. In fact, one chef told me he was "absolutely certain" he lost *Le Grand Concours* (a venerable French chef competition) due to too much garlic. To each their own. Garlic is one of my favorite aromatics, and I've found that frying garlic softens its "burn" (if you can call it that) and appeals to my biased French guests. I always make as large a batch as I can manage. To make quick work of this recipe, use already peeled garlic cloves in a jar straight from the supermarket. **MAKES ABOUT 1½ CUPS**

1.   Pour enough oil to come about ½ inch up the sides of a large, wide skillet. Heat over medium-high heat until the oil is shimmering. In batches, without crowding, carefully sprinkle in the garlic, and fry until a pale golden brown, about 1 minute. (Do a small first batch as a trial run.) Immediately remove the garlic with a slotted spoon to the prepared plate. (The garlic tends to overbrown quickly, before you know it. Err on the side of cooking too lightly, as it will continue to brown more outside of the oil from retained heat.)

2.   Sprinkle the garlic with a pinch of salt. As the garlic cools, the chips will become addictively crispy.

3.   The chips can be stored in an airtight container at room temperature for up to 2 weeks. (But in my house they last barely two hours!)

- *Medium bowl with ice water*
- *Tongs*
- *Medium saucepan*
- *Blender*
- *Coffee filter lined with a paper coffee filter, or a wire sieve lined with paper towels or cheesecloth*

1 bunch or 2 of fresh, tender-leafed herbs, such as parsley, cilantro, basil, dill, tarragon, or a combination (about 1 cup loosely packed leaves, and you can include some thin stems)

1 cup neutral-flavored oil, such as grapeseed or canola oil (do not use an assertive oil such as olive or sesame)

Universal Herbed Oil

I think of this oil as the classic gold earrings of my pantry—the elegant and somewhat simple thing to dress up almost any dish. It's straightforward to make, and keeps for a few weeks. It can be considered a sauce because it is a great way to elevate plain grilled meat, poultry, seafood, or vegetables. Does your soup need a lift? Give it a taste, and drizzle the oil onto each serving. Use it in place of plain oil in salad dressing or on roasted vegetables. MAKES ABOUT 1 CUP

1.   Place the ice water near the stove. Bring a medium saucepan full of water to a boil over high heat. Using tongs, add the herbs to the water and blanch for 15 seconds. This will affix the chlorophyll, so they will remain vibrant green. Remove with tongs, and transfer the herbs to the ice water. This stops them from cooking and becoming mushy. Allow the herbs to cool completely in the ice water.

2.   Use your hands to lift the cooled herbs out of the water and squeeze them well, but gently, to extract excess water. Wrap in paper towels and press gently to remove more water.

3.   Put the herbs in a blender. Add the oil and blend until the herbs are very finely minced, almost a purée.

4.   Line a coffee filter with a paper filter and place over a cup. (Or line a wire sieve with paper towels or cheesecloth placed over a bowl.) Pour in the herb oil and let it drip. Allow gravity to do this; do not press or stir until the bright green, richly flavored oil has passed through into the receptacle and only a bright green residue remains in the filter. This will take at least 30 minutes.

5.   The oil can be stored in a bottle and refrigerated for up to 2 weeks. Bring to room temperature before using.

OEUFS EN COCOTTE

Baked eggs, *oeufs en cocotte*, shirred eggs: they have many names, but mean the same thing. Eggs baked with a liquid are simply delicious. And the ability to make this is a delightful trick to have up your sleeves, whether you're cooking for one or many. *Oeufs en cocotte* are always cooked individually in small ramekins, which increases the adorable and wow factors.

A single baked egg is a great option for breakfast (the French would never do that, but you could!). They are also perfect for lunch or as a starter for a special dinner. I love to serve the classic *oeufs en cocotte* on a bed of foie gras as an extravagant start to a meal. It's also a bit of a surprise to get a personal egg dish at dinner. If serving as a meal, accompany baked eggs with a simple salad, as you would for an omelet.

All *oeufs en cocotte* require a few of the same things:

- A seasoned liquid, usually heavy cream, but try the tomato sauce variation on page 67.

- A bain-marie, which is a fancy term for a water bath. Choose a roasting pan large enough to hold the ramekins. It adds steam to the oven, keeping the tops of the eggs from drying. The water also insulates the ramekins to help the eggs cook more evenly.

- Ramekins (about 4-ounce or ½-cup capacity) for each serving.

On the following pages, you will find two variations: the classic and an *oeufs en cocotte* in a tomato base.

- *Roasting pan or baking dish*
- *Ramekin or small ovenproof dish (such as a Pyrex custard cup)*
- *Tongs*

Softened butter, for the ramekin

2 tablespoons heavy cream

Fine sea salt and freshly ground black pepper

Pinch of finely chopped fresh thyme

1 large egg

Crostini (page 60) or toast points, for serving

Classic Oeufs en Cocotte

Here is the classic version of *oeufs en cocotte* that every French *maman* knows how to make for a quick meal. The combination of eggs and cream is luscious, and of course, you can use another favorite herb for the thyme. SERVES 1, SCALE UP AS NEEDED

1. Preheat the oven to 350°F. Place the roasting pan in the oven and pour in enough hot water to come about halfway up the sides. Heat the filled pan for 5 minutes.

2. Lightly butter a 4-ounce ramekin. Pour in the cream, season with salt and pepper, and add the thyme. Crack the egg on top, being careful not to break the yolk. Place the ramekin in the water in the baking dish.

3. Bake until the egg whites are set, 10 to 13 minutes. Check if they need more time at 10 minutes. Be careful not to overbake, as they will be hard-cooked with firm yolks after 15 minutes. Runny yolks are essential to this dish. Using tongs, remove the ramekin from the water. Place the ramekin on a plate and serve hot. Eat straight from the ramekin with a spoon and serve with crostini to dip into the egg, or unmold the egg on toast points.

- *Roasting pan or baking dish*
- *Ramekin or small ovenproof dish (such as a Pyrex custard cup)*
- *Medium skillet*
- *Tongs*

Olive oil, plus extra for the ramekin

½ shallot, sliced

½ teaspoon cumin seeds, crushed with a mortar and pestle or with a skillet

½ teaspoon coriander seeds, crushed with a mortar and pestle or with a skillet

¼ cup diced tomatoes, fresh or canned

Pinch of ground cardamom

Pinch of garlic powder, or a few grates of fresh garlic (use a Microplane)

Harissa or hot sauce (optional)

1 large egg

Fine sea salt and freshly ground black pepper

Crostini (page 60) or toast, for serving

Oeufs en Cocotte with Moroccan Tomatoes

Shakshuka, or eggs poached in spiced tomato sauce on top of the stove, is one of my go-to breakfast dishes. This single-serve *en cocotte* variation is even better, as you can control the risk factors of an inconsistent oven. I make this dish as a first course for dinner parties; the warm seasonings are an appetite teaser. SERVES 1, SCALE UP AS NEEDED

1. Preheat the oven to 350°F. Place the roasting pan in the oven and pour in enough hot water to come about halfway up the sides. Heat the filled pan for 5 minutes.

2. Lightly oil a 4-ounce ramekin. Heat a splash of the oil in a skillet over medium-low heat. Add the shallot and cook, stirring often, until tender, about 5 minutes. Add the cumin and coriander and allow them to bloom (release their aromas) for 2 minutes. Add the tomatoes and bring to a simmer. Cook until the juices thicken slightly, about 5 minutes. Stir in the cardamom, garlic powder, and harissa, if using. Cook to blend the flavors for about 1 minute more. Spoon into the ramekin, make a well for the egg with the back of a spoon, and crack in the egg, being careful not to break the yolk. Season with salt and pepper.

3. Bake until the egg whites are set, 10 to 13 minutes. Check at 10 minutes to see if they need more time. Be careful not to overbake, as they will be hard-cooked with firm yolks after 15 minutes. Runny yolks are essential to this dish. Using tongs, remove the ramekin from the water. Place the ramekin on a plate and serve hot. Eat straight from the ramekin with a spoon and serve with crostini or toast.

GALETTES FOR ALL SEASONS

The South of France is defined by *rustic elegance*. And nothing feels more elegantly rustic than a galette. In France, a galette is one of two things: 1) a pancake or 2) a round-ish, free-form tart that is frequently made at home, but can occasionally be found in restaurants.

There are endless variations, and they are a year-round thing and served as a savory starter, perfect for *l'apéro*. Or as a gorgeous main course with a side salad. They can also be a perfect dessert.

I have included a few galette recipes and here are general guidelines for making an ideal galette that will enable you to make almost any variation:

- **A HOT OVEN:** Preheat the oven to 425°F (or the temperature recommended on store-bought dough).

- **PASTRY:** I recommend the Flaky Buttery Pastry on page 72. But you can also use thawed frozen puff pastry, refrigerated pie dough, or even refrigerated croissant dough (the kind in a can). It should be rolled into a 10-inch round about ½ inch thick. You may have to trim it into shape, or keep it in a square if that is more convenient.

- **A HALF-SHEET PAN, LINED WITH PARCHMENT PAPER:** You need a rimmed baking sheet to hold your dough and to prevent the filling's juices from leaking into your oven. Parchment paper will guard against sticking.

- **FILLING:** Cooked fillings should be cool, if not chilled before they are spread in the pastry, leaving a 2-inch border. Raw fillings can just be added directly, but beware of super wet fillings—they can create soppy pastry.

- **GLAZE, OR NOT:** For the crispiest pastry border, beat an egg well and brush it on in a thin glaze before baking. I do not always do this. It's nice but not critical. Usually, the high heat of the oven provides the right color and texture on its own without any glaze, so I consider it an optional step.

- **A QUICK, HOT BAKE:** Bake for 35 minutes, or until golden brown.

Almost anything, sweet or savory, can be a potential galette filling. Here are a few ideas:

- **HARICOTS VERTS AND MUSHROOMS GALETTE:** Repurpose leftovers of the side dish on page 276 as a galette. For a real beauty, top with a poached egg.

- **CARROT-HUMMUS GALETTE:** Toss 2 or 3 narrow carrots, cut into thin rounds, with 1 teaspoon honey, a squeeze of lemon juice, and a drizzle of olive oil in a small bowl. Spread about 1 cup of hummus (perhaps the Roasted Beet Hummus with Cumin on page 83) on the pastry round. Scatter the carrots over the hummus, leaving any liquid behind in the bowl. Finish with flaky salt, pepper (if you must), and a smattering of fresh thyme leaves.

- **BOEUF BOURGUIGNON GALETTE:** Mix about 1 cup of leftover braised beef (see page 253) with ¼ cup of crème fraîche or sour cream, top with salt and pepper, and spoon into a galette. When it emerges from the oven, garnish it with a few sprigs of fresh thyme leaves and a hit of lemon zest.

- **MUSHROOM GALETTE:** Use leftover Mushroom Carpaccio with Sumac and Olive Oil (page 144) as the topping (you need at least a cup, and it needs to be drained of excess dressing/liquid), and the seasoned mascarpone from the Ratatouille Galette on page 75.

- **CHÈVRE AND OLIVE GALETTE:** The Bubbling Baked Chèvre and Olive Spread on page 84 makes a terrific galette. You'll need about ½ cup.

- **KUMQUAT AND POMEGRANATE GALETTE:** Spread the ricotta base from the Citrus Galette on page 76 onto the pastry, and top with 1 cup of the relish from page 273.

- **FIGGY GALETTE:** Spread with about ½ cup Figgy, Dippy, Jammy Spread on page 92, top with about a dozen halved figs, and a ½ cup crumbled feta or goat cheese.

- **PISSALADIÈRE-STYLE GALETTE:** Pissladière is a famous onion and olive tart and a Provençal specialty. Cut 5 yellow onions into thin half-moons. Heat a good glug of olive oil in a large nonstick skillet. Season with salt and pepper. Add the onions and cook over medium-low heat, stirring occasionally, until they are very tender, and caramelize to golden brown, about 40 minutes. Cool completely. As your base, spread ¼ cup Dijon mustard and ½ cup of My Tapenade (page 103) on the pastry, and top with the cooled onions. Add as many white or canned anchovy fillets as you like. Bake.

- **WHITE BEAN AND FENNEL GALETTE:** Spread White Bean Dip (page 101) on the pastry, then top with a couple of handfuls of shaved fennel and thinly sliced onion.

- **ZUCCHINI BLOSSOMS GALETTE:** Use about 1 dozen Stuffed Zucchini Blossoms (page 130) for the base. Top with about 6 chopped zucchini blossoms and sprinkle with shelled pumpkin seeds (pepitas).

Cherry Tomato Tarte Tatin
with Balsamic Glaze
page 161

Ratatouille Galette
page 75

Citrus Galette
page 76

MISE EN PLACE
- *Medium bowl*
- *Large fork*
- *Glass measuring cup
  with ice water*
- *Rolling pin*

1½ cups (3 sticks) cold salted butter

3½ cups all-purpose flour

½ cup ice water, as needed

Flaky Buttery Pastry

I like pastry to be buttery, flaky, and a bit salty, which is not French-traditional. You can substitute unsalted butter, if you prefer, but then you'll miss out on the flavor lift that salt always brings to the table, even with sweet dishes. I double or triple this recipe and freeze individual disks of about 5 inches across, and 1½ inch thick or so. This means I always have pastry on hand. You'll be glad you have it when you want to turn leftovers into galettes or whip up a quick dessert. **MAKES 3 PASTRY DISKS**

1. Cut the butter into ½-inch cubes. Place on a plate and freeze for 5 to 10 minutes so it is quite cold.

2. Sift the flour into a bowl, or simply it pour in and whisk it to add some loftiness. Add the butter and toss to coat the cubes. Using your fingertips, rub the butter into the flour mixture, occasionally letting it "rain" between your fingers, until it resembles coarse breadcrumbs with some pea-size bits of butter. (These bits are the secret to flaky pastry—don't let the mixture get too finely textured.)

3. Stirring with a large fork, gradually stir in enough of the ice water until the dough clumps together. You may need more or less water. Gather up the dough in the bowl and press into a ball.

4. Transfer the dough to a lightly floured surface. Cut the dough into three equal pieces. Shape each piece into a thick disk and wrap in plastic wrap or waxed paper. Refrigerate for at least 30 minutes or up to 1 hour. Use the dough chilled, but not rock hard.

5. The dough can be double-wrapped in more plastic wrap and frozen for up to 3 months. Thaw in the refrigerator overnight and let stand at room temperature for about 10 minutes before rolling out. When the dough cracks during rolling out, it is usually because the dough is too cold. Let it stand for a few minutes, and try again.

- *Half-sheet pan*
- *Parchment paper*
- *Mandoline*
- *Small bowl*
- *Medium bowl*
- *Serving platter*

1 narrow eggplant, about 1 pound, sliced into thin rounds about ¼-inch thick

3 medium zucchini, cut into ¼-inch rounds

Fine sea salt or kosher salt

⅓ cup (¼-inch dice) ripe, fresh diced tomatoes, or use canned drained

1 tablespoon herbes de Provence

2 garlic cloves, grated on a microplane

Freshly ground black pepper

8 ounces (1 cup) mascarpone cheese, at room temperature

1 disk (one-third of recipe) Flaky Buttery Pastry (page 72)

All-purpose flour for rolling the pastry

Extra-virgin olive oil

1 small, bell pepper, seeded and very thinly sliced, for garnish

Ratatouille Galette

Here is another way to use the beloved Provençal trio of eggplant, tomatoes, and zucchini, this time encased in pastry as a galette. You won't have any trouble thinking of when to serve this beauty—brunch, lunch, *l'apéro*, or dinner. . . . It is welcome any time. SERVES 4 TO 6

1. Preheat the oven to 425°F. Line a half-sheet pan with parchment paper.

2. Toss the eggplant and zucchini with a few hearty pinches of salt in a medium bowl or colander over a sink, and let stand for about 30 minutes to draw out some juices. Rinse the vegetables under cold water and pat dry with paper towels.

3. In a small bowl, mix the diced tomatoes with the herbes de Provence, garlic, and a pinch of salt and pepper. Season the mascarpone with salt and pepper.

4. On a lightly floured surface, roll out the pastry into a 10-inch round about ⅛ inch thick. Transfer the pastry to the prepared pan. Spread the mascarpone in a round on the pastry, leaving a 2- to 3-inch border. Reserving 2 tablespoons for finishing, scatter the tomatoes on top, and swirl them in.

5. Overlap the eggplant and zucchini rounds, working in a spiral from the outside in, beginning with the larger rounds and working down to the smaller ones. I generally use 2 or 3 zucchini rounds followed by 1 slice of eggplant. Brush the vegetables with oil.

6. Bake until the pastry is golden brown, 30 to 35 minutes. Slide the galette off the pan onto a serving platter. Scatter the raw bell pepper and reserved tomatoes on top for a splash of fresh color. Serve hot, warm, or cooled to room temperature.

- Half-sheet pan, lined with parchment paper
- Small bowl

8 ounces (1 cup) ricotta, preferably whole milk

1 tablespoon honey

Finely grated zest of 1 small lemon

Pinch of fine sea salt

½ teaspoon fresh lemon juice (optional)

Flour for rolling out the dough

1 disk (one-third of recipe) Flaky Buttery Pastry (page 72)

1 pound of mixed citrus (oranges, blood oranges, lemons, limes, grapefruit), peeled, cut into ¼-inch rounds

1 teaspoon raw sugar

1 teaspoon confectioners' sugar (optional)

Citrus Galette

This galette works with any citrus. It can be made throughout the year, but it is especially welcome in the winter when citrus is at its peak and good berries are nowhere to be found. The best combination is a mix of citrus, some sweeter than others, such as lemons, limes, and oranges. While it is great unaccompanied, you can also serve it with the Not-Too-Sweet Whipped Cream on page 59. Thank goodness for small miracles!
SERVES 6

1. Preheat the oven to 425°F. Line a half-sheet pan with parchment paper.

2. In a small bowl, mix the ricotta, honey, and lemon zest with a pinch of salt. For a touch more acidity, add the lemon juice, if desired.

3. On a lightly floured surface, roll out the pastry into a 10-inch round about ⅛ inch thick. Transfer the pastry to the prepared sheet pan. Spread the ricotta in a round on the pastry, leaving a 2- to 3-inch border. Arrange the citrus rounds in a beautiful pattern that strikes your eye, but try to avoid overlapping the rounds. Sprinkle with the raw sugar.

4. Bake until the pastry is golden brown and the citrus edges are beginning to brown, 30 to 35 minutes. Slide the galette off the pan onto a serving platter. Sift the confectioners' sugar on top (if using). Serve hot, warm, or cooled to room temperature.

CHAPTER 4
L'APÉRO!

Sundays are my favorite days. That's when our guests arrive at La Peetch. They pull in from the Nice airport around 3:00 p.m., and for the next three hours, we welcome them with what else? local specialties and plenty of wine.

One by one, platters arrive on the patio. First, there's a charcuterie board piled high with sausages, Alpine dried hams surrounded by plump fresh figs plucked from our trees, and olives—briny and hard, wrinkly and salty, in every shade of green, brown, and black-blue.

There are creamy mushroom pâtés, pork terrines, and our own Chicken Liver Mousse with Pickled Shallots (page 87). A parade of spicy seed-specked mustards adorns our table. You might say we have a fetish; we never leave a new market without a jar of . . . something.

The pièce de résistance is the cheese board: we have at least eight different cheeses, from cave-aged Roquefort to Époisses, a cheese so pungent that my cheesemonger calls it a cheese that moves as it melts out of its wine-washed rind. Sometimes we pick up a sharp aged cheddar sent

over from the UK. And finally, we never forget a tangy silky chèvre—from the goat farm just down the road, so fresh it still tastes of fresh cut grass.

And depending on the season: ripe fruit tarts, stone fruit sticky with ricotta; and of course tangy slow-fermented breads and fresh-from-the-vine whirred Dairy-Free Tomato "Cream" with Basil (page 162).

L'apéro is a way of life, even if it's not nearly as elaborate as the spread I just described.

I have included some seasonal apéro favorites on the following pages. A few caveats, though—because, well, I am still an American in many ways—I take what I love from the French while espousing my own American flair here and there. For example, my apéro is often the *entire dinner*, not just the starter to the dinner.

Also, I've added cheese boards, because in my world of *l'apéro*, cheese is always on the menu. This is a catastrophic misstep in the eyes of the French, who prefer their cheese after dinner. I like cheese before the meal, like a typical American cocktail hour.

- *Parchment paper*
- *Roasting pan or half-sheet pan*
- *Blender*
- *Spatula*
- *Serving bowl*
- *Microplane*

1 (14-ounce) can chickpeas (garbanzo beans), drained, liquid (aquafaba) reserved

1 small beet, cooked according to the instructions for Whole Roasted Beets (page 212)

¼ cup tahini

1 lemon, juiced and zested

1 teaspoon ground cumin, plus extra for serving

2 garlic cloves, crushed and peeled

Fine sea salt

Olive oil for garnish

Crostini (page 60), for serving

Roasted Beet Hummus with Cumin

One of the best parts about being on the French Mediterranean is the marriage of French and Mediterranean flavors and dishes. You can't leave a grocery store without seeing hummus or other dips in the take-out aisle. But, unlike in North American markets, there isn't a lot of variety. So, I have become adept at making hummus in many iterations. You might want to reserve a roasted beet from the recipe on page 212 to make this.
MAKES ABOUT 2 CUPS

1.   Purée the chickpeas, beet, tahini, lemon juice, cumin, and garlic in a blender. Once it comes together, add a pinch or two of salt, then the aquafaba, a tablespoon at a time, until the texture resembles a thick sour cream. Taste and adjust the seasoning with more salt or lemon juice.

2.   Transfer to a serving bowl. Top with a pinch of ground cumin, a swirl of olive oil, and a bit of lemon zest. Serve with crostini or eat it with a spoon. I've done it all!

MISE EN PLACE

- *Small, deep, round flameproof casserole dish, about 1 quart capacity, or a small ovenproof skillet*
- *Spoon or spatula*

Olive oil

2 small shallots, minced

2 garlic cloves, grated

2 cups cherry tomatoes

1 teaspoon dried thyme

1 teaspoon dried basil

Juice of ½ lemon

1 cup pitted kalamata olives, cut in halves

8 ounces soft, rindless chèvre cheese

Crostini (page 60) or bread sticks

Bubbling Baked Chèvre and Olive Spread

When I lived in San Antonio, I frequented an Italian restaurant that served a version of this dip. I never really thought about this dip again until I moved to France. Then I started craving it because . . . well . . . chèvre is abundant here. I crafted a version of this dip to make it very Provençal, easy, fast, and, of course, highly munchable. You might even end up eating it all yourself before putting it on the table. Not saying I've done that. . . . SERVES 4 TO 6

1. Preheat the oven to 425°F. In the casserole dish, heat a glug of olive oil over medium heat. Add the shallots and cook until softened, about 5 minutes, add the garlic, and let cook until fragrant, about 3 minutes. We're looking to add some color here. The bitterness that a bit of char lends provides a nice balance to the sweet tomatoes.

2. Add the tomatoes, thyme, basil, and lemon juice, and increase the heat a bit. The goal here is to encourage the tomatoes to burst without burning, give off some juices, and then allow about one-fourth of the tomato liquid to evaporate. Cook for about 15 minutes, or until you've achieved jammy tomato magic. Fold in the olives and remove from the heat.

3. Nestle or crumble the chèvre on top of the olive mixture. Bake until bubbling, about 10 minutes. Serve hot with crostini or bread sticks, and share with others . . . if you want to.

- Medium bowl
- Wooden spoon
- Large skillet
- Blender, preferably high-power, or a food processor
- Wire sieve
- Silicone or rubber spatula
- Electric mixer or whisk
- Small bowl
- Small (2- to 4-ounce) ramekins, small bowls, or small jars for serving (You can also serve this in one dish, but it's not as pretty and doesn't keep quite as well)

FOR THE MOUSSE

1 pound chicken livers, rinsed and drained

Whole milk, as needed

Olive oil

6 shallots, finely sliced

2 garlic cloves, grated

¼ cup sherry, brandy, or port

¼ cup peeled, cored, and chopped quince or Granny Smith apple

5 sprigs fresh thyme or savory, or 1 to 2 sprigs fresh rosemary

5 dried bay leaves

10 to 12 juniper berries, coarsely crushed (optional)

¼ teaspoon ground mace, could substitute nutmeg

¾ cup (1½ sticks) salted butter, at room temperature, cut into tablespoons

Fine sea salt and freshly ground black pepper

¾ cup heavy cream

ingredients continue

Chicken Liver Mousse with Pickled Shallots

Chicken liver is not the cocktail party must-have in North America the way that it is in France. But I urge you to give this a shot. It is buttery and light, with a mousse-like texture. The soaking process mellows the liver and makes this more accessible to offal resisters. It calls for tart quince, but the mousse won't suffer if you use Granny Smith apples.

SERVES 6 TO 8

1. **MAKE THE MOUSSE:** Trim any excess white tissue from the livers, leaving the deep red parts. Place the trimmed livers in a medium bowl, and pour in milk to cover. Refrigerate for at least 10 minutes or up to overnight. This will mellow some of the strong liver flavor.

2. Heat a glug of olive oil in a skillet over medium heat. Add the shallots and cook for 5 to 8 minutes until they are tender, deeply colored, and even burnished in some places. Stir in the garlic and let it cook until fragrant without browning, 2 to 3 minutes. Pour in the sherry and stir with a wooden spoon to scrape up any browned bits in the skillet. Stir in the quince, herb sprigs, bay leaves, juniper berries, if using, and mace. Bring to a simmer and cook to blend the flavors, about 3 minutes.

3. Strain the livers, discarding the milk. Add the livers to the skillet. Cook, uncovered, until the livers show no sign of pink when pierced with the tip of a small sharp knife, about 10 minutes. Discard the herb sprigs and bay leaves.

4. Strain the mixture remaining in the skillet through a sieve over a bowl, reserving the cooking liquid. Allow the liver mixture to cool until warm, and then transfer it to a blender. With the machine running, add the butter, 1 tablespoon at a time, and process until very, very smooth. If the blender is struggling, add a bit of the cooking liquid to thin it out. The mixture should be thick and creamy. Season with salt and pepper.

5. Using a silicone spatula, rub the mixture through a wire sieve into a bowl to eliminate any unblended bits.

6. Whip the cream in a chilled bowl with an electric mixer at high speed until stiff peaks form. Fold the liver mixture into the cream. Stir slowly, so as to not lose too much loft from the cream.

recipe continues

FOR THE PICKLED SHALLOTS

3 shallots, sliced

1 teaspoon sumac

1 teaspoon yellow mustard seeds

½ cup red wine vinegar, as needed

Baguette slices or Crostini (page 60), for serving

7. Divide among ramekins or small jars. Cover and refrigerate until chilled and firm, at least 1 hour. (The mousse can be refrigerated for up to 2 days or frozen for a month.)

8. **MAKE THE PICKLED SHALLOTS:** Place the shallots in a small bowl with the sumac and mustard seeds, and cover with the vinegar. Let stand uncovered for at least 30 minutes. (The shallots and liquid can be transferred to a covered container and refrigerated for a couple of weeks.)

9. Serve the mousse chilled, with the pickled shallots, and baguette for spreading with the mousse.

MISE EN PLACE
- Skillet
- Bowl
- Blender or food processor
- Serving bowl or ramekins
- Plastic wrap
- Plate

1 cup walnuts, plus extra finely chopped walnuts for garnish

Olive oil

3 shallots, sliced

1½ pounds virtually any variety mushrooms, although I prefer oyster or baby portobellos (cremini), coarsely chopped or torn

3 garlic cloves, grated

Fine sea salt

½ pound (2 sticks) unsalted butter, at room temperature

4 sprigs fresh herbs, such as rosemary, savory, or thyme, stems removed

Sherry vinegar (optional)

Freshly ground black pepper

Paprika, for garnish

Crackers or baguette slices, for serving

Mushroom Walnut Pâté

Every once in a while, I want a meat-free spread. And this is that magical thing. It tastes meaty and creamy, without either. I like it best in winter when mushrooms are abundant in the South of France. It can also be prepared vegan by substituting the butter for an oil-based, butter-like spread (e.g., margarine or other "vegan butter"). This makes a lot, but it is easier to process in a large amount, and it keeps very well, even frozen. Serve this with small toasts or crostini right from a serving bowl or in individual ramekins (unmolded or not). Or, if you're feeling fancy, prepare it in a loaf pan and unmold it onto a platter. MAKES 3 CUPS, SERVES 8 TO 12

1. Spread the walnuts in a cold skillet and heat over medium-high heat. Cook, tossing occasionally, until they take on some color, 5 to 7 minutes. Watch them carefully to avoid burning. Transfer to a bowl to cool completely.

2. Heat a glug of the olive oil in the same skillet over medium heat. Add the shallots and cook, stirring occasionally, until browned and even slightly charred (which does wonders here for the flavor), about 6 minutes. Add to the bowl with the walnuts.

3. Heat another glug of olive oil in the skillet over medium-high heat. Stir in the mushrooms, garlic, and a generous pinch of salt (this releases a bit more moisture, and too much moisture is the enemy of a good mushroom pâté). Cook, stirring infrequently, until the liquid evaporates, about 5 minutes more. Transfer to the bowl with the shallots and walnuts and let cool.

4. Transfer the mushroom mixture, butter, and herbs to a heavy-duty blender. Blend slowly at first, and once the mixture starts to come together, add the vinegar, if using. Then blend on high until very smooth, about 3 minutes. Season with salt and pepper. The pâté should be tangy. If you wish, blend in a little more vinegar, tasting as you go.

5. Transfer the pâté to a serving bowl or ramekins and cover with plastic wrap. Chill until set, at least 3 hours or overnight.

6. To mold the pâté, rinse a medium bowl, loaf pan, or individual ramekins with water, and line with plastic wrap. Drape the excess wrap hanging over the sides. Fill with the pâté, and cover with the plastic wrap. Chill until set, 3 hours or overnight (or about 2 hours for the ramekins). To unmold, pull back the wrap, place a plate, platter, or serving board over the vessel, and invert the bowl and base together to unmold the pâté. Remove the vessel and plastic.

7. Sprinkle with chopped walnuts and paprika and serve chilled with crackers.

- *Rimmed baking sheet*
- *Serving platter big enough to hold cheese, bread, and apples for dipping*

1 (450-g) round Mont d'Or or other washed-rind cheese, preferably in a wooden box (see headnote)

3 garlic cloves, sliced lengthwise into slivers

1 shallot, sliced into thin rounds

5 sprigs fresh rosemary and/or thyme

Dry white wine (optional)

FOR SERVING

Crusty bread, sliced or left whole for ripping apart at the table

Tart apples, such as Granny Smith, cut into wedges

Mont d'Or, aka Big Melty

Digging into a strikingly ripe, baked cheese elicits immediate glee. The Big Melty is prepared like fondue, without the fondue pot. At La Peetch, we use French or Swiss Mont d'Or, which comes in an adorable, rustic spruce box. We bake the cheese right in its container—it won't burn because wood combusts at over 500°F, and you'll be baking at a lower temperature.

Many excellent North American cheesemongers, such as Murray's, sell it online, and Jasper Hill, a terrific Vermont cheese farm, makes two soft cheeses that work well here, Harbison and Winnimere. Uplands Cheese, a farm in Wisconsin, makes Rush Creek Reserve, which is a near-duplication of Mont d'Or, preserved in a wooden ring rather than a box. Brie and Camembert also work well, and you can bake one of these, boxed or not, in a small Dutch oven or casserole that is about the same size as your cheese.

This can be served either as a to-share starter, an apéro snack, or as a meal. This recipe works well for dinner à deux, served with a crisp salad.

SERVES ABOUT 6

1.   Preheat the oven to 425°F. Remove any paper or wrapping from the cheese itself, and replace the cheese in the box, discarding the lid. Make small slits across the top of the cheese and stuff with the garlic, shallot, and rosemary, leaving the tops sticking out like you just planted a delicious garden.

2.   Place the dressed cheese onto a rimmed baking sheet and, if you want to go all out, drizzle 1 to 2 tablespoons of white wine over it. (The wine adds a nice bit of acidity to balance the rich cheese.) Bake for 45 minutes, or until the cheese is completely melted and bubbly.

3.   **TO SERVE:** Transfer the box of cheese to a platter. Surround it with the bread and apples for dipping. Eat the glistening, melted cheese heartily and directly from the container. Once melted, the cheese won't keep, so you might as well polish it off.

8 ounces slab bacon, rind removed, cut into strips (lardons) about 1 inch long and ¼ inch thick

1 medium yellow onion, minced

12 ounces fresh figs, such as Mission or Brown Turkey, quartered

1 sprig fresh rosemary or thyme

2 dried bay leaves (optional)

2 tablespoons honey

2 teaspoons balsamic vinegar

Fine sea salt and freshly ground black pepper

Figgy, Dippy, Jammy Spread

Is this a dip, a spread, a jam? Is it all three? Well, that depends on what temperature you serve it. Think of it as a savory dip if served hot, and a righteous jam/spread when served at room temperature or cold. La Pitchoune and my home in Grasse are full of fig trees, and I make this dippy, jammy beauty to raves all the time. Try it as a condiment with roast pork. MAKES ABOUT 2 CUPS, SERVES 8 TO 10

1. Spread the bacon in a cold medium saucepan and place over medium heat. This method slowly melts the bacon fat, adding more of its flavor to the jam. Cook for about 10 minutes, until the bacon is only about halfway to brown and crispy. Increase the heat to medium-high. The bacon should sizzle loudly but not pop.

2. Don't hover over the bacon. Give it time on each side until you have reached the three-quarters point (the bacon should just start to brown, but be nowhere near finished), 3 to 5 minutes. Pour off about half of the bacon fat into a small bowl and cool and refrigerate for another use.

3. Add the onion to the saucepan and cook, stirring occasionally, until it begins to brown, about 5 minutes. Stir in the figs, rosemary, and bay leaves, if using, and mix well until it is a mostly homogenous mixture.

4. Reduce the heat to medium-low and cook, stirring often, until the mixture has reduced by about half, 20 to 30 minutes. Stir in the honey and vinegar. Simmer, stirring often, until richly colored and a beautiful jammy consistency, 5 to 10 minutes more. Remove the rosemary and bay leaves and let cool. Season with salt and pepper. Serve warm or let cool completely.

CHARCUTERIE BOARDS

Building a beautiful charcuterie board does not have to be high touch. Nor does it have to be photograph worthy to be delicious. In fact the charcuterie boards can be and should be one of the best parts of a *l'apéro*. I approach them as deconstructed sandwiches.

My vision and mission when it comes to charcuterie? Craveable and approachable. My family and I love to play with the concept of a charcuterie board, and when it's just the three of us, we eat directly from the paper wrapping and straight from the jars. It makes for an expedited dinner.

- **MEATS (THE BOARD'S FOUNDATION):** In general, you want a minimum of three meat-based products on the board, even if you're only serving one person. One product isn't a board, it's just meat on a plate, two is in teasing territory, and with three we're in "three's a crowd" mode, which is not great for middle-school friendships but delightful when it comes to serving meat on a platter.

  When choosing the meat products to have on your board think about the following: texture (thinly sliced, thickly sliced, spreadable, creamy, etc.), flavors (some are smoked, some not, some have aromatics like fennel added), and type of meat (pork, beef, poultry, wild game). You could have three different pork products, such as pork pâté from France, Ibérico ham from Spain, and finocchiona from Italy—a fennel-based salami. They are all different in texture and flavor, even though they are made from the same type of meat. This contrast is what makes the board sing.

- **QUANTITY:** If what you're serving after *l'apéro* is on the heavier side, meaning you've got a few courses ahead of you or you invited people over before they head to another location for dinner—

you'll want about ¼ to ⅓ pound of meat total per person, about 8 slices of thinly sliced, cured deliciousness per person.

If your main course is on the lighter side—or your *l'apéro* is meant more to be the main event—you'll want to up that to about ½ pound (16 slices) total.

- **ACCOUTREMENTS:** Mustard—either in a ramekin or spooned straight onto the board—is always a welcome addition. Depending on what I have in my own pantry and what kinds of meat I am serving, I might have more than one mustard on the board or next to it. A quick Microplane of garlic with some salt as a spread brings a spicy note. Horseradish either full strength or mixed with some crème fraîche, provides the same bite. A sprinkle of flaked chiles will bring color and flavor.

  Cornichons or other pickled products (olives, sweet and sour pickles, chutneys) make a bright pairing with cured meats.

  Pairing meat with additional fats creates depth, which is where mayonnaise and butter can be the stars on your board. A drizzle of olive oil over an item or two is a fun addition.

  Beautiful garnishes can include fresh herbs and colorful spices. A rosemary sprig, a pinch of herbes de Provence, or a tiny bowl of spices lets people make their own herb butter.

- **BREAD, CROSTINI, AND CRACKERS:** There is no right or wrong. I prefer to have one crunchy thing (like a crostini or a cracker) and at least one softer bread.

  Breadsticks are always a crowd-pleaser as you can wrap thin meats around the sticks and dip them in the various things on the board.

CHEESE BOARDS

When it comes to constructing a cheese board, much of the philosophy for me is similar to that of a charcuterie board. One cheese isn't enough, two is a tease, and three is when you're starting to get into cheese board territory. Like charcuterie, we want to have variance in texture (creamy, soft, medium, hard), flavor (sweet, understated, strong, pungent), and the type of milk animal (cow, goat, sheep). You can also have fun with color.

- **CHOOSE A FEW CHEESES THAT LOOK NOTHING ALIKE:** Orange mimolette, Morbier with its gray line of ash, chèvre rolled in green herbs, or golden Comté, all contrasting with the bright white rind of a Brie or St.-André. I won't even read the labels until I've gotten the color difference out of the way.

- **CONSIDER DIFFERENT TEXTURES:** Make sure you are not buying only hard cheeses or only soft cheeses.

- **YOU WANT ABOUT 4 OUNCES OF CHEESE PER PERSON:** Cheesemongers will say that every piece of cheese that someone tastes should have the "full length" of that cheese in the serving size. They mean that the piece should have the rind (if edible) all the way to the middle of the cheese in the serving. Cheese changes flavor as you eat from the inside to the outside, or vice versa. I think this is key if you are

hosting a cheese tasting. But for a pre-dinner cheese board—where often guests will be found aimlessly hacking away at the cheese to eat it heartily and there is no chance in god's green earth that I will be able to mitigate the chaos—I throw that notion out the window.

Because no one wants to be chastised by the cheese czar at a party, and whoever is opening their home to friends frequently doesn't want to be said cheese czar.

- **CONSIDER THE CUT:** I serve cheese with one small wedge removed, which signals to guests that they are invited to eat it, and can cut their own wedge.

- **SERVING SUGGESTIONS:** Make sure any rind is facing toward the interior of the platter so that everyone has access to the cheeses and no one has to cross their arms weirdly over the center of the platter to access cheese.

- **ACCOUTREMENTS:** A cheese platter needs extras, especially nuts of any kind, honey and honeycomb (if you have it), sweet and savory jams (check out Figgy, Dippy, Jammy Spread on page 92), herbs and spices sprinkled directly on an item or placed into little mounds on the board, and fresh and dried fruit. All make great accoutrements for cheese boards.

VEGGIE CRUDITÉS

The most thrilling thing in the world to me? Alluring and resplendent bright crudités that will wow even your most particular guests.

There are three keys to a great crudités platter:

- **GORGEOUS PRODUCE:** I'm talking crunchy, colorful, begging to be consumed, adorable (if you can call a romanesco floret or baby carrot adorable, I sure can), rainbow-colored produce. You want variety, you want pretty, but it doesn't have to be fancy (whatever that means to you). The specifics and volume are up to you, but I like to think ¼ pound per person. And, if all you can find is a prepackaged bag of baby carrots or mixed vegetables, bring it on.·

- **BOARDS AND/OR BOWLS:** Presentation is key to very alluring crudités. I like to nestle all the produce into a large bowl (or a myriad small bowls) or place it all on a large wood board.

- **DIPS:** All these crudités need to be supported by a good dip (or three).

My approach is unfussy, but looks fussy. You can cut up the produce as much as you'd like, into whatever shapes you like, serve it as is, and there is no doing it wrong. You can pull together a plate like this in less than 5 minutes if you pre-buy the dips. Want to make three dips? We're moving into somewhat fussier territory.

But the good news is that the leftovers give you flavorful crunchy sides for a couple days. Or you can turn leftovers into Vinegar-Roasted Veggies (page 243).

White Bean
Dip, *page 101*

Ranch-y Dip
(and More),
page 102

- *Blender or food processor*
- *Microplane*
- *Serving bowl*

1 (12-ounce) can white beans, drained

1 cup loosely packed fresh herbs (tender or leafy herbs, such as mint, tarragon, chervil, parsley, chives, and cilantro are best, and use strong woody herbs like rosemary and thyme judiciously, about 1 teaspoon per cup)

¼ cup extra-virgin olive oil

1 tablespoon minced onion or shallot

Zest and juice of 1 lemon

Kosher salt

Freshly ground pepper

White Bean Dip

I love a good hummus, but in the name of variety, I often substitute white beans (cannellini or Great Northern) for the garbanzo beans. The approach is flexible, and focused on the using herbs and alliums you have on hand, especially those that need to be used before they expire. This dip should be nice and green and creamy. SERVES 6 TO 8, MAKES ABOUT 2 CUPS

1. Place the beans, herbs, oil, and onion in the blender. Start on low and begin to blend. Once it stops coughing, turn it up to medium. Turn off the machine and scrape down the sides every now and then.

2. Add half of the lemon zest and half of the juice to the blender. Whir in the blender another minute, or until creamy. Taste. The dip should be bright, lemony, and distinctly herbaceous. If you'd like it to be more lemony, add some more zest and juice. For a smoother texture, add water, a couple of tablespoons at a time, and blend until it is the creaminess you like. Season with salt and pepper and blend to combine. Serve warmish from the friction of the blender.

3. The dip can be refrigerated in a covered container for up to a week.

1 cup sour cream or plain Greek yogurt

½ cup mayonnaise (store-bought is fine)

Bunch of fresh chives, chopped very finely, about ⅓ cup

1 teaspoon garlic powder, or to taste

1 teaspoon kosher salt

Ranch-y Dip (and More)

I am often asked what I miss most about the United States. At first, the answer was always ranch dressing. For years, any American friend who made the trip across the pond to visit me would bring me a container of ranch. Eventually I devised my own version of something that tastes *remarkably* similar to use in different guises—dip, dressing, and marinade. I think garlic powder gives the dressing its ranchness, but you could substitute grated fresh garlic, if you prefer. Serve the dip with crudités, potato chips, or even on Fondant Potatoes (page 236). MAKES ABOUT 2 CUPS

Whisk together the sour cream, mayonnaise, chives, garlic powder, and salt in a medium bowl. The dip can be refrigerated in a covered container for up to 5 days.

HERBY RANCH DRESSING: This salad dressing is great atop any green salad, but especially the Herbaceous Bibb Salad with Parmesan Crisps and Dream Vinaigrette on page 143. Simply replace the ½ cup of the sour cream with ½ cup of buttermilk to make the dip more of a dressing, and proceed with the recipe. It can be refrigerated in a covered container for up to 1 week. Makes about 2 cups.

HERBY RANCH MARINADE: Here the dressing is transformed into a marinade that gives a spicy deliciousness to any meat when marinated and refrigerated for at least 4 hours and preferably overnight. Whisk together 1 quart buttermilk, 1 cup sour cream, and 1 bunch fresh chives, minced (about ⅔ cup), in a large bowl. Add 2 teaspoons garlic powder and 2 teaspoons fine sea salt and whisk well. Reserve 1 cup to use as a baste during grilling. Makes about 5 cups.

My Tapenade

MISE EN PLACE

- *Blender*
- *Serving bowl*

2 cups drained oil-packed sun-dried tomatoes, with oil reserved

2 cups pitted kalamata olives

1 teaspoon capers

3 anchovies, oil packed

Crostini (page 60) or crackers, for serving

When I was in college, there was a gourmet grocery store just over the Connecticut River from campus called Bread & Circus, which was a Whole Foods–type place before that chain became an international behemoth. I fell in love with Bread & Circus's very pricey tapenade. It was garlicky, rich with olives and sun-dried tomatoes, salty, and smooth. Eventually, I became so addicted to it that I had to figure out how to make my own for the sake of convenience and economy. This is not the traditional Provençale tapenade, which can have ingredients such as capers, mustard, lemon juice, garlic, crushed red pepper, and mashed anchovies. But this four-ingredient version is delicious and whips up in no time. SERVES 8, ABOUT 3 CUPS

Process the tomatoes, olives, capers, and anchovies together in a blender or food processor until puréed. Drizzle in the reserved oil until you reach your ideal texture. That's it. Serve at room temperature with crostini or crackers. The tapenade can be refrigerated in a covered container for up to 2 weeks.

4 cups baby arugula

¼ cup extra-virgin olive oil

Juice and zest of 1 lemon

Flaky salt

Freshly ground black pepper

24 Crostini (page 60)

2 garlic cloves, peeled

3 (3.5 ounce) containers white anchovies (boquerones), marinated in oil, about 24 fillets

Anchovy and Arugula Toasts

Anchovy-lovers will be thrilled with these simple toasts, or miniature tartines (French open-faced sandwiches), that take less than 15 minutes from start to finish. I am especially fond of boquerones, the white Spanish anchovy fillets found refrigerated at specialty shops. If you don't like these "gourmet" anchovies, go for the standard oil-packed canned ones, or even sardines. **SERVES 6 TO 8, MAKES ABOUT 24 TOASTS**

1. Toss the arugula, oil, and lemon juice in a bowl. Season with salt and pepper and toss again.

2. Rub the crostini with a garlic clove for a breath or two. Top each one with a small pile of arugula and follow with a few anchovy fillets. Garnish with the lemon zest over the top, and add a pinch of flaky salt. Serve fairly soon after making so the crostini stay crisp.

MISE EN PLACE

- *Roasting pan*
- *Spatula*
- *Serving bowl*

2 pounds cherry tomatoes or grape (other types work, too, but the smallest sizes will get beautifully jammy)

Zest of 1 lemon, removed in strips with a vegetable peeler

4 to 8 garlic cloves, peeled

5 sprigs fresh rosemary, thyme, or savory (a mix is lovely), or ½ teaspoon dried

¼ cup olive oil

Fine sea salt

Freshly ground black pepper to taste

Chile flakes (optional)

24 Crostini (page 60)

Roasted Cherry Tomato "Jam"

As the summer winds down, and fall descends on Provence, we sadly have to say goodbye to summer tomatoes. It's warm enough for a few heirlooms to stick around through fall, but the cherry tomatoes are the first to droop and wrinkle. These last-gasp tomatoes are great slow roasted and transformed into an irresistible spread perfect for schmearing onto crostini for a bruschetta or just in a bowl as a dip. It is also an umami-rich addition to soups (such as the Roasted Fresh Tomato Soup with Grilled Cheese on page 224), sauces, and tarts (try it in the Ratatouille Galette on page 75). **SERVES 6 TO 8, MAKES ABOUT 2 CUPS**

1. Preheat the oven to 275°F. Spread the tomatoes in a roasting pan and scatter the lemon zest, garlic, and rosemary on top. Drizzle with the oil, toss to coat, and sprinkle evenly with a few pinches of salt.

2. Bake, stirring occasionally, until the tomatoes have burst and turned into a jammy concoction with reduced, sticky juices, about 2 hours. Let cool. Remove the lemon zest and rosemary sprigs, or keep them in the jam as garnishes. Season with salt and pepper. Serve with crostini.

3. The jam can be refrigerated in a covered container for up to 1 week. Serve at room temperature.

6 ripe plums, pitted

Ground allspice

Sparkling wine, preferably prosecco

Fresh thyme leaves for garnish

Plum and Thyme Bellinis

I frequently adjust summer recipes for cooler weather cooking, and vice versa. Bellinis are always a delicious cocktail, especially in the drippy heat of August, when peaches explode from the trees. Later, when plums start to arrive, and fall's kiss of cool arrives, I am ready for this version, which is made with the flowers of wild thyme that come in the fall.

This recipe uses a 750-milliliter bottle of sparkling wine. Assuming one per person, that is six servings. But . . . I will not make these assumptions for you. Your math on cocktails is your business. **SERVES 6**

1. Purée the plums with a tiny pinch of allspice in a blender. This should take about a minute. Pour through a wire sieve into a bowl to remove the skins.

2. For each serving, add about 1 teaspoon purée into a champagne flute. Fill each with sparkling wine. Add a thyme sprig and serve immediately. Reserve the remaining purée for another use; it will keep in the refrigerator for about 2 days. Try it with your morning yogurt or over vanilla ice cream.

- *Saucepan*
- *Sieve*
- *Punch bowl*

½ cup packed fresh lemon verbena leaves, or 6 lemon verbena tisane bags

½ cup dried hibiscus flowers

1 (12- to 16-ounce) bag frozen raspberries (the frozen berries make the punch cold; if you use fresh and add ice cubes, the drink will be diluted)

2 cups chilled sparkling water (increase to 4 cups for nonalcoholic punch)

2 cups chilled lemon-lime soda (increase to 4 cups for nonalcoholic punch)

1 (750-ml) bottle chilled vodka or gin (optional)

5 citrus fruits, such as oranges, lemons, or limes, in any combination, cut into thin rounds or suprêmes (see page 34)

Hibiscus Verbena Punch

When it comes to clear spirits, I almost always pick gin. But this vodka and verbena punch is a keeper, and it is just as good with gin, or booze-free as a fancy little mocktail. However you enjoy it, it is a worthy addition to your warmer days. Its beautiful magenta color is too good to miss, so skip the red party cups for this one, and make the effort to serve in clear glasses. SERVES 12 TO 18, MAKES ABOUT 3 QUARTS

1. Bring 2 quarts of water to a boil in a large saucepan. Remove from the heat. Add the verbena and hibiscus flowers, stir, and steep for 30 minutes. Transfer to the fridge for at least 1 hour or up to overnight. You want the infused base to be very cold.

2. Pour the raspberries into a punch bowl. Strain the hibiscus/verbena mixture through a wire sieve straight into the bowl. Add the sparkling water and soda and stir gently. Add the vodka, if using, and then the citrus. Ladle into clear glasses over ice.

- *Ice cube trays*
- *Beer (pilsner) glass*

About 1 (12-ounce) bottle raspberry lambic (or other fruity lambic flavor of choice; fruit beers are not an equivalent)

4 to 6 (12-ounce) bottles chilled white beer (witbier), preferably a cloudy variety, such as Hoegaarden or Allagash White

Witbier with Raspberry Lambic Ice Cubes

When I was in college, my favorite place to study was the Bookmill, a used bookstore with the motto "Books you don't need in a place you can't find." It's hidden in an old grist mill above the Sawmill River in Montague, Massachusetts. The Lady Killigrew Café on the store's lower level was my respite. This cocktail is adapted from one of their old summer specials. Pale ale is a good substitute for the witbier. Lambics are pretty easy to find at most decent liquor stores; they are heavy Belgian fruit beers. In lieu of lambic ice cubes, you can make raspberry purée and freeze it. SERVES 6, DEPENDING ON THE AMOUNT OF ICE CUBES USED

1. The day before you plan to serve these, pour enough lambic to fill two ice trays and freeze overnight. Alcohol slows down the freezing process, so you'll want to give them plenty of time to freeze, I tend to freeze them overnight. If you're struggling to freeze them (some freezers aren't quite cold enough), try adding 2 ounces water to help dilute the lambic.

2. Add 4 to 6 lambic ice cubes to a tall beer glass. Gradually pour in the witbier. Serve immediately.

Pink-Swirled Margaritas

MISE EN PLACE
- Blender, preferably heavy-duty
- Wire sieve
- Small bowl
- 4 margarita glasses, simple cocktail glasses, or stemless wineglasses
- 1 small plate, for the salt

6 prickly pears, peeled, or
½ cup prickly pear purée, or 1 cup pomegranate arils, raspberries, or strawberries

4 cups ice cubes

1 cup fresh lime juice (about 6 limes, hulls reserved)

¼ cup fresh orange juice (1 large orange)

8 ounces blanco tequila or silver

1 to 2 ounces triple sec, preferably Cointreau

Honey, as needed

½ cup flaky or kosher salt, as needed

One of my (many) favorite things about Bramafam is that prickly pear cacti grow well in our challenging clay soil. Come the end of February, we have abundant prickly pear fruit. If you can't find prickly pear, pomegranate juice will work well in this recipe, as will raspberry or strawberry purée. You can make it without alcohol easily; just double the citrus juices. SERVES 4

1. Blend the prickly pears for 30 seconds. The seeds will remain whole. Pour the purée through a wire sieve into a bowl and discard the seeds. (You should have about ½ cup purée.)

2. Process the ice, lime juice, and orange juice in the blender on high speed for 10 to 15 seconds, until slushy. (If using a standard blender, make in batches.) Add the tequila and triple sec and blend until combined, about 15 seconds. Add as much honey as you like, and process to blend.

3. Spread the salt on a small plate. Cut the reserved lime hulls in half and run the flesh side around the rim of each glass. Then turn the glasses upside down into the salt so that the rim picks up the salt.

4. Pour the margarita mixture into the glasses, leaving a ½-inch gap at the top of the glass. Spoon a few tablespoons of the purée on top of each and swirl it in so it creates a dazzling ripple effect. Serve immediately.

MISE EN PLACE
- *Saucepan*
- *Pitcher*
- *Ice for pitcher*
- *Highball or wineglasses*

6 ounces bourbon or rye

2 cinnamon sticks, or 1 teaspoon ground cinnamon

½ vanilla bean, split lengthwise, or 2 teaspoons vanilla extract

2 green apples, unpeeled and cored

2 oranges, preferably blood oranges

Arils (seeds) from 1 pomegranate

1 (750-milliliter) bottle of fruity red wine, such as Merlot or a blended red wine

Anytime Spiced Sangria

When I think of sangria, I think of summer patios and ice cubes. But even when the weather is cool, I still want a cold drink that is also delightfully spiced and iced. After a fair amount of trial and error, I landed on a bourbon-based, red wine sangria. It's fast, it's yummo, and it's simple and great all year round. **MAKES 4 AMPLE GLASSES OF SANGRIA**

1. Heat the bourbon in a medium saucepan over medium-low heat until it is steaming. Remove from the heat. Add the cinnamon and vanilla and steep for 10 minutes.

2. Slice the apples and oranges horizontally into rounds of varying diameters. Set aside 4 apple rounds, 8 orange rounds, and half of the pomegranate arils for garnish. Place the remaining fruit in a large serving pitcher.

3. Add the wine and bourbon mixture to the pitcher and stir with a wooden spoon to knock some juice out of the fruit.

4. In each wineglass, place 1 reserved apple round, 2 orange rounds, and 1 tablespoon or so of pomegranate arils. Add a couple of ice cubes. Fill each glass with the sangria.

- *Lowball (old-fashioned) cocktail glass*
- *Cocktail muddler or wooden spoon*

1 thick slice blood orange, peeled

Ice cubes

2 ounces gin

Tonic water, preferably Fever-Tree

1 sprig fresh rosemary

Blood Orange Gin and Tonic

I didn't know it when I moved here, but gin is the spirit of the Mediterranean. It was a happy surprise: I love gin and come from a family of gin drinkers. I learned that the main reason for the vast selection of gin is the abundance in the area of incredible citrus fruits, which makes for some darn good gin. You can use any gin in this cocktail, and if you can get your hands on Fever-Tree tonic, I recommend it. It's less sugary than most tonics and has a lovely, complete flavor. MAKES 1 DRINK

1. Take the naked blood orange round, and place it at the bottom of a glass. Muddle it a bit with a wooden spoon. You want it to hold its shape, but release enough juice that it actually gives the beverage tartness and a bit of a red hue.

2. Add ice cubes and pour in the gin. Fill to the brim with tonic water. Pop in the sprig of rosemary, and delight in the fact that you're imbibing the taste of summer with a cooler weather flavor profile.

PART TWO

Warmer Weather Recipes

I love big warmer weather meals: In spring, the air is fresh and dry and perfect for a long meal outside. The terrace at La Peetch is shaded by wisteria, which bursts to life in April and makes the spring meals even more idyllic. (We keep a watchful eye on the plants, though; it threatens to take over the roses and the nearby olive tree that Paul Child planted and obsessed over.)

A new vegetable appears each week at the market, while at home we are plucking strawberries off the vine and gathering zucchini blossoms to quick fry. Nasturtiums explode in a cacophony of pink, red, and orange and lend bright color and sweetness as a garnish to salads and other dishes; their leaves are edible, too, and add a peppery flavor.

The Riviera summer is a Technicolor season that deserves the romanticized, glamorous 1960's St. Tropez chic that is so often associated with the region. Summer is about playing by the shore, plunging in the pool, and drinking rosé all day. The Riviera begs to be experienced this way.

The summer sea air is hot and thick. Villages swell with life. There are blazing beach days, dripping Popsicles and sticky hands, and food trucks parked along the shore that serve sandwiches and ice-cold beverages to barefoot kids and adults alike at prices that don't shock the wallet. It is so humid that your glasses will fog moving from the oppressive heat into an air-conditioned shop where you might wander just to cool off (if you're lucky enough to find one with A/C, they are rare). In the late afternoon, refreshing swimming pools and the sea swell with humans—tucked into clear blue water before plopping down to nap on a plush chaise.

The most beautiful part of summer is the achingly long, relaxed and languorous days. The sun sets at nearly 11:00 p.m., which provides ample time for late-afternoon-into-evenings-bleeding-to-nearly-midnight parties. My approach to summer is especially loose.

I typically start meals indoors (with air-conditioning as my sidekick) and purée splashy gazpachos (pages 152 to 156) into a canvas of yellow, green, orange, and red. If I am hosting a gathering, I fill cocktail glasses with ice cubes as people arrive and scootch everyone outdoors. No one wants to stay in the air-conditioning in the late afternoon (except perhaps me), when we can relax in the shade of olive trees and dive into the shimmering mosaic pool. I stand nearby at the grill with zucchini and eggplant doused in olive oil and sprinkled with fresh herbs and seasoned with smoked salt; unhusked corn waiting to be covered in butter and fresh cracked pepper; spicy, succulent merguez and chipolata sausages from just down the road; marinated duck and beef; and spatchcocked chickens that friends dive into with aplomb.

If that doesn't invite you to sidle up to the picnic table, I am not sure what will.

CHAPTER 5

WARMER WEATHER STARTERS, SOUPS, SALADS, AND SIDES

1 cantaloupe, honeydew, or canary melon

2 tablespoons chiffonade of mint

2 teaspoons sumac (optional)

Flesh from ½ caviar lime, or juice from 1 lime

2 teaspoons flaky salt, preferably smoked

Freshly ground black pepper (optional)

Minted Melon

I grew up all over the United States—in California, Colorado, and the Northeast. Regardless of the region, on a good day, there were only three summertime melons at the typical grocery store. Watermelon (not technically a melon but rather a berry), cantaloupe, and honeydew. I was shocked when I moved to France and saw the vast array of available melons.

French melons come in many shapes, colors, and sizes and they are all just simply called melons. The most famous is called a Charentais melon. (It looks like a small cantaloupe and its aroma is distinctly more fruity, and is almost sugar-sweet.) It is sometimes also called by the town of its frequent origin, Cavaillon, not far from us. For this recipe, you can use any type of melon that has seeds in the center (so that leaves out watermelon). Spring for the very best melons of the season at your local produce stand. Caviar lime, if available at your local specialty produce store, is wonderful in this recipe. Inside its oblong green skin are tiny balls filled with tart juice. But regular lime wedges are fine. SERVES 6

1. Using a sharp knife, cut the melon into 6 wedges. Scoop out and discard the seeds. Cut the flesh of the melon from the rind keeping the round shape as much as possible. Discard the rind. Cut the melon into ½-inch pieces. Transfer to a large bowl.

2. Top with the mint, sumac, if using, and caviar lime, sprinkle with the salt, and add a few cracks of pepper, if using. Toss and serve.

- *Large saucepan*
- *Bowl of ice water*
- *Medium bowl*
- *Microplane*
- *Ring mold, for serving (optional)*
- *Serving plates*

8 ounces small red-skinned potatoes, scrubbed but unpeeled

Fine sea salt

8 ounces green beans, trimmed, and cut at an angle into ¼-inch lengths

½ cup pitted and coarsely chopped kalamata olives

1 shallot, minced

½ teaspoon chile flakes of choice, plus more for garnish

3 garlic cloves, finely grated

3 tablespoons olive oil

3 tablespoons soy sauce

6 cherry tomatoes, cut into quarters

Dash of red wine vinegar

1 tablespoon minced fresh parsley

1 teaspoon mashed black garlic flesh (optional)

1 pound sashimi-grade tuna

Freshly ground black pepper

1 lemon

Tuna Tartare

There are few things I enjoy on a hot sunny day more than tuna tartare. This one is bright and bold, with pops of warm-weather flavors. The classic French tuna tartare tends to lean into Asian-inspired flavors, and mine is no exception. But kalamata olives and red pepper flakes give this a Mediterranean nod, along with the notable Niçoise elements (like potato and green beans) that harken to the namesake salad (see page 178). When it comes to tartare, always keep the tuna cold and cut it up as close to serving as possible. **SERVES 4**

1. Put the potatoes in a large saucepan, add enough salted water to cover, and bring to a boil over high heat. Cook until they are fork tender, about 20 minutes. Drain the potatoes and transfer them to a bowl of ice water. Let cool completely. Drain again. Cut into ½-inch dice.

2. Mix the potatoes, green beans, olives, shallot, chile flakes, and garlic together in a medium bowl. Add the oil and soy sauce and mix again.

3. For a garnish, toss the cherry tomatoes and vinegar in a small bowl. Add the parsley, chile, and black garlic, if using, and mix well.

4. Remove the tuna from the fridge, and cut ½-inch vertical slices, then slice those into ½-inch thick sticks, and finally cut them crosswise into ½-inch dice. Since we're dicing here, going with the grain is less important, as we'll have created a tender dice no matter the direction you start in. Transfer the tuna to a bowl. Stir in the potato mixture. Season with more vinegar, oil, soy sauce, salt, and black pepper, as needed.

5. I like to put the tartare into an oiled ring mold, and invert it onto a large serving platter. Or you can make smaller circles on each serving plate.

6. Sprinkle the cherry tomato garnish over the tartare (either on the platter or plates). Add a few pulls of lemon zest on top. Serve cold.

THE MAGIC OF THE HUMBLE ZUCCHINI BLOSSOM

From April until late October, you will find zucchini or pumpkin blossoms at French village markets. In the US, you can often find them in the spring at farmers' markets. Here are three recipes that show off these beauties at their best. The flavor sensibilities are based in Provence, but with global influences.

TO PREP ZUCCHINI BLOSSOMS: Whether you are pickling, stuffing, or frying them, zucchini blossom prep is the same. To clean zucchini blossoms, gently brush off any debris with a vegetable brush. If they really need to be washed, dip each blossom, one at a time, into a bowl of cold water. Shake off excess water and place on paper towels to drain. Carefully pat them dry with more paper towels. They are delicate, and you want them to keep their shape.

If the pistil inside the flower is thin and shorter than about ½ inch, leave it be, but if it looks thick and tough, pluck the pistil and stamens out.

- *Mixing bowl*
- *Whisk*
- *Large, deep skillet at least 10 inches in diameter*
- *Tongs*
- *Slotted spoon*
- *Paper towel–lined plate*

About 18 zucchini blossoms, prepared as on page 128, but with about ½ inch stem left attached

FOR THE BATTER

3 large egg whites (keep your yolks, and make good use of them later by making Hollandaise, page 54)

⅓ cup mild-flavored beer, such as light or pilsner

6 tablespoons cornstarch

1 teaspoon fine sea salt, plus more for garnish

Vegetable or canola oil, for deep-frying, as needed

Pumpkin Seed Dip (page 130), for serving

Tempura-Fried Zucchini Blossoms

Often, when you see fried zucchini blossoms in Provence (and Italy), they are served stuffed with cheese, but not always. I prefer to actually taste the zucchini blossom, which is challenging with a rich stuffing. This recipe is a little more simple: dip the flowers into a light beer batter, then frying them for the full benefit of their delicate flavor. I suggest a pumpkin seed dip, based on the stuffing for the Stuffed Zucchini Blossom Salad on page 130. But for a very easy dip, mix soy sauce with a generous squeeze of fresh lime juice. SERVES 6

1. Preheat the oven to 200°F.

2. **MAKE THE BATTER:** Whisk the egg whites and beer well in a medium bowl until thoroughly combined and foamy (this can take a couple of minutes). Gradually whisk in the cornstarch, 1 tablespoon at a time, being sure that each addition is dissolved before adding more. Whisk in the salt.

3. Add enough oil to come about 1 inch up the sides of the skillet and heat until the oil is shimmering. Do not let it heat so much that it smokes. To test the oil temperature, drop a small shmoop of batter into the oil. It should bubble and fry to a golden color in about 2 minutes. If it takes longer, the oil isn't hot enough and needs to be heated more. If it browns too quickly, the oil is too hot, so add a few glugs of oil to cool it down.

4. One at a time, holding by the stem end, dip a blossom into the batter. Drag it gently along the side of the bowl to remove excess batter, and gently place it in the skillet. Continue with more blossoms, but do not crowd them in the skillet. Fry for about 1 minute, then turn and continue cooking until golden, about 1 minute more. Using a slotted spoon, transfer to the paper towel–lined plate and keep warm in the oven until all of the blossoms are fried. Sprinkle with salt and serve immediately, with the dip or soy sauce and lime juice.

FOR THE STUFFING

2 cups shelled pumpkin seeds (pepitas)

½ cup tahini

½ cup olive oil

½ cup packed fresh parsley leaves

2 shallots, coarsely chopped

4 garlic cloves, crushed under a knife and peeled

One 2-inch knob of ginger, peeled and coarsely chopped

3 tablespoons apple cider vinegar

Fine sea salt

2 lemons

12 squash blossoms, prepped (see page 128)

FOR THE SALAD

5 to 6 ounces arugula

1 pint cherry tomatoes, preferably of mixed colors, cut into quarters

Extra-virgin olive oil

1 lemon

Flaky salt

¼ cup shelled pumpkin seeds (pepitas), coarsely chopped

Hemp seeds (optional)

Stuffed Zucchini Blossom Salad

Sometimes (often, if we're being honest) I don't want my zucchini blossoms fried. But I do, in fact, want them. This salad is an utter crowd pleaser. Most people have never had a non-fried zucchini blossom, so they are frequently quite excited to try one. You will likely have leftover stuffing, because you need to make a greater quantity than you need for it to blend. I've provided a great little dip recipe to use the rest. **SERVES 4**

1. **MAKE THE STUFFING:** Blend the pumpkin seeds, 1 cup water, the tahini, oil, parsley, shallots, garlic, ginger, vinegar, and salt in a blender until it makes a thick purée. If you have a standard blender, you may have to do this in batches. Add a few pulls of the lemon zest, squeeze in the lemon juice, and blend again to combine.

2. Transfer the mixture into a piping bag or plastic resealable bag. If using a resealable bag, cut a ¼-inch opening in one corner. Pipe a generous amount of the stuffing into each blossom (it should seem overstuffed), and seal the top by twisting closed. Transfer the blossoms to a plate.

3. **MAKE THE SALAD:** Add a quarter of the arugula to each serving plate. Scatter equal amounts of the tomatoes on top. Drizzle with oil, then add a squeeze of lemon, and a pinch of flaky salt. Top with 3 zucchini blossoms, sprinkle with crushed pumpkin seeds, and hemp seeds, if using, and serve.

PUMPKIN SEED DIP: If you have leftover stuffing, make a dip with one part sour cream to two parts stuffing, seasoned with additional salt. It is terrific with crudités, pita crisps, and Crostini (page 60), but also with the Tempura-Fried Zucchini Blossoms on page 129.

- *Medium saucepan*
- *Sieve*
- *Large bowl*
- *Blender, preferably high-power*
- *Small bowl or large ramekin*
- *Shallow soup bowls*

FOR THE SOUP

3 pounds zucchini, cut into 1-inch chunks

3 cardamom pods, lightly crushed with a mortar and pestle or skillet

2 garlic cloves, smashed under a knife and peeled

Fine sea salt

FOR THE ZUCCHINI BLOSSOM PICKLES

12 zucchini blossoms, prepped (see page 128)

White wine vinegar, as needed

1 teaspoon ground coriander

½ teaspoon honey

Flaky salt

Extra-virgin olive oil

Freshly ground pepper, preferably white if you have it

Zucchini Soup with Pickled Zucchini Blossoms

This zucchini soup has just a few carefully chosen ingredients, and the final soup sings with vegetables and the surprising flavor of cardamom. The pickled zucchini blossoms function as a tart, palate-rousing counterpoint to the mellow squash purée. **SERVES 6 AS A STARTER**

1. **MAKE THE SOUP:** Put the zucchini, cardamom pods, garlic, and 1 teaspoon salt in a saucepan, and add enough cold water to cover. Bring to a hard simmer (not a boil) over high heat. Reduce the heat to medium so the liquid remains at a hard simmer. Cook until the zucchini is very tender but not obliterated, about 8 minutes.

2. **MEANWHILE, MAKE THE ZUCCHINI BLOSSOM PICKLES:** Trim the green stems and cut each blossom in half lengthwise. In a large bowl whisk together about 3 tablespoons vinegar with the coriander, honey, and a pinch of salt. Add the blossoms and mix gently. If they aren't just covered with the liquid, add more vinegar and adjust the other ingredients accordingly. Set aside while finishing the soup, about 15 minutes.

3. Drain the zucchini in a colander set over a bowl, reserving the liquid. Discard the cardamom pods and garlic, then blend the zucchini on high for 3 minutes in a high-speed blender, longer for a standard blender. The soup should be supremely smooth. Season with salt. If you would like a thinner soup, gradually blend in some of the reserved cooking liquid. Strain the soup through a wire sieve, discarding the solids in the sieve.

4. To serve hot, reheat the soup in the saucepan until simmering. To serve cold, let the soup cool to room temperature, then cover and refrigerate until chilled, at least 2 and up to 12 hours. Or serve at room temperature. In any case, serve in shallow bowls, topped with a drizzle of oil, a few zucchini blossom pickles, a sprinkle of flaky salt, and a few cracks of pepper.

Note: If you are serving the soup chilled or at room temperature, hold off on pickling the zucchini blossoms until about 15 minutes before serving, as the blossoms are delicate and shouldn't be over-pickled.

MISE EN PLACE

- *Small bowl*
- *Half-sheet pan*
- *Metal spatula for transferring the asparagus to the platter*
- *Serving platter*
- *Microplane*

FOR THE MAYONNAISE

3 black garlic cloves, peeled

½ cup Mayonnaise (page 52)

1 garlic clove, grated

2 pounds asparagus (try to buy stalks of the same diameter)

Olive oil

1 lemon

Smoked flaky salt

Freshly ground black pepper

Roasted Asparagus with Black Garlic Mayonnaise

One morning during our first winter in the tiny village of Valbonne, my husband, Chris, was out hiking in the hills and encountered a local with fistfuls of tender, tiny asparagus. He excitedly explained that he had found them *dans la forêt* ("in the forest"). On our subsequent foraging hikes, we found that the stalwart villagers of Valbonne had already picked the hills clean of this late winter treat. A few winters later, we couldn't believe it when we found the terraced gardens of La Peetch rife with wild asparagus, literally growing in our backyard. I don't expect you to make this with wild asparagus, but do use thin, fresh-as-you-can-find local asparagus during its short but glorious season. And if you have access to purple asparagus, definitely use it here. SERVES 4 TO 6 AS A SIDE DISH

1. Preheat the oven to 450°F.

2. **MAKE THE MAYONNAISE:** Mash the black garlic in a small bowl. Add the mayonnaise and garlic and stir well.

3. Cut the woody asparagus stems off just where they meet the more tender stalk. (Some people peel the stems of their asparagus, but I do not. It's too much work for too little payoff. Just buy tender, thin asparagus in the first place.) Spread the asparagus on a half-sheet pan. Drizzle all over with oil and toss to coat.

4. Roast, occasionally rolling the asparagus over in the pan for even cooking, until they are crisp-tender, about 10 minutes, or longer, for very tender spears.

5. Transfer the asparagus to a platter. Grate the zest of the lemon on top, sprinkle with the salt, and add a few cracks of pepper. Cut the lemon in half, and squeeze the juice of one half over the asparagus. Serve hot.

6 ripe tomatoes, a mix of colors and heirloom varieties

2 ripe peaches, cut into thin wedges

8 ounces strawberries, hulled, halved or quartered

1 large ball mozzarella or burrata

2 tablespoons extra-virgin olive oil

Flaky salt, smoked or unsmoked

Freshly ground black pepper

About 12 basil leaves

1 lemon

1 lime

Caprese with Peaches and Strawberry

Caprese salad, named for Capri, isn't really a salad. It is the spirit of warm, bright summers itself. The combination of tomatoes and mozzarella is second to none. In Provence, people are tomato fanatics—so much so that they believe that the only tomatoes worth eating should be sun-soaked and vine-ripened. It therefore follows that many local cheesemongers do not sell mozzarella out of tomato season. I made this fruity variation on the old theme as a lark, and, lo, it was delightful. And I absolutely had to share it with absolutely everyone. SERVES 4 TO 6

1. Slice the tomatoes into a variety of shapes—crosswise, lengthwise, and wedges. This makes them all the more beautiful, and the light catches each differently, and provides a captivating and varying mouthfeel. Place on a platter. Nestle the peaches among the tomatoes, and sprinkle with the strawberries.

2. If you're using mozzarella, tear it into bite-size pieces. If using burrata, place the beauty in the center of your plate and leave it be.

3. Drizzle the oil over the whole thing. You don't want pools of olive oil, but you do want each piece to get some green, spicy olive oil love.

4. Sprinkle with about ½ teaspoon salt. Crack some pepper over everything. Stack and roll up the basil leaves into a cylinder, and cut crosswise with a sharp knife into thin shreds (chiffonade). Do this at the last minute so the basil doesn't discolor.

5. Using a Microplane, zest the lemon and lime over all. Cut the lemon and lime in half and rain the juice of half a lemon and half a lime on top. Serve, letting each person cut a portion of the burrata, if using.

1 pound of unripe tomatoes, the harder the better for this recipe

1 to 2 tablespoons extra-virgin olive oil

1 lemon, cut in half

Fine sea salt

Sumac

Freshly ground black pepper

Unsprayed edible flowers, such as rose or marigold petals (optional)

Tomato Carpaccio

We've all eaten underripe tomatoes, and generally speaking they aren't all that enjoyable. (Unless we're talking fried green tomatoes, and then we're in business!) Like farmers everywhere, we at Bramafam and La Peetch often have a number of underripe tomatoes at the end of the season. So what does one do with a few dozen underripe, green tomatoes that will never really ripen? You make this. It's great any time your tomatoes are not up to par. SERVES 4

1. Slice the tomatoes incredibly thin, as thin as your mandoline or knife skills will allow. We want a stained glass tomato that holds its shape, but ideally allows you to see through to the bottom of the plate.

2. Arrange the tomatoes in overlapping spirals on each plate. I start from the outside, working toward the interior. Fill the middle with a couple of slices.

3. Drizzle each with olive oil, about 1 to 2 teaspoons per plate. Squeeze the juice from each lemon half over each plate and follow with a sprinkle of salt.

4. Let the dressed tomatoes stand at room temperature for 20 to 30 minutes. This allows the flavors to penetrate, and creates bright and briny juices that soften the under ripe tomatoes.

5. Just before serving, finish each plate with a pinch of sumac, a crack or two of pepper, and garnish with flowers, if you're feeling fancy.

2 tablespoons apple cider vinegar or distilled white vinegar

Fine sea salt

6 large eggs, at room temperature

⅓ cup walnuts, toasted and coarsely chopped (see Note)

½ cup plain Greek yogurt

½ cup finely diced celery

½ cup finely diced Granny Smith apple, peeled or unpeeled (pick your poison)

½ yellow onion, minced (about 3 tablespoons)

⅓ cup caperberries, quartered, or 2 tablespoons nonpareil capers, plus their brine as needed

2 tablespoons coarsely chopped celery leaves

Small pinch of ground allspice

10 to 12 basil leaves (¼ cup after cutting)

Egg Salad with Basil, Caperberries, and Apple

When it comes to sandwiches, I have very specific tastes. I do not do classic meat/cheese/vegetable sandwiches. I prefer a spreadable filling, along the lines of tuna or egg salad. So, I've made this grown-up, full-flavored egg salad smooth and chock-full of all kinds of surprises. The secret to easy-to-peel eggs is vinegar and salt in the cooking water—the vinegar softens the shell a bit. **SERVES 4**

1. Bring a medium saucepan of water to a boil over high heat. Add the vinegar and 3 tablespoons salt. Using a slotted spoon, carefully slide the eggs into the boiling water. Reduce the heat so the eggs aren't bouncing around. Boil for exactly 7 minutes, and not a second more. This will get you an exemplary egg with a jammy yolk. If you prefers eggs with firmer yolks, let them cook for 12 minutes.

2. Using a slotted spoon, transfer each egg to a bowl of ice water. Let them cool for at least 5 minutes. Peel the eggs, then chop them coarsely.

3. Mix the walnuts, yogurt, celery, apple, onion, caperberries, celery leaves, and allspice in a medium bowl. Fold the eggs into the mixture. Instead of salt, I like to season this with the brine from the caperberries. Start by adding a teaspoon and taste. I use a full tablespoon, but you may prefer less. Taste for acidity, salt, and texture. Add some salt if you don't get the salt level you want from the brine alone. Cover with plastic wrap and refrigerate until chilled, about 1 hour, or up to 3 days if you wish.

4. Just before serving, roll the basil leaves into a cylinder. Using a sharp knife, cut crosswise into thin shreds (chiffonade). Stir into the salad and serve chilled.

Note: To toast the walnuts, heat an empty skillet over medium-high heat. Add the walnuts and cook, stirring often, until toasted and fragrant, about 5 minutes. Do not let these beauties burn, please! Transfer to a plate and let cool. Coarsely chop the walnuts.

MISE EN PLACE
- *Medium saucepan*
- *Small plate*
- *Wooden spoon*
- *Sieve*
- *Mixing bowl*
- *Microplane*
- *Individual serving bowls*

Olive oil

3 shallots, minced

½ teaspoon yellow mustard seed, crushed with a mortar and pestle or under a skillet

3 garlic cloves, grated

½ teaspoon minced fresh thyme

1 teaspoon smoked paprika

1 tablespoon salted butter

1 cup French green lentils, preferably lentilles du Puy, rinsed, drained, and sorted for stones

3 cups Almost-from-Scratch Stock (page 45), other stock, or low-sodium canned beef or chicken broth, as needed

½ teaspoon fine sea salt

2 tablespoons black vinegar, or to taste

1 teaspoon soy sauce

3 dashes fish sauce

Garnishes: Lime, plain Greek yogurt, mint or cilantro leaves, and Garlic Chips (page 62) (optional)

Vinegary Green Lentil Salad

Lentils have been cultivated in France for hundreds of years, and the French revere them. The most famous are green *lentilles du Puy* from a region in the central part of the country. Petite, with thin, green skins, they retain their shape beautifully during cooking. In fact, they bear little resemblance to the starchy brown American variety. Lentilles de Puy are a respected protected "product of designated origin," and must be grown in Puy to get the appellation, just as any sparkling wine cannot be called Champagne unless it is from that particular region. This can be served cold, room temperature, or warm. I like it all ways, but my preference is room temperature as I find the flavors the most appealing at that point.

SERVES 3 AS A MEAL, 4 TO 6 AS A SIDE DISH

1. Heat a glug of olive oil in a medium saucepan over medium-high heat until the oil shimmers. Add the shallots and cook, stirring occasionally, until they turn gold, about 3 minutes. Transfer one-third of the shallots to a plate and set aside. Let the remaining shallots cook in the skillet until they turn deep gold with bits of brown, about 2 minutes more. Stir in the mustard seeds. Add the garlic and stir well.

2. Stir in the thyme and paprika. Add the butter and stir with a wooden spoon to loosen any browned bits in the pan. Add the lentils and stir well. Cook until the lentils smell toasty, about 3 minutes. This develops their very appealing flavor.

3. Pour in the stock and bring to a boil over high heat. Stir in the salt. Reduce the heat to low and simmer for 30 minutes. Taste for doneness—they should be just tender and not too soft. Remember, these lentils cook more quickly than the American variety, so don't overcook them! Strain in a sieve to remove any excess cooking liquid. Transfer the lentils to a serving bowl and let them cool.

4. Add the thinnest veil of oil into the saucepan and heat over medium-high heat. Add the reserved shallots and cook, stirring occasionally, until they are crisp on the edges and very dark brown on the point of burning, 4 to 5 minutes. Scrape the browned shallots onto a plate so they stop cooking.

5. Stir the vinegar, soy sauce, and fish sauce into the lentils, tasting and adjusting for acidity and salt. Use a Microplane to zest the lime over the lentils, then cut the lime in half and squeeze its juice on top. Serve in individual bowls, add a dollop of yogurt, a sprinkle of herbs, some crispy shallots, and a scattering of garlic chips, if using.

- *Half-sheet pan*
- *Parchment paper*
- *Microplane for grating the cheese*
- *Large serving bowl*

1 cup freshly grated Parmesan cheese

Freshly ground black pepper

2 heads Bibb lettuce

About ½ cup lightly packed fresh, delicate herb leaves, e.g., dill, tarragon, parsley, cilantro, chervil, a mixture is especially nice

2 tablespoons Your Dream Vinaigrette (page 55) with ½ garlic clove, grated into the dressing

Zest of 1 lemon or lime

Herbaceous Bibb Salad with Parmesan Crisps and Dream Vinaigrette

Here's a slightly more complex version of a simple side salad, for when you want to get fancy. The sweet, large, and tender leaves of Bibb lettuce act as ideal little cups to catch your vinaigrette. Go strong on the fresh herbs, and balance the aromatics with salty, peppery, easy-to-chomp, umami-bomb Parmesan crisps. This is a great way to use leftover herbs, and this salad is both easy to put together and tasty, yet delivers on a special presentation. SERVES 4

1. Preheat the oven to 400°F. Line a half-sheet pan with parchment paper. Sprinkle the cheese onto the parchment. It doesn't have to be sprinkled evenly— it should look lacy, with some thicker and thinner areas, and plenty of overlap. Crack a generous amount of black pepper on top.

2. Bake until the Parmesan turns a crispy, knockout golden brown, 6 to 8 minutes. Let the crisp cool in the pan.

3. Wash and dry your lettuce, keeping the leaves whole. This is a fork-and-knife kind of salad.

4. Cut the herbs into myriad sizes: Mince some, tear some into pieces, and coarsely chop others. Set a hearty pinch or two aside for a final garnish.

5. Mix the lettuce and remaining herbs together in a large serving bowl. Drizzle in the vinaigrette and toss with your hands to coat evenly.

6. Top with the remaining herbs, and grate the lemon zest over all. Break the Parmesan crisp into cracker-size pieces, scatter over the salad, and serve.

- *Mandoline or sharp knife*
- *1 small bowl*
- *Appetizer-size serving plates*

12 ounces dense mushrooms

2 tablespoons sherry vinegar

¼ cup extra-virgin olive oil

1 teaspoon fresh thyme leaves, or ½ teaspoon dried thyme, plus extra fresh thyme for serving

2 teaspoons sumac, plus extra for serving

3 tablespoons minced sun-dried tomatoes in oil

Flaky salt

Freshly ground black pepper

Mushroom Carpaccio with Sumac and Olive Oil

Carpaccio once referred only to thinly sliced beef with a white dressing, but it has now come to mean any food that is prepped paper-thin and served as an appetizer. I've provided a few variations at the end of the recipe to give you some ideas. Choose dense mushrooms for this recipe, such as baby bellas (cremini), king, or white button; shiitakes or portobellos are too soft and don't hold up well to the mandoline slices of this recipe. **SERVES 4**

1. Slice the mushrooms as thinly as possible on a mandoline or with a knife. You're going for paper-thin mushrooms here. Set aside.

2. Whisking the vinegar in a small bowl, gradually add the oil. If you're using dried thyme, rather than fresh, add it here to hydrate and release its flavor. Whisk in the sumac. Let stand for about 5 minutes, and taste for seasoning. If the thyme flavor isn't coming through, add a bit more. Taste as you cook! The dressing can be made a few hours ahead, but whisk again before using.

3. Divide the mushrooms among the plates, mounding them in the center and taking care not to smoosh them—they are delicate! (At this point, you can set aside the mushrooms for an hour or so at room temperature. Do not dress them until just before serving.) Drizzle with the dressing, starting with a gentle drizzle as not to overdress the mushrooms and make them soggy.

4. Sprinkle with the sun-dried tomatoes, dispersing them equally. Season with flaky salt and a few cracks of pepper. Finish with a sprinkle of fresh thyme, if using, and a couple of pinches of sumac. Let stand for a few minutes to allow the mushrooms to absorb the dressing. Serve immediately.

MUSHROOM CARPACCIO WITH SHALLOT AND LIME: Omit the vinegar and thyme. Cut 1 shallot into thin rounds and place in a small bowl. Add enough fresh lime juice (about 2 limes) to cover. Macerate for at least 30 minutes. Gently toss the mushrooms in oil, using a little at a time so they don't get soggy. Add the shallots and lime juice, adjusting to taste.

MUSHROOM CARPACCIO WITH CILANTRO AND CHILE: Omit the thyme. Plate the mushrooms and top each with freshly grated garlic, chopped fresh cilantro, and a sprinkle of chile powder, all according to your taste.

*   *Sharp knife*
*   *Mandoline (optional)*
*   *Mixing bowl*
*   *Small bowl*
*   *Immersion blender or whisk*
*   *Mortar and pestle*

FOR THE SALAD

2 pounds (about 2 heads) celery with the leaves attached

2 shallots, sliced into paper-thin rounds

FOR THE DRESSING

¼ cup extra-virgin olive oil

3 tablespoons celery vinegar, preferably Tart Vinegar brand, or other vinegar of choice

3 drained anchovy fillets packed in oil

1 teaspoon Dijon mustard

1 garlic clove

½ teaspoon celery seed

½ teaspoon fish sauce (optional)

Pinch of Korean chile threads (*silgochu*) or other chile flake, for garnish (optional)

Freshly ground black pepper

Celery Salad Gone Wild

I love the crisp texture of the ribs and the parsley-like flavor of celery leaves, all held together with a bold vinaigrette. It is a staple at the neighborhood traiteur (or caterer, similar to a deli with a case filled with take-out items), but it can be a little mundane, as all salads can be. I perk it up with some of my favorite not-so-French ingredients. When it comes to celery vinegar, it is not easy to find, but you can mail order it from a manufacturer in Brooklyn called Tart Vinegar. Other vinegars work just as well. **SERVES 6**

1. **MAKE THE SALAD:** Cut off the woody, pale ends of the celery. (Reserve the trimmings in a bag in the freezer for making stock.) Cut off the leafy tops and set aside separately. Cut the celery, with the knife held at a slight angle, into diagonal slices about ¼ inch thick. Keep the slices as even as possible. (Once you make that first diagonal slice, you can use a mandoline.) Transfer to a bowl. Add the shallots and half of the leaves to the celery and toss together.

2. **MAKE THE DRESSING:** Process the oil, vinegar, anchovies, mustard, garlic, celery seed, and fish sauce, if using, in a small bowl with an immersion blender. (Or whisk until combined. If using a whisk, mince the anchovies into a paste and grate the garlic.)

3. Pour the dressing over the salad and toss lightly. (The salad can be covered and refrigerated for up to 1 day before serving.)

4. Chop the remaining celery leaves and sprinkle over the salad. Top with a sprinkle of chile threads, if using, and a couple of cracks of black pepper.

MISE EN PLACE

- 3 small bowls, one lined with paper towels
- Large, deep skillet
- Perforated spoon
- Colander
- Large bowl
- Serving platter

2 pints cherry tomatoes, preferably mixed colors, cut lengthwise

Fine sea salt

1 teaspoon cumin seeds, crushed with a mortar and pestle or under a skillet

1 teaspoon coriander seeds, crushed with a mortar and pestle or under a skillet

1 shallot, sliced thinly crosswise

Red wine vinegar

¼ cup cornstarch

½ cup drained but unrinsed canned chickpeas (garbanzo beans)

Safflower or canola oil, for frying

1 teaspoon ground turmeric

1 to 2 tablespoons extra-virgin olive oil

¼ cup loosely packed fresh cilantro leaves

1 teaspoon chile flakes, such as Urfa biber

Garnishes: Flaky salt, mint leaves, chive blossoms (optional), and Garlic Chips (page 62) (optional)

Spiced Tomato Salad with Turmeric Fried Chickpeas

This dish tastes exactly like summer. It is hot, sweet, and a bit crunchy, and I love it as a side dish with barbecued or grilled foods. The earthy chickpeas mingle with tart, spiced onions, while fit-for-a-jewelry-box tomatoes bring bright summer bounty to the plate. You'll likely want to eat the crispy turmeric chickpeas all by their lonesome. In fact, you might want to make a double batch and use the whole can of chickpeas so you can have some for later. They make a welcome road-trip snack. SERVES 6

1. Mix the tomatoes with 1 teaspoon salt in a colander and place in your sink. Let stand for at least 10 and up to 30 minutes to give off some juices.

2. Mix the cumin and coriander in a small bowl with a pinch of salt. Add the shallot and pour in enough vinegar to cover. Set aside for 15 to 45 minutes.

3. Spread the cornstarch in another small bowl. Add the chickpeas, toss well, and set aside for about 3 minutes so the mixture forms a moist coating.

4. Toss the chickpeas in your hand, letting the excess cornstarch fall into the bowl. Transfer the chickpeas to a plate.

5. Pour enough oil to come about ½ inch up the sides of a large skillet and heat over high heat until the oil is shimmering. To test the oil temperature, add a chickpea. It should sizzle but not pop. If it does not sizzle, heat the oil longer. If the chickpea spits back at you, add a glug or two of oil to the skillet to lower the temperature a bit.

6. Carefully add the chickpeas to the oil and do not move them for 15 seconds. Then, using a perforated spoon, gently stir the oil so the chickpeas roll over. Cook, stirring occasionally for even cooking, until the chickpeas are crisp, about 1 minute. Using the perforated spoon, remove the chickpeas from the oil and transfer to a paper towel–lined bowl. Let stand for about 30 minutes to absorb excess oil. Remove the paper towels. Sprinkle the turmeric over the chickpeas and toss so the chickpeas get brightly colored.

7. Drain the tomatoes in a colander, discarding the liquid, and transfer them to a bowl. Gently stir in enough oil to coat the tomatoes. Put the tomatoes on a serving platter. Drain the shallots, shake off any clinging spices, and scatter over the tomatoes. Sprinkle with the chickpeas, and top with the cilantro. Finish with a pinch of flaky salt and some mint leaves, followed by the chive blossoms and garlic chips, if using.

Green Gazpacho, *page 156*

Magenta Gazpacho, *page 153*

Classic-ish Red Gazpacho, *page 152*

GAZPACHO, FOUR WAYS

When temperatures swell, a big batch of cold gazpacho is guaranteed to refresh even the fussiest humans. For this delightful blend, the brighter the color the better. The key is to use ingredients that are similar in color. For a gazpacho that awes and inspires, color reigns supreme, but the flavor is right up there.

The following recipes are designed to create four basic gazpacho color schemes: red (*la classique*), magenta, yellow or orange, and green. Start with a bell pepper as the flavor and color base of the soup. Next add an allium (they have a range of colors, too). Then bring in the acidic/sweet component of tomatoes. Be careful not to do too much mixing of tomato/pepper colors, as a discordant combination will give you a muddy color. For example if you're using a yellow pepper, a red tomato will turn your gazpacho brown. Seedless cucumber (if you use standard cucumbers, peel and scoop out their seeds first) and olive oil are must-haves. Whether you peel the seedless cucumber depends on the final color you want—a red gazpacho won't stay red with an unpeeled cucumber.

You may want to add a fruit for sweetness to balance the tomatoes' acidity or the pepper's spice. Take care when experimenting with leafy green herbs like cilantro or basil. They might sound good, but their chlorophyll will quickly throw off your desired color, unless you're going for green soup. Even vinegar (dark sherry vinegar works in red and magenta, but white wine vinegar would be a better choice for green and yellow) can be a culprit when trying to keep the color bright. Oil will lighten the color as air is incorporated, and when it emulsifies into the gazpacho, it will thicken it.

Garnishes add a final flourish. You can include cherry tomatoes of a contrasting color, a drizzle of olive oil, citrus peel zest, chopped nuts, or crumbled cheeses such as feta or goat.

Whatever gazpacho you make, be sure to allow plenty of time for it to chill. Make it in the morning and let it stand in the fridge until it is nice and cold, at least 2 hours.

MISE EN PLACE
- Blender, preferably heavy-duty
- Glasses or bowls, for serving
- Microplane

Classic-ish Red Gazpacho

SERVES 4 TO 6

1 red bell pepper, stemmed, seeded, and cut into large pieces

2 red tomatoes, about equal in weight to the bell pepper, cored and cut into thick wedges

½ seedless (English) cucumber, or 1 standard, peeled, seeds scooped out of the standard cucumber

About 1 cup seedless and chunked red watermelon (or remove seeds from seeded watermelon if that's what you have)

½ small red onion, coarsely chopped

4 garlic cloves, crushed under a knife and peeled

⅓ cup extra-virgin olive oil

Juice from ½ lemon

1 teaspoon sherry vinegar

1 teaspoon fresh thyme, or ½ teaspoon dried

Fine sea salt

Pinch of crushed hot red pepper

Hearty pinch of smoked paprika

Garnishes: Smoked paprika, crushed hot red pepper, lemon, and fresh thyme leaves

1. Add the bell pepper, tomatoes, cucumber, watermelon, onion, garlic, oil, lemon juice, vinegar, thyme, salt, red pepper, and paprika to a blender and process until very smooth. Season with with more salt to taste and blend well to combine. (If using a standard blender, blend the ingredients in batches and combine in a bowl.) Pour into a medium bowl.

2. Cover and refrigerate until well chilled, at least 2 hours. Serve chilled, topping each serving with paprika, hot pepper, a few pulls of lemon zest, and some thyme.

MISE EN PLACE
- *Blender, preferably heavy-duty*
- *Glasses or bowls, for serving*
- *Microplane*

1 red bell pepper, stemmed, seeded, and cut into large pieces

1 medium beet, raw or roasted (see page 212), cut into large chunks (For the smoothest gazpacho, use a roasted beet, although raw works well, too.)

½ seedless (English) cucumber, or 1 standard, peeled, seeds scooped out of the standard cucumber

½ red or yellow onion, coarsely chopped

4 to 6 strawberries, hulled

3 to 4 garlic cloves

¼ cup extra-virgin olive oil, plus extra for serving

2 tablespoons white balsamic vinegar or sherry vinegar

Pinch of ground cumin

Smoked flaky salt

Garnishes: Coarsely chopped toasted walnuts (see Note, page 139) and crumbled feta

Magenta Gazpacho

SERVES 4 TO 6

1. Add the bell pepper, beet, cucumber, onion, strawberries, garlic, oil, vinegar, and cumin to a blender and process until very smooth. Season with salt and blend well to combine. (If using a standard blender, blend the ingredients in batches and combine in a bowl.) Pour into a medium bowl.

2. Cover and refrigerate until well chilled, at least 2 hours. Serve chilled, topping each serving with sprinkles of walnuts and feta, and a drizzle of oil.

1 yellow bell pepper or orange, stemmed, seeded, and cut into large pieces

2 yellow tomatoes, about equal in weight to the bell pepper, stemmed and cut into thick wedges

½ seedless (English) or 1 standard cucumber, peeled, seeds scooped out of the standard cucumber

About 1 cup seeded and chunked cantaloupe

½ white onion or yellow, coarsely chopped

4 garlic cloves

⅓ cup extra-virgin olive oil

1 teaspoon turmeric

Juice of ½ lemon

Fine sea salt

Garnishes: Halved cherry tomatoes, smoked paprika, and freshly ground black pepper

Yellow or Orange Gazpacho

With the colors of bell pepper available today, it is easy to make a beautiful gazpacho that is outside of the red-magenta spectrum. And here it is. SERVES 4 TO 6

1. Add the bell pepper, tomatoes, cucumber, cantaloupe, onion, garlic, oil, turmeric, lemon, and more salt to taste to a blender and process until very smooth. Season with salt and blend well to combine. (If using a standard blender, blend the ingredients in batches and combine in a bowl.) Pour into a medium bowl.

2. Cover and refrigerate until well chilled, at least 2 hours. Serve chilled, topping each serving with some cherry tomatoes, a pinch of paprika, and a crack or two of pepper.

Green Gazpacho

MISE EN PLACE

- *Blender, preferably heavy-duty*
- *Glasses or bowls, for serving*
- *Microplane*

1 green bell pepper, stemmed and seeded, cut into large pieces

2 to 3 green tomatoes, about equal in weight to the bell pepper, stemmed

½ seedless (English) cucumber, or 1 standard, peeled, seeds scooped out of the standard cucumber

About 1 cup seeded and chunked honeydew melon or yellow watermelon

½ white onion or yellow, coarsely chopped

½ cup packed fresh cilantro leaves

3 garlic cloves

¼ cup extra-virgin olive oil

1 jalapeño pepper, seeded and coarsely chopped

Fine sea salt

Garnishes: Crumbled queso fresco or feta cheese, fresh oregano leaves, and thinly shaved radish (use a mandoline or vegetable peeler)

Green gazpacho is a classic Spanish recipe. A jalapeño chile gives the soup a bit of heat. If you want it spicier, include the seeds and ribs when blending. SERVES 4 TO 6

1. Add the bell pepper, tomatoes, cucumber, melon, onion, cilantro, garlic, oil, and jalapeño to a blender and process until very smooth. Season with salt and blend well to combine. (If using a standard blender, blend the ingredients in batches and combine in a bowl.) Pour into a medium bowl.

2. Cover and refrigerate until well chilled, at least 2 hours. Serve chilled, topping each serving with some cheese, a sprinkle of oregano, and a scattering of radish.

MISE EN PLACE

- *Soup pot*
- *Large Dutch oven*
- *Large skillet*
- *Blender*
- *Wide soup bowls*

FOR THE BROTH

Olive oil

1 yellow onion, cut in half

4 garlic cloves, smashed under a knife and peeled

About 6 ounces Parmesan cheese rinds

1 bouquet garni (see page 25)

FOR THE SOUP

Olive oil

3 leeks, white and pale green parts only, rinsed well and thinly sliced

Fine sea salt

2 carrots, cut into ½-inch rounds

½ cup dry white wine

1 large baking potato, such as russet, cut into ½-inch cubes

4 pounds (about 4 cups) shelling beans, such as fava or cranberry beans, shelled and peeled as needed, or 3 (14-ounce) cans white (cannellini) beans, drained and rinsed

3 to 5 ripe tomatoes, diced, or 1 (28-ounce) can diced tomatoes, drained

1 pound zucchini or other summer squash

8 ounces green beans, cut into ½-inch lengths

ingredients continue

Pistou (Not Pesto) Soup

Pistou is practically synonymous with Provence and the Riviera. It uses the very best of the abundant summer vegetables in the South of France and elevates them from ordinary roadside produce to culinary delight. This soup is typically made with water, but I prefer a Parmesan-based broth that brings umami depth to the dish. Collect a rind or two from Parmesan as the cheese is used up and refrigerate or freeze them until you make this broth. Or simply cut the rind off a hunk of Parmesan and use even if you haven't used the cheese yet. . . . If you don't have Parmesan rinds, you can substitute any vegetable broth, and add a couple dashes of fish sauce to the broth for umami.

In France, pistou refers to a soup and the basil paste itself. Pistou and pesto are basically synonymous, and start from the same base of garlic, olive oil, and fresh basil. Pistou stops there and morphs into pesto with the addition of Parmesan and pine nuts. Here I play with that by making the Parmesan broth. This soup is intended as a complete meal. SERVES 6

1. **MAKE THE BROTH:** Heat a glug of oil in a large pot over medium-high heat until the oil is shimmering. Add the onion, cut side down. Cook, without turning or disturbing, until the undersides are very dark brown and on the verge of charring, about 5 minutes. Add the garlic and stir. Reduce the heat and cook until the garlic softens, about 3 minutes more. Keep your eye (and nose) on this process.

2. Add the Parmesan rinds and the bouquet garni to the pot, then pour in 5 quarts of water. Bring to a boil over high heat. Reduce the heat to medium-low heat
and simmer until the liquid is reduced by about one-third. This will take about 1½ hours. You should end up with about 3½ quarts of broth. Remove and discard the onion, visible garlic, rinds, and the bouquet garni.

3. **MAKE THE SOUP:** Heat a glug of oil in a large skillet over medium heat. Add the leeks and a pinch of salt and cook, stirring occasionally, until the leeks begin to soften and deepen in color, 5 to 8 minutes. Stir in the carrots and cook until they soften a bit, another 3 to 5 minutes. Stir in the wine and dislodge any browned juices from the bottom of the pan. Stir the vegetable mixture into the broth.

recipe continues

FOR THE PISTOU

Extra-virgin olive oil

2 cups packed basil leaves

3 garlic cloves

Pinch of fine sea salt

Zest of one lemon

Freshly ground black pepper, for serving

Lemon wedges, for serving

4. Increase the heat to medium-high and bring the soup to a strong simmer. Add the potatoes and adjust the heat to maintain the steady simmer. If using fresh beans, add them now. Simmer until the potatoes are almost tender, about 15 minutes. Stir in the tomatoes, zucchini, green beans, and canned beans, if using. Continue to simmer until the green beans are tender, about 10 minutes. Season the soup with salt.

5. **MAKE THE PISTOU:** Add a couple of glugs of olive oil into a blender. Add the basil, garlic, salt, and lemon zest and process, adding more oil to make a spoonable paste.

6. Serve the soup in wide bowls, and top with a few cracks of freshly ground pepper. Serve with the pistou and lemon wedges passed so each guest can add their own to taste.

PISTOU WITH DRIED BEANS: Rinse and sort through 1 cup dried cannellini or White Northern beans. Place in a large bowl and add enough cold water to cover by 2 inches. Let soak overnight. (If it is warm, refrigerate.) Drain well. Put the beans in a large saucepan and add enough water to cover well. Stir in 2 teaspoons salt. Bring to a boil over high heat. Reduce the heat to medium-low and simmer until tender, about 1 hour (but the exact time depends on the age of the beans). Drain and substitute for the canned beans.

- *10-inch, oven-safe skillet (wrap the handle in aluminum foil if in doubt)*
- *Good pot holders*
- *Serving platter*

12 to 14 garlic cloves, peeled

6 sprigs fresh thyme

Olive oil

2 pints cherry tomatoes

Fine sea salt and freshly ground black pepper

1 tablespoon balsamic vinegar

1 teaspoon honey

Flour for rolling out the dough

1 disk (one-third of recipe) Flaky Buttery Pastry (page 72)

Cherry Tomato Tarte Tatin with Balsamic Glaze

This is a relative of the beloved galette (see page 68). The Tatin sisters became famous for their apple tarte Tatin, essentially an upside-down apple galette in which the juices have pooled during the cooking. My version is savory, yet still upside-down. It is another way to enjoy the super-sweet, small cherry tomatoes that abound during the summer and into fall. Bake it in the morning when the weather is cooler for a perfect lunch with a cold glass of rosé. SERVES 4 TO 6

1. Bring ¼ cup water to a simmer in a medium, nonstick oven-safe skillet. Add the garlic and thyme and adjust the heat so the water simmers steadily. Cook until the water evaporates completely, 3 to 5 minutes. This mellows the garlic's bite.

2. Add a glug of oil, followed by the tomatoes, and season with salt and pepper. Cook over medium heat until the tomatoes burst and the juices begin to reduce, about 8 minutes. Add the vinegar and honey and gently stir just until the honey melts. Cook until the juices thicken into a syrup and the tomatoes look jammy, about 10 minutes. Season with salt and pepper. Remove from the heat and let cool until warm, about 10 minutes.

3. Preheat the oven to 425°F. On a lightly floured surface, roll out the dough into a 10-inch round about ⅛ inch thick, and then trim it into a round that fits inside the pan. (The pan lid is the perfect template.)

4. Drape the pastry over the tomatoes in the skillet and tuck the edges into the pan. Pierce the dough about a dozen times with the tip of a sharp knife to let the steam escape while it bakes. Bake until the pastry is rich golden brown, 30 to 35 minutes. Remove from the oven and let cool for 10 minutes.

5. To unmold the tarte, you need some courage and good pot holders. Find a serving dish that matches the size of the pan and place the plate upside over the skillet. With the handle facing away from you, grasp the plate and skillet together with both hands, and in a swift motion, flip them so the plate is on the bottom to unmold the tarte. If the tomatoes look messy, just rearrange them, but the rustic look is part of this tarte's charm. Remove any loose thyme sprig twigs, leaving the leaves on the tarte. Serve immediately, while the crust is crisp.

MISE EN PLACE
- *Paring knife*
- *Blender, preferably heavy-duty*
- *Soup bowls of stemless wineglasses*

2 pints cherry tomatoes (about 2 pounds), or 3 to 4 large, ripe tomatoes, all the same color (cherry tomatoes work best here due to their lower water content, and higher seed ratio, which aids in the emulsion)

½ cup extra-virgin olive oil, as needed

Fine sea salt

Handful of fresh basil leaves (about ½ cup packed), plus extra for garnish

Juice of ½ lemon

Universal Herbed Oil (page 63) (optional)

Dairy-Free Tomato "Cream" with Basil

This not-quite-a-recipe is a summertime essential. While it's straightforward, a true recipe doesn't really work here. It requires tasting, trust, and lots of blending. This emulsion comes together because of tomato seeds. The seed quantity, the ripeness and sweetness of the tomato, the ratio of skins and flesh, the juiciness of the fruit—these change with each batch. Playing with it, to get it right, results in tomato-basil-lemony heaven. Taste as you go, adjusting the lemon, oil, salt, and basil as you go. My guests drink it straight from the glass, and within seconds ask sheepishly, "Can I have a bit more?" No one can tell that it is vegan or so, so easy to prepare. Impress everyone, eat bountifully. SERVES 4 TO 6

1. Using a paring knife, cut away the stems and any tough seams or spots from the tomatoes. Cut large tomatoes into quarters. (No need to chop cherry tomatoes.) Transfer to a blender (skin, seeds, and all) and blend on low speed to break up the tomatoes.

2. Add a glug of the oil and about 1 teaspoon of the salt. Blend on low speed until chopped more finely, then increase the speed to high and whirl until smooth. This could take up to a minute.

3. Add another glug of oil and process on high speed until it is incorporated into the mixture. Keep adding the oil, with the machine running, until the mixture is thicker, paler, and looks like tomato soup to which someone has added just a touch of cream. You're looking for a creamy, bright summer in a sip. It should feel luxuriously thick and airy without being dense. This will take a few minutes, so be patient.

4. Add the basil and lemon juice (no seeds—if blended, they will make the "cream" bitter). Blend again just until the basil is very finely minced. Taste and season carefully with salt, more lemon juice, and basil as needed. Serve immediately or transfer to a bowl, cover, and refrigerate until chilled, at least 2 hours or up to 8 hours. Whisk before serving.

5. Pour the mixture into shallow bowls or stemless wineglasses. Drizzle with some of the herbed oil, if you wish. Garnish with a few basil leaves and serve.

CHAPTER 6

WARMER WEATHER BIGGER DISHES

2 lemons, sliced into thin rounds

2 yellow onions, cut into thick slices

6 garlic cloves, smashed under a knife and peeled

1 tablespoon ground sumac

2 chickens, 3 to 4 pounds each, giblets reserved for gravy/stock/etc., spatchcocked (see page 36)

Olive oil

Kosher salt

Rosemary sprigs

Freshly ground black pepper, for finishing

Roast Chickens with Lemon and Sumac

I'm a sucker for a whole roasted bird, mostly because of the uses *after* it's been made into a resplendent meal. But roasting a whole bird can be a time suck, for which I am *not a sucker*. So unless I am going for perfect presentation, in which a whole untouched bird is worth making, I will spatchcock my birds. Some argue that this process is time consuming, but there are only *two cuts to make*. And once you've practiced a few times, it is less time constraining than stuffing a chicken/trussing/etc., and you don't risk *overcooked* breasts and *undercooked thighs*. Even if you're cooking for fewer people than eight, go ahead and make two at a time. Then you'll have meat for later and plenty of carcass and herbs for stocks, too. **SERVES 8, 4 PER CHICKEN**

1. Preheat the oven to its highest setting, around 500° to 550°F.

2. On a sheet tray, create a bed of lemons, onions, and garlic. Sprinkle with the sumac. Lay the chickens on the bed of aromatics, skin side up. Drizzle olive oil over the chickens and sprinkle one teaspoon of salt over each chicken. Top the mixture with a few rosemary sprigs.

3. Put the chickens in the oven, quickly! Let's not lose heat! Reduce the temperature to 500°F. Roast for 15 minutes. Reduce the temperature to 450°F and cook for 20 minutes more, or until the chicken is crispy and the legs wiggle easily in the joints, for a total of 35 minutes. If you want to check for doneness with a thermometer, insert an instant-read thermometer in the thickest part of the breast—it should read 165°F.

4. Transfer to serving platters or a chopping board. Let stand for about 5 minutes and add pepper to finish. Carve the chickens and serve with the cooked aromatics and pan juices.

MISE EN PLACE
- *2 plates, one lined with paper towels*
- *Dutch oven*
- *Slotted spoon*
- *Microplane*
- *Shallow serving bowls*

8 ounces bacon slices, cut into 1-inch lengths (If you think you are going to snack on the bacon, make extra!)

4 chicken leg quarters, or 4 each chicken legs and thighs (about 2½ pounds)

Fine sea salt

1 white onion, chopped

8 ounces parsnips, cut into ½-inch dice

1 large leek, white and pale green parts only, rinsed well and cut into ½-inch dice

2 cups dry white wine

1 teaspoon ground coriander

¼ teaspoon fish sauce

3 cups Chicken Broth (page 46), or use canned chicken broth, as needed

4 dried bay leaves

2 clementines, peeled and separated into segments

FOR THE GREMOLATA

Cooked bacon (from above)

1 whole preserved lemon, skin minced, flesh reserved for its juice

2 garlic cloves, grated

4 tablespoons minced fresh cilantro

About 8 raw radishes, finely diced, or burnished radishes (see page 231)

Freshly ground blackpepper

Braised Chicken in White Wine with Bacon-Radish Gremolata

Coq au vin translates literally to "rooster (cockerel) in wine." It was traditionally made with red wine so the tannins could break down the tough old meat. These days we are much more likely to use a well-plumped, tender chicken from the grocery store and thus, tannins are no longer necessary. The lighter wine also makes this recipe more appealing in the warmer months. SERVES 4

1. Preheat the oven to 425°F. Put the bacon in the cold Dutch oven and place over medium-high heat. Cook, stirring occasionally, until the bacon is crisp and browned, about 8 minutes. (You want to render as much bacon fat as possible—starting in a cold pan works best.) Using a slotted spoon, transfer the bacon to a paper towel–lined plate, leaving the fat in the pan.

2. Season the chicken with salt. In batches, without crowding, add the chicken to the Dutch oven, skin side down, and cook until the underside is browned, about 5 minutes. Flip the chicken and cook the other side for about 3 minutes. Move the chicken to the other plate.

3. Pour all but 2 tablespoons fat out of the pan, and scoop out as many brown bits as you can. Too many will discolor the sauce. Reduce the heat to medium-low. Add the onion and cook, without stirring, until softened but not browned, about 5 minutes. Stir in the parsnips and leek and cook until softened, about 5 minutes. Add the wine and increase the heat to medium-high. Bring to a boil and let the wine reduce for about 3 minutes. Stir in the coriander and fish sauce.

4. Return the chicken to the pot, skin side up, nestled closely together. This placement will help keep the chicken moist. Pour in enough of the broth to barely cover the chicken. Add the bay leaves. Bring the broth to a simmer and cover the Dutch oven.

5. Bake for 45 minutes. Uncover the pot and cook to lightly brown the exposed chicken and reduce the broth, about 15 minutes. During the last 10 minutes, add the clementines.

6. MAKE THE GREMOLATA: Gently mix the reserved bacon, preserved lemon skin, garlic, and cilantro in a small bowl. Add the radishes and gently mix again. Season with a little salt and a few cracks of black pepper. Squeeze in the juice from the reserved preserved lemon flesh (press the flesh in a sieve over the relish).

7. Divide the chicken among serving bowls. Top each serving with some of the gremolata and serve hot.

MISE EN PLACE

- *Chilled bowl for whipping the cream*
- *Electric mixer*
- *1 or 2 half-sheet pans*
- *Medium saucepan*
- *Large bowl*

FOR THE BLUE CHEESE WHIP

1 cup heavy whipping cream

½ cup strong blue cheese, such as Stilton or Roquefort (generic blue cheese is too mild), crumbled

FOR THE WINGS

2 pounds chicken wings

Olive oil

1 teaspoon fine sea salt

½ cup (1 stick) salted butter

¼ cup mild hot sauce, such as Frank's RedHot

1 teaspoon Urfa biber or chipotle chile flakes (optional)

Hot Wings à les Américains with Blue Cheese Whip

In general, the French don't like super-spicy food, and hot wings don't exist at all in France. But my French friends love these. At first, they look like I've set their mouth on fire, but when I pass the cool blue cheese whipped cream, they bravely give it another go. You can also use the Ranch-y Dip (and More) (page 102) instead of the whip. My favorite hot sauce is Frank's RedHot, which is on the mild side. I know there are hotter sauces, but that is the brand used in the original recipe from Buffalo, New York. SERVES 6 TO 8, EXCEPT IN MY HOUSE (MORE LIKE 4)

1. **MAKE THE BLUE CHEESE WHIP:** Whip the cream in a chilled medium bowl with an electric mixer set on high speed until soft peaks form. Add the blue cheese and continue whipping until the mixture is stiff and the blue cheese is mostly absorbed. Refrigerate until ready to serve.

2. **MAKE THE WINGS:** Preheat the oven to 475°F. Arrange the wings on a half-sheet pan, leaving as much space as you can between them. If they seem crowded, use two sheets. Drizzle with olive oil, season with the salt, and toss on the sheet to coat. (Do not add pepper, as it will burn in the hot oven.) Bake until the wings are crisp and deep golden brown, 25 to 30 minutes.

3. Melt the butter with the hot sauce in a medium saucepan over medium heat. Whisk to combine. Pour into a large bowl, add the wings, and toss together. For spicier wings, sprinkle with the chile flakes and toss again. Serve the wings hot, with the whip for dipping.

4 small zucchini or yellow squash, about 2 pounds, tops and bottoms trimmed, cut in half lengthwise

2 eggplants, on the small side, about 12 ounces each, tops and bottoms trimmed, cut in half lengthwise

3 large bell peppers, mixed colors, quartered lengthwise and seeded

4 large ripe tomatoes, cut in half lengthwise

Extra-virgin olive oil

Fine sea salt

FOR THE TOMATO SAUCE

1 can crushed tomatoes

2 tablespoons tomato paste

1 teaspoon honey

2 teaspoons apple cider vinegar

1 teaspoon herbes de Provence

½ teaspoon kosher salt

Freshly ground black pepper

½ cup freshly grated Parmesan cheese

Flaky salt

Grilled Ratatouille

Ratatouille, with its main components of zucchini, eggplants, bell peppers, and tomatoes, is another Provençal specialty that I have found can be much more interesting to modern palates if lightened up a little. The original is a stew that can be on the heavy side. But when the ingredients are grilled, it really comes to life. SERVES 6 TO 8 AS A SIDE DISH

1. Preheat a gas grill to 500°F. For a charcoal grill, let the coals burn until they are covered with white ash. Move the coals to the edges of the grill, leaving the center empty. Brush the grill grates clean.

2. Combine the zucchini, eggplants, bell peppers, and tomatoes in a large bowl. Drizzle with oil, season with salt, and toss well to coat.

3. **MAKE THE TOMATO SAUCE:** Whisk together the crushed tomatoes, tomato paste, honey, vinegar, and herbes de Provence in a small bowl, and season with the salt and black pepper.

4. Remove the vegetables from the oil, letting any excess oil drip off into the bowl. Place them on the grill, cut sides down, and cover the grill. Grill until the undersides are charred with grill marks, about 3 minutes. Flip the vegetables over. Cover the grill and continue cooking until the vegetables are tender, 3 to 5 minutes more.

5. Transfer the vegetables to a platter. Sprinkle with the Parmesan and a hearty sprinkle of flaky salt. Serve with the tomato sauce on the side. This dish can be served hot, warm, or at ambient temperature.

- *Large bowl*
- *Serving platter*

2 whole chickens, spatchcocked
(see page 36)

Herby Ranch Marinade (page 102)
with 3 tablespoons salt added

Grilled Chicken with Ranch Marinade

I always spatchcock chicken (see page 36), because it results in the most even cooking. I especially love this because it can be multiplied to feed a crowd, depending on how much space you have on your grill. You'll want about one bird for every four people. **SERVES 8**

1.   Place the chickens in a large bowl. Reserve 1 cup of the marinade for later, and pour the remaining marinade over the chicken. Cover and refrigerate, turning the chicken occasionally, for at least 12 hours and up to 48 hours.

2.   Preheat a gas grill to 500°F. For a charcoal grill, let the coals burn until they are covered with white ash. Move the coals to the edges of the grill, leaving the center empty. Brush the grill grates clean.

3.   Remove the chickens from the marinade. Place, skin side down, on the grill. For a charcoal grill, place the chicken in the empty center part of the grid. Close the grill and cook for 15 minutes. If the chicken flares up, turn off a burner or two and move the chickens to the cooler area.

4.   Flip the birds over, skin side up, and pour the reserved marinade on top. Close the grill and cook until an instant-read thermometer inserted in the thigh reads 165°F, 20 to 25 minutes more.

5.   Transfer the chicken to a carving board. Let stand for 5 minutes, cut into serving pieces, transfer to a platter, and serve.

2 heads napa cabbage

Olive oil

Fine sea salt

½ cup (1 stick) salted butter, thinly sliced

2 tablespoons finely chopped fresh thyme or savory

Freshly ground black pepper

1 lemon, cut into wedges, for serving

Grilled Napa Cabbage "Steaks"

If I had to pick one recipe from this book to serve over and over, it would be this one. It's simple, it's stupid delicious, and it makes you look fancy, even though it's not really fancy at all. The idea is to cut "steaks" from a big head of napa cabbage, but to do that, you need to tie the head crosswise with string to hold the layers in place. Another tip—do not use tongs to turn the steaks. A large spatula (like the one you use to flip burgers) works much better. SERVES 4 TO 6

1.   Preheat a gas grill to 500°F. For a charcoal grill, let the coals burn until they are covered with white ash. Move the coals to the edges of the grill, leaving the center empty. Brush the grill grates clean.

2.   Rinse each cabbage well under cold running water. Tie three tight (but not digging into the head) loops of kitchen twine around the circumference of the cabbage, starting about 1 inch from the top and tying them equally apart. Use a large knife to trim off the top and bottom of the cabbage. Cut between the loops on the cabbage to make three slabs, each about 1½ inches thick, with the twine in the center of each slab. The twine will hold the leaves in place; tie them tighter, if necessary. Cut away any hanging twine. Repeat with the second cabbage. Drizzle the cabbage all over with oil and season with salt, rubbing it in as you might with a beef steak. Transfer the cabbage to a half-sheet pan.

3.   Place the cabbage steaks on the grill. Cover and cook until the undersides are charred with grill marks, about 5 minutes. Using a spatula (not tongs!), flip each cabbage over.

4.   Cover and grill for about 2 minutes. Scatter the butter over the cabbages, distributing it evenly, and top with the herbs. Close the grill and continue cooking until the undersides are charred with grill marks and the cabbage is softened, about 3 minutes more.

5.   Transfer each cabbage steak to a dinner plate. Remove the twine. Add a few cracks of pepper to each. Serve hot, with the lemon wedges.

- *2 medium bowls, 1 with ice water*
- *Large pot*
- *Large bowl*
- *Medium skillet*
- *Cutting board*
- *Four small bowls, for accoutrements*
- *Serving platter*

4 ounces cherry tomatoes, cut in halves lengthwise

Fine sea salt

3 tablespoons white distilled vinegar or apple cider vinegar

4 large eggs, at room temperature

½ pound small boiling potatoes, such as fingerlings or red-skinned

Olive oil

1 large red onion, cut into thin half-moons

8 ounces green beans, sliced on a bias into ¼-inch lengths

1 pound tuna steaks, cut about 1 inch thick, at room temperature

Freshly ground black pepper

¼ cup sesame seeds, black or white, preferably half of each, or substitute nigella seeds for the black sesame

Vegetable or canola oil

3 tablespoons Your Dream Vinaigrette (page 55)

2 tablespoons mayonnaise

1 tablespoon Dijon mustard

6 ounces mixed salad greens

¼ cup white anchovies (boquerones)

1 (2-ounce) can anchovy fillets in olive oil

¼ cup finely chopped fresh chives

Warm Salade Niçoise

I've realized that yes, indeed, there is room for a new version of Salade Niçoise. The "correct" way to make it is important to the unofficial Salade Niçoise Police and woe to those who miss the mark. The background to how this came to be is all a bit murky; the original Niçoise was tomatoes with anchovies, and was a *far cry* from the composed salad that is readily available throughout the world these days by the same name. My recipe would get me into Salade Niçoise Jail because I've added all sorts of extra ingredients and prepare them differently, giving gorgeous contrast.
SERVES 4

1. Season the cherry tomatoes with salt in a small bowl and set aside.

2. Fill a medium saucepan about three-quarters full with water and bring to a boil over high heat. Add the vinegar and 2 tablespoons salt. Using a slotted spoon, carefully slide the eggs into the boiling water. Reduce the heat so the eggs aren't bouncing around, and boil for exactly 7 minutes, for jammy yolks. While the eggs cook, prepare a bowl with ice water. Use a slotted spoon to transfer the eggs to the ice water and let stand until ready to peel.

3. Rinse the pot, and add the potatoes, cover with water, add a handful of salt, and bring to a boil over high heat. Reduce the heat to medium-low and cook until the potatoes are fork-tender, 10 to 15 minutes. Drain and place in a large bowl. Cover with a kitchen towel to keep warm.

4. Heat a glug of olive oil in a medium skillet over medium heat. Add the onion and cook, stirring occasionally, until it is tender and deep purple, about 10 minutes. Add the onion to the bowl with the potatoes. Wipe out the skillet and reserve for the tuna.

5. Peel and halve the eggs and add them to the bowl, along with the green beans. Re-cover with the towel to keep the mixture warm.

6. Season the tuna with salt and pepper. Spread the sesame seeds on a plate and coat the tuna on both sides, pressing the seeds in gently to adhere to the fish.

7. Heat a glug of vegetable oil in a large skillet over medium heat until it begins to shimmer. Add the tuna and cook, adjusting the heat as needed so the seeds don't burn, until the seeds are toasted on the underside, about 2 minutes. Flip the tuna and cook to toast the other sides, about 2 minutes more, for rare tuna. (Cook longer, if desired, if you want the tuna cooked more, but well-done tuna can be dry.) Transfer the tuna to a cutting board and cut across the grain into ½-inch strips.

8. Add the vinaigrette with the mayonnaise and mustard to the bowl with the potatoes, eggs, and green beans, and transfer to a platter. Top with the greens, then the tuna. Put the tomatoes, both types of anchovies, and chives in individual small bowls and serve with the salad so guests can add what they want to their portion. Dive in.

- *Blender*
- *Half-sheet pan*

FOR THE SALMON

1 salmon fillet, with skin, 2 to 3 pounds

Fine sea salt

8 ounces hulled strawberries (about 2 cups chopped)

1 teaspoon chile flakes, preferably chipotle, or Urfa biber

1 lime

1 small shallot, coarsely chopped

½ teaspoon ground coriander

FOR THE GARNISH

8 ounces cherry tomatoes, cut into halves

4 ounces strawberries, hulled and chopped

½ cup chopped fresh cilantro or basil, alone or in combination

Fine sea salt and freshly ground black pepper

Sweet Chile Glazed Salmon with Strawberry Sauce Vierge

At first, this audacious combination of strawberries and salmon was hotly contested by everyone at the Courageous Cooking School. But after enlisting friends and students to test many variations, we hit on this beautifully glazed recipe with a distinct bite of chiles. You might want to make extra glaze to whisk with some olive oil and a splash of vinegar to make into a fruity salad dressing. **SERVES 4**

1. **MAKE THE SALMON:** Preheat the oven to 450°F. Place the salmon on a half-sheet pan and season both sides with salt. Allow it to come to room temperature while you prepare the glaze.

2. Combine the strawberries and chile flakes in a blender. Grate in lime zest from the entire lime, cut the lime in half, and add about 1 tablespoon of the juice. Add the shallot, coriander, and a hearty pinch of salt, and process until smooth. Set aside.

3. Move the salmon to one side of the half-sheet pan. Pour about half of the sauce, in a strip the same length as the salmon, onto the center of the pan. Place the salmon on top. Smother the remaining glaze over the top of the salmon. Bake for 5 minutes to set the glaze.

4. Reduce the temperature to 425°F. Continue baking until the salmon is rare (the flesh looks rosy when prodded in the center with the tip of a sharp knife), about 10 minutes more. For medium-rare (the flesh is pink with a rosy center), bake for 15 minutes. For fully cooked salmon (the flesh is pink and opaque), allow 20 minutes.

5. **MAKE THE GARNISH:** Mix the tomatoes, strawberries, and herbs in a small bowl and season with salt and pepper.

6. You can cut the salmon into portions and serve on plates, but honestly, we eat it right off the sheet pan, with the garnish on the side.

2 tablespoons coarse-ground mustard

2 tablespoons maple syrup

3 whole cloves, very finely crushed with a mortar and pestle, or ¼ teaspoon ground cloves

1 garlic clove, grated

Fine sea salt

1 pound pork tenderloin, silver skin trimmed

1 tart apple, such as Granny Smith, cut crosswise cored, and sliced into 6 to 8 rings

¼ cup apple cider or juice

2 tablespoons dry white wine

2 dried bay leaves

Freshly ground black pepper

Maple-Mustard Pork

This exciting recipe is strangely suited for warm temperatures. While it has what I consider cold weather flavors of maple and apples, its acidic edge has a brightness that feels very summery. And is delicious served with a big side salad. SERVES 3 TO 4

1.   In a large bowl, whisk the mustard, maple syrup, cloves, and garlic with a pinch of salt. Smear the mixture all over the pork, place on a plate, cover, and let stand at room temperature for 30 minutes to 1 hour. (The pork can be refrigerated for up to

8 hours, but let it stand at room temperature for 1 hour before cooking.)

2.   Overlap the apples in the center of the baking dish in a row about the length of the tenderloin. Place the pork on the apples. Bake for 8 minutes. Pour in the cider, wine, and bay leaves and bake for 8 minutes more. Turn off the oven and let the pork continue to cook for about 15 minutes in the residual heat until an instant-read thermometer reads 145°F, about 15 minutes.

3.   Remove from the oven and let rest for about 5 minutes. Cut crosswise into thick slices, top with a few cracks of freshly ground pepper, and serve with the cooked apples.

MAKING AN OMELET INTO A MEAL

The perfect omelet (or *omelette* in French) is one of those things that many people claim to have the answer to, as if the answer they stumbled upon was heralded from the sky and written on stone tablets.

A marvelous omelet is far less complex or mysterious. The keys are speedy preparation, a reasonable amount of excellent eggs (skip the enormous five-egg omelet), and good butter. When you are cooking with so few ingredients, be sure they are top quality. Pasture-raised, organic eggs truly matter. You'll notice the difference immediately. It will be love at first bite.

Omelets make a filling breakfast, but they are so versatile they deserve to be on the table throughout the day. Omelets for lunch or a light dinner are transcendent, because soft, barely-held-together eggs and fresh herbs have a natural balance. The herbs will offset the creamy, decadent nature of the eggs and butter. A bright flavorful side salad with a homemade vinaigrette (see page 55) rounds out the meal. Simple salads are best in this case, as their freshness provides even greater balance to the eggs.

Making an omelet is one thing, but what to fill it with? You can keep it simple with shredded cheese, bacon or ham, and sautéed vegetables from asparagus to zucchini. But, as I do with my galettes, look to leftovers from recipes in this book to transform into omelets. Some suggestions include:

ASPARAGUS: Use the Roasted Asparagus on page 132.

CHÈVRE: Use the Bubbling Baked Chèvre on page 84.

FIG: Use the Figgy, Dippy, Jammy, and Smoky Spread on page 92.

ROASTED MUSHROOM: Use the Roasted Mushrooms with Escargot-Style Butter on page 235.

RATATOUILLE: Use the Grilled Ratatouille on page 172.

ROASTED CHERRY TOMATO "JAM" (page 106)

STUFFED ZUCCHINI BLOSSOMS (from the salad recipe on page 130)

MY TAPENADE (page 103)

FOR THE FILLING

Olive oil

8 to 10 cherry tomatoes, cut in half

½ shallot, finely chopped

Fine sea salt and freshly ground black pepper to taste

FOR THE OMELET

2 large eggs, preferably pasture-raised and organic

Fine sea salt and freshly ground black pepper

1 tablespoon salted butter, plus extra for serving

1 ounce rindless soft goat cheese, syche as chèvre, crumbled

4 large basil leaves, cut into chiffonade (see page 33), or other fresh herbs you have on hand

Large pinch of flaky salt, for finishing

Summer Omelet with Cherry Tomatoes, Chèvre, and Basil

Everyone needs to know how to make a simple omelet. In the summer, when the produce is bountiful, your filling choices are enormous, but the classic combination of tomatoes and basil is a great place to start practicing your omelet skills. For more ideas throughout the year and omelet basics, see page 184. **MAKES 1 OMELET, CAN EASILY BE SCALED TO SERVE MORE**

1. **MAKE THE FILLING:** Heat a glug of oil in a medium nonstick skillet over medium heat. Add the tomatoes and shallot. Cook, stirring occasionally, until the shallot softens and the tomatoes begin to give off juices, about 2 minutes. Season with salt and pepper. Transfer to a small plate. Wipe out the skillet.

2. **MAKE THE OMELET:** Whisk the eggs briskly in a medium bowl. Add two pinches of salt and a crack of pepper and whisk again, being sure to combine the whites and yolks, but don't overbeat them. Overbeating toughens the eggs, and we want tender eggs here.

3. Melt the butter in a skillet over medium-high heat until the butter foams up and then subsides. Pour all of the beaten eggs at once into the skillet. Let the eggs bubble up.

4. Let the eggs cook until they are just beginning to set around the edges, about 1 minute. Using a silicone spatula, lift up an edge of the omelet and tilt the skillet, so the uncooked eggs on top flow underneath. Continue cooking, occasionally lifting up the omelet edge and tilting the skillet, until the eggs are almost set on top, about 1 minute. The omelet is done when the eggs are barely set. The top will still look shiny. French omelets are supposed to be very moist.

5. Scrape the filling in a vertical column on the side of the omelet opposite the handle and sprinkle with the cheese. Remove the skillet from the heat. Turn the skillet so the handle is facing the three o'clock position. (Or nine o'clock if you are left-handed.) Using an underhanded grip, grab the skillet handle in one hand, and a dinner plate in another. Slide the omelet out of the skillet so it is about halfway onto the plate. Turn the skillet bottom-side up so the omelet rolls and folds over on itself to cover the filling, sliding the omelet entirely onto the plate. Sprinkle with the basil and flaky salt and . . . voilà!

Fine sea salt

½ cup walnuts

Semolina Pasta (page 188), cut for fettuccine, or 1 pound store-bought fresh pasta

3 tablespoons extra-virgin olive oil

About ¼ cup chopped fresh herbs, such as parsley, chives, tarragon, thyme, rosemary, basil, mint, and oregano, in any combination

¼ cup freshly grated Parmesan cheese, plus a chunk of Parmesan for serving

Freshly ground black pepper

Homemade Pasta with Toasted Walnuts and Fresh Herbs

Making homemade pasta into a simple dinner is a fun thing to master. This recipe is very straightforward, and if you have the Universal Herbed Oil (page 63) on hand, you are golden. (Just use it in place of the olive oil and skip the fresh herbs.) While a small portion of pasta is a welcome starter in the Italian tradition or presented as a side dish elsewhere, I love to serve this as a light main course, as the olive oil and egg-rich pasta make it feel more substantial. It is the perfect recipe to show off your handmade pasta. The delicate sauce lets the pasta shine. **SERVES 4 TO 6**

1. Bring a large pot of salted water to a boil over high heat.

2. Meanwhile, heat an empty skillet over medium-high heat. Add the walnuts and cook, stirring often, until toasted and fragrant, about 5 minutes. Do not let these beauties burn, and they can burn quickly! Transfer to a plate and let cool. Coarsely chop the walnuts.

3. Add the pasta to the water and cook until al dente, about 3 minutes. Drain.

4. Heat the oil in a large skillet over medium heat. Stir in the herbs and walnuts and let them wilt for about 15 seconds. Add the pasta, followed by the cheese. Mix gently to coat with the herbed oil. Season with salt and pepper. Serve hot, with a chunk of Parmesan passed on the side for grating.

2 cups semolina flour, plus extra for sprinkling

3 extra-large eggs, or 3 large eggs plus 1 large egg yolk

Semolina Pasta

I think many Americans tend to shy away from handmade pasta. It comes off as involved, and therefore is reserved for special occasions. I was once that person.

I experimented with many recipes before landing on this one, which I consider foolproof. This can be done on a wood board or in a bowl. I prefer channeling the grandmothers of yore and doing it on a board. But if you prefer less flour on your counter top, a bowl is fine. I recommend doubling the recipe and freezing one batch to have another meal on hand in a snap.

SERVES 4, MAKES ABOUT 1 POUND PASTA

1. Pour the semolina onto a board or into a medium mixing bowl. Use a fork to make a wide, shallow well in the center about 6 inches wide and 1 inch deep. Crack the eggs into the well. Using the fork, mix the eggs in the well until they are combined. Next, start moving the fork out from the center to the walls of the well, pulling a bit of the semolina from each turn of the fork into the eggs, eventually bringing all of the semolina into the central mass. When you have made a dough, gather it up into a moist cohesive ball with your hands. If it is sticky, work in a little more semolina, a tablespoon at a time. If it is too dry and crumbly, do the same with a few sprinkles of water.

2. Sprinkle a work surface with semolina. Knead the dough on the surface until the dough bounces back when indented with your thumb, about 5 minutes.

3. Shape the dough into a ball, return it to the bowl, and cover with a damp cloth. If using immediately, let rest at room temperature for 30 minutes. If you're using a bit later, place in the refrigerator and let relax for at least 1 hour and up to 24 hours. Let the dough stand at room temperature for about 20 minutes to lose its chill before rolling.

4. Divide the dough into quarters. Set the pasta machine with the rollers at the widest setting. Sprinkle the work surface with a bit more semolina.

5. Working with one piece of dough at a time, roll it out with a rolling pin into an oblong shape about ½ inch thick. The dough should roll out easily, not snap back when rolled out, and should not stick to the rolling pin. Run the dough through the machine. Do not worry about flouring the dough unless it is sticking, and then just add a sprinkling on both sides.

6. If all is well after your initial run, you're ready to rock. Simply run the pasta through the machine, each time lowering the setting a notch so the opening gets progressively smaller and the pasta becomes thinner. When the pasta is about

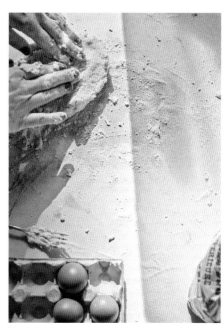

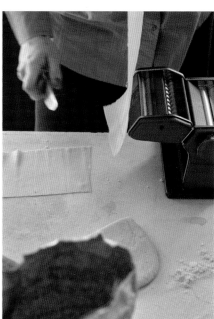

2 feet in length, cut it in half and continue to run the pieces through separately.

7. When the pasta is thin enough to see light through it, stop rolling. This is usually the second or third notch from the last. To cut, run the pasta through the cutters. Or roll up each piece of dough into a cylinder and cut crosswise into the widths you want.

8. Sprinkle a baking pan with semolina. Make mounds of the pasta on the pan and sprinkle with more semolina. (Covered with plastic wrap, the pasta can be refrigerated for up to 2 days.)

FOR THE RICE

¼ cup olive oil

1 white onion or yellow, diced

4 garlic cloves, grated

2 cups short-grain brown rice

3 cups Rich Stock (page 43) or water

4 or 5 roasted beets (see page 212), cut into ½-inch dice

1 tablespoon salted butter

FOR THE DRESSING

⅓ cup olive oil

¼ cup dark soy sauce or regular with a pinch of brown sugar

¼ cup sherry vinegar or balsamic vinegar

1 garlic clove, grated

2 teaspoons gochujang, or
2 teaspoons maple syrup and
1 teaspoon Urfa biber (optional)

6 cups mesclun or baby spinach

8 ounces small, raw broccoli florets

6 scallions, white and green parts, thinly sliced on the bias

Warm Brown Rice Salad

The Bookmill in Montague, Massachusetts, is one of my very happy places. I try to visit it annually. Their Witbier with Raspberry Lambic Ice Cubes (page 109) is one of my favorite summer beverages and their warm brown rice salad is *legendary*.

Short-grain brown rice is grown locally in Provence, a mere hour away in the Camargue, an area known for salt, rosé wine, rice, and pink flamingos (whole lotta pink). I have taken some of the flavor profiles from the Bookmill's salad, and Frenchified it. It inadvertently honors the flamingos where the rice is grown because the roasted beets turn the rice a true shade of pink. My daughter calls it pink rice, I just call it hearty comfort food. **SERVES 4**

1. **MAKE THE RICE:** Heat the oil in a medium saucepan over medium heat. Add the onion and cook, stirring occasionally, until golden, about 5 minutes. Stir in the garlic and cook until beginning to brown, 1 to 2 minutes more. Stir in the rice, followed by the stock. Cover and bring to a boil over high heat. Reduce the heat to medium-low and simmer until the rice is tender, 30 to 40 minutes, depending on the origination of the rice. (French rice is especially hearty.) During the last 5 minutes, stir in the beets. Drain the rice if necessary. Transfer the rice to a large bowl. Add the butter and stir until melted.

2. **MAKE THE DRESSING:** Process the oil, soy sauce, vinegar, garlic, and gochujang, if using, in a blender until smooth. Stir about ¼ cup of the dressing into the warm rice.

3. Toss the greens and broccoli with the remaining dressing. For each serving, spoon a portion of the rice onto a plate. Top with a handful of the salad, and sprinkle with the scallions.

4. This can be served warm or at room temperature.

CHAPTER 7

WARMER WEATHER SWEETS

MISE EN PLACE
- *10-inch pie dish or 9-inch square baking pan*
- *Medium bowl*
- *Flour sifter or wire mesh sieve*
- *Wire cooling rack*

Softened butter, for the baking dish

1 pound cherries, pitted (2½ to 3 cups)

4 large eggs, at room temperature

½ cup granulated sugar

1¾ cups whole milk

2 teaspoons vanilla extract, or 1 teaspoon vanilla extract and 1 teaspoon orange liqueur, such as Cointreau

½ teaspoon freshly grated orange zest

¾ cup all-purpose flour

½ teaspoon smoked chile flakes, such as Cobanero or chipotle, or Urfa biber, finely ground in a spice grinder, plus extra unground flakes for sprinkling (optional)

¾ teaspoon kosher salt

¼ teaspoon ground cinnamon

2 tablespoons confectioners' sugar for garnish

Not-Too-Sweet Whipped Cream (page 59), for serving (optional)

Cherry Clafoutis with Cobanero Chile

I adore clafoutis (pronounced klah-foo-TEE) because it's like a pancake without the fuss. Perfect for either dessert or a breakfast dish, it is more of a technique than an actual recipe because it can be applied to so many different fruits, such as peaches, plums, apricots, berries, and thinly sliced apples and pears. Here, I've taken one of the most popular versions, with cherries, but added a spicy element to change things up a bit. Cobanero chile flakes are perfect because their heat contains a pronounced fruity note. SERVES ABOUT 8

1. Preheat the oven to 400°F. Butter a 10-inch pie dish or 9-inch square baking dish. Scatter the cherries in the bottom of the dish.

2. Whisk together the eggs and sugar well in a medium bowl. Whisk in the milk, vanilla, and orange zest. Sift in the flour, chile flakes, salt, and cinnamon and whisk until smooth. (Add any chile flakes left in the sifter.) Pour the batter evenly over the cherries.

3. Bake until the clafoutis is golden brown and puffed along the edges. This can take anywhere from 35 to 60 minutes, so check it after 35 minutes and then again in five minute intervals. Let cool slightly on a wire rack until warm.

4. Sift confectioners' sugar over the top, sprinkle with additional chile flakes, if using, and serve with the whipped cream, if using.

- *Small saucepan*
- *Fine mesh sieve*
- *Medium saucepan*
- *Mixing bowl*
- *8 ramekins*
- *Large rimmed baking dish*
- *Tongs*

1½ cups (12 ounces) fresh strawberries, hulled and sliced, divided

¾ cup granulated sugar, divided

1 cup heavy cream

1 cup whole milk

1½ teaspoons ground cardamom

8 large egg yolks

1 teaspoon vanilla extract

Pinch of salt

Mint leaves for garnish

Strawberry Cardamom Pot de Crème

Pot de crème is a simple dessert that is generally *not all that flavorful*. Strawberry and cardamom here take it up a couple notches. This is best when strawberries are at their peak; when made with off-season strawberries the flavor just doesn't come through as well. You can substitute strawberries for blueberries, blackberries, or raspberries and this will be just as delightful. Just make sure you strain the purée well regardless of the berry. SERVES 8

1. Preheat the oven to 325°F.

2. In a small saucepan, heat 1 cup of the strawberries over low heat with 2 tablespoons of the sugar until they become soft and release their juices. This should take about 5 minutes. Remove from heat and let it cool slightly.

3. Blend the cooked strawberries until smooth using a blender or food processor. Strain the mixture through a fine-mesh sieve to remove any seeds. Set the strawberry purée aside.

4. In a medium saucepan, combine the cream, milk, and cardamom. Heat over medium heat until it begins to steam, but don't let it come to a boil. Remove from heat and set aside.

5. In a separate bowl, whisk together the egg yolks, the remaining sugar (about ½ cup), vanilla, and salt until well combined.

6. Slowly pour the warm cream mixture into the egg yolk mixture while continuously whisking. This is to temper the eggs and avoid curdling. Mix until well combined.

7. Stir the strained strawberry purée into the egg and cream mixture, ensuring it's thoroughly incorporated.

8. Divide the mixture evenly among the 8 ramekins in the baking dish. (See Note)

9. Pour hot water into the baking dish until it reaches about halfway up the sides of the ramekins. This creates a water bath and helps the custards cook evenly.

10. Carefully transfer the baking dish to the preheated oven and bake for 30 to 35 minutes, or until the custards are set around the edges but still slightly jiggly in the center.

11. Using tongs, remove the ramekins from the water bath and allow them to cool to room temperature. Then, refrigerate for at least 4 hours or overnight to let them fully set.

12. When ready to serve, garnish each pot de crème with the remaining fresh strawberry slices and mint leaves, and a bit of Not-Too-Sweet Whipped-Cream (page 59) if desired.

Note: Fill ramekins in the oven first, then fill water into deep baking dish. This method prevents the dance of spilling the custard into the water or even worse, the water into the custard (instant scrambled egg dessert).

FOR THE SHORTCAKES

2¼ cups all-purpose flour, plus extra for rolling

1 tablespoon baking powder

3 teaspoons granulated sugar, divided

¼ teaspoon fine sea salt

8 tablespoons (1 stick) cold salted butter

1 cup whole milk, as needed

FOR THE BERRIES

2 tablespoons granulated sugar

3 cups roughly chopped mixed berries, about 18 ounces

2 to 4 tablespoons brandy, Cognac, or bourbon, to taste

½ teaspoon lemon juice

FOR THE WHIPPED CREAM

1 cup heavy cream

3 tablespoons confectioners' sugar

¼ cup crème fraîche or sour cream

½ teaspoon vanilla extract

Pinch of fine sea salt

Shortcakes with Boozy Berries and Cream

One of my favorite desserts growing up was store-bought shortcakes, the small divot filled in with strawberries covered in half-and-half. In France, sponge cakes are sold everywhere, but biscuits are unusual, so I make the biscuit version when I'm feeling nostalgic. When I am in the US, I will buy the golden, cakey shortcakes for old times' sake. **SERVES 8**

1. Preheat the oven to 425°F. Line a half-sheet pan with parchment paper.

2. **MAKE THE SHORTCAKES:** In a large bowl, whisk together the flour, baking powder, 2 teaspoons of the sugar, and the salt. Grate the butter right into the dry ingredients and toss everything together. Toss to coat, and use your fingertips to rub the ingredients together until the mixture looks like coarse breadcrumbs with some pea-size bits. Stir in enough of the milk to make a shaggy dough. Do not overmix; that makes the biscuits dense, and you're going for light and fluffy.

3. Transfer to a lightly floured surface and press into a rough rectangle. Flour the top and roll into a 12 by 8-inch rectangle. Fold the dough in half onto itself, brushing off excess flour. Roll a second time into a 12 by 8-inch rectangle, and fold in half. Flour the top and roll into an 9 by 6-inch rectangle about ½ inch thick.

4. Use a biscuit cutter or a drinking glass dipped in flour and cut out six 3-inch rounds. Arrange on the prepared baking sheet, placing them an inch or so apart. Gently press the scraps together into a rectangle about ½ inch thick. Cut out 2 additional rounds and transfer to the baking sheet. If you wish, press the remaining scraps together to get a "bonus" biscuit, although this one won't rise as well as the others.

5. Refrigerate the biscuits for 15 to 30 minutes. Sprinkle the tops with the remaining teaspoon of sugar. Bake until risen and golden brown, 16 to 18 minutes. Transfer to a wire cooling rack and cool completely.

6. **MAKE THE BERRIES:** Bring the sugar and 1 tablespoon of water to a boil in a medium saucepan over medium heat, stirring to dissolve the sugar. Add the berries and simmer, stirring occasionally, until the berries have begun to soften and liquid is syrupy, 3 to 4 minutes. Remove from the heat, stir in the brandy and lemon juice. Transfer to a bowl and let cool.

recipe continues

7. **MAKE THE WHIPPED CREAM:** Whip the cream and confectioners' sugar in a chilled medium bowl with an electric mixer on high speed (or use a whisk) until soft peaks form. Add the crème fraîche, vanilla, and salt and whip just until stiff.

8. **TO ASSEMBLE:** Cut the biscuits in half. For each serving, place a biscuit bottom on a dessert plate. Top with a generous spoonful of berries and a dollop of the cream. Place the top of the biscuit, cut side down, in the bowl of berries and let it soak up some of the syrup. Turn the biscuit syrup-side down to make a berry sandwich. Top with a dollop of cream. Serve immediately and smile.

- *Large bowl*
- *Whisk*
- *Large bowl with ice water*
- *6 ramekins*

2 preserved lemons

FOR THE FILLING

4 large eggs

1 cup granulated sugar

1 cup heavy cream

1 teaspoon vanilla extract

¼ cup butter

Store-bought Oreo Cookie Crust
(optional)

FOR SERVING (OPTIONAL)

Confectioners' sugar

Fresh mint leaves

Preserved Lemon Custard

I'm a sucker for anything savory and sweet in combination. And this is no exception. Using preserved lemons gives this custard a distinctive pucker, but also lends a ton of umami and salt to the final dessert. You can either pour the custard into a premade Oreo Cookie Crust (which is delicious and my first choice) or pour into small ramekins and serve crust free.
SERVES 6

1. Preheat the oven to 325°F.

2. Rinse the lemons under cold water to remove excess salt. Cut the lemons in half and remove the seeds. Finely chop the lemon peels.

3. **MAKE THE FILLING:** In a large bowl, whisk together the eggs and sugar until well combined. Add the cream and vanilla, and continue to whisk until the mixture is smooth. Mix the cream and egg mixture in a double boiler, constantly whisking until thickened. What you will notice is that the mixture will "foam" then all of a sudden the foam will be gone. This is a sign you are close to finished. Keep the mixture moving as letting it sit still will turn this into lemon scrambled eggs partially, which also is what happens when it's cooked too long.

4. Remove from heat, and add the butter into the mixture.

5. Place over an ice bath, and gently fold in the chopped preserved lemon peels into the egg mixture.

6. Place the premade cookie crust on a rimmed baking sheet to catch any spills. Pour the preserved lemon filling into the crust. If going crust free, pour into the ramekins, spreading it out evenly, then fill the baking sheet with water until it reaches about a third of the way up the ramekin. Bake in the oven for 30 to 35 minutes until the custard is barely set.

7. **FOR SERVING:** Remove the tart from the oven and let it cool to room temperature. Once the tart has cooled, you can sift confectioners' sugar over the top for a nice finishing touch. You can also add some mint for a pop of color and flavor. You can refrigerate this for up to 3 days.

8. Slice the preserved lemon tart into 8 equal portions. Serve and enjoy!

MISE EN PLACE
- *Half-sheet pan*
- *Parchment paper*
- *Electric mixer*
- *Soup spoon*
- *Wire rack for cooling*

FOR THE MERINGUES

4 large egg whites, at room temperature

1 cup granulated sugar

2 teaspoons cornstarch

1 teaspoon fresh lemon juice

⅛ teaspoon fine sea salt

FOR A FIG TOPPING

8 ounces sliced figs

2 tablespoons honey

½ teaspoon ground cardamom

FOR A TROPICAL FRUIT TOPPING

3 kiwis, peeled and roughly chopped

1 cup pineapple, cut into ½-inch dice

¼ cup sweetened coconut flakes

FOR A STRAWBERRY-CHOCOLATE TOPPING

3 tablespoons coconut oil

1 cup semisweet chocolate chips

10 ounces strawberries, sliced, about 2 cups sliced

Miniature Meringues with Seasonal Fruit

I make these frequently because I often have leftover egg whites due to the amount of egg yolks in French cooking (thank you, hollandaise!). For such an elegant dessert, meringue is pretty easy. I've included a few different topping options, depending on the season/what you have on hand. Try to avoid making this when the weather is damp or humid, as the meringues can be a bit dense and chewy rather than light and crisp. All of these variations would benefit from a dollop of Not-Too-Sweet Whipped-Cream (page 59) and topped with a few fresh berries, but it's not a requirement. SERVES 8

1. **MAKE THE MERINGUES:** Preheat the oven to 250°F. Line a half-sheet pan with parchment paper. Beat the egg whites in a medium bowl with an electric mixer set on medium speed until they form soft peaks. Gradually beat in the sugar, about a tablespoon at a time, beating until the whites form stiff, glossy, marshmallow-like peaks. Add the cornstarch, lemon juice, and salt and beat for an additional 30 seconds to incorporate.

2. Using a large soup spoon, drop 8 mounds of meringue (about ½ cup each), onto the baking sheet, spacing at least 2 inches apart. Use the back of the spoon to create a well with ½-inch sides in the center of each meringue.

3. Bake until the meringues are firm to the touch, about 1¼ hours. Turn off the oven and let the meringues stand, with the door closed, for 1 hour. Transfer the meringues to a wire rack to cool completely.

4. Meanwhile, prepare one of the toppings.

5. **FOR THE FIG:** Mix the figs, honey, and cardamom gently in a bowl. Divide among the meringues and serve.

6. **FOR THE TROPICAL FRUIT:** Mix the kiwi, pineapple, and coconut. Divide among the meringues and serve.

7. **FOR THE STRAWBERRY-CHOCOLATE:** Melt the coconut oil in a small saucepan over medium heat. Remove from the heat and add the chocolate chips. Let stand for 2 to 3 minutes to soften the chocolate, then whisk until smooth. Divide the strawberries among the meringues, top with chocolate sauce (which will harden as it cools!), and serve.

- *12-cup fluted tube pan*
- *Whisk*
- *3 medium bowls*
- *Small bowl*
- *Wire cooling rack*
- *Small saucepan*
- *Blender*

FOR THE CAKE

Nonstick baking spray or standard cooking spray with flour

1½ cups plus 1 tablespoon all-purpose flour, plus more for the pan, if needed

1 cup almond flour, preferably blanched

2 teaspoons baking powder

1 teaspoon kosher salt

5 large eggs, at room temperature

1¼ cups granulated sugar

¾ cup olive oil

1 teaspoon vanilla extract

Finely grated zest of 1 lemon

2 ripe fresh or frozen peaches, peeled and cut into ½-inch dice (about 1½ cups)

FOR THE GLAZE

1 cup fresh or frozen blueberries

1½ cups confectioners' sugar, plus more as needed

2 teaspoons lemon juice

Pinch of kosher salt

¼ cup sliced almonds, raw or toasted (optional)

Peach Olive Oil Cake with a Lemon Blueberry Glaze

This little number is heavenly. When baking during the summer, I want to be sure that my time in a warm kitchen is well spent, and this cake is pretty with a deep fruit flavor. Peaches are one of summer's ultimate treats, and while this is at its best with fresh fruit, I've used frozen peaches, too, with delectable results. SERVES 8 TO 10

1. **MAKE THE CAKE:** Preheat the oven to 350°F. Spray the inside of a 12-cup fluted tube pan with nonstick baking spray. (Or use standard cooking spray and dust the inside of the pan with flour, and tap out the excess.)

2. Whisk 1½ cups of the all-purpose flour, almond flour, baking powder, and salt together in a medium bowl.

3. Beat the eggs and sugar in a medium bowl with an electric mixer set on high speed until pale and triple in volume, about 5 minutes. Beat in the oil, vanilla, and lemon zest and mix for about 30 seconds to incorporate.

4. In three additions, gently fold the flour mixture into the beaten eggs, just until combined.

5. Toss the peaches with the remaining 1 tablespoon of flour in a small bowl and fold them into the batter.

6. Pour the batter into the prepared pan and smooth the top. Bake until a wooden toothpick inserted in the center comes out clean, 50 to 55 minutes. Cool in the pan on a wire cooling rack for 15 minutes. Invert the cake onto the rack and cool completely.

7. **MAKE THE GLAZE:** Add the blueberries and 1 tablespoon water to a small saucepan over medium heat, and cook, stirring often, until the berries have burst and release their juice, about 5 minutes. Purée in a blender, making sure you leave a bit of room for steam to escape as you do. Pour the blueberry purée into a medium bowl. Add the confectioners' sugar with the lemon juice and salt. If needed, whisk in more confectioners' sugar until the glaze has the consistency of melted ice cream.

8. Place the rack over a plate to catch the drips. Pour the glaze over the cake, letting the excess run down the sides. Sprinkle with the almonds, if using. Let the glaze set. (The cake can be refrigerated in an airtight container for up to 3 days.)

PART THREE

Cooler Weather Recipes

I know the summer rush has mellowed when Parisian accents disappear from the village, the English pubs become homey rather than swollen with people, and Scandinavian languages aren't picked up in every corner of the local restaurants. When parking at the *marché paysan*, or our local produce market, is no longer a fraught game of Tetris.

Fall in the Riviera is a hat tip to a life without plans. It is slipping into a restaurant without a reservation. The Courageous Cooking School reopens for guests in the La Pitchoune kitchen. We casually invite friends to dinners at home without making it a party.

The garden groans with produce this time of year. The tomato vines droop heavily. We are overrun with watermelons that yield sweet pink juice. I am usually overwhelmed by the bounty and almost always have enough butternut squash larger than most infants to fill three to four baskets full to the brim. (I've been known to snuggle a butternut squash as if I am holding a child while walking through the garden.)

Our hens produce abundant eggs when fall arrives; I think the shift in weather offers the entire region's inhabitants a small boon in joy. By fall, zucchini has been coming in heavy for months, I've made every squash dish possible, and olives appear. I count down the days until we thwack our trees (and that of our neighbors) with twenty-five-foot poles, combing branches for green and black fruits that tumble to our feet on one-hundred-foot nets. We always think of our daughter's birth around this time. She came crashing into the world on November 9, pretty much the ideal day for an olive harvest party and get-together with friends. Fall is measured by abundance, gatherings, and the reappearance of red wine as a staple of the dinner table.

Fall is a labor of love in the Riviera. And that labor is very much worth all the fruit.

Fall is famously wonderful on the Riviera, but winter is resplendent, and marked by a very strange friend. The arrival of snow. Not so much on the beach, but just a mere thirty miles away into the hills of the Alps. The region is still very much considered the French Riviera, and there are ski resorts there. Mornings can start with cool water swims in the Mediterranean, and by lunch you can be strapped to skis and on a chairlift.

I am almost loathe to write this, because we cherish this quiet time, but I would be remiss if I didn't share the ultimate hot tip: come to the Riviera in the winter.

Sure, the breeze is a tad gustier. The weather is a bit more temperate and sometimes . . . temperamental. But Grasse and the surrounding areas shine in the winter. Granted, there aren't swimsuits or lounges by a pool. Winter here doesn't scream "rosé all day." But it's the season of sunlight skittering among racing clouds, cups of tea, and a blanket on the terrace, which is just as magical as the warm weather routines.

The food during this season is sublime. Beef stews drowned in wine, bean dishes with tied bundles of pork, and roasted chickens prepared every which way. It's never really cold and is absolutely the most divine time for pizza ovens and outdoor hearths. Wood-fired grills lend life to fish, lamb, vegetables, and pretty much anything else that needs to be cooked. The markets teem with dense produce, and there's no traffic. In other words, winter is the best time for cooking outside, extending the seasons of beautiful food prepared simply and easily.

So, come in the winter, but don't tell anyone just how sumptuous the Riviera is from December through February. (Please! Keep it our petite secret.) I'll happily meet you on the terrace of a restaurant with a sea view. We can have a glass or two of a light, red Burgundy.

CHAPTER 8

COOLER WEATHER STARTERS, SOUPS, SALADS, AND SIDES

6 whole beets, about 5 ounces each, without greens, unpeeled but scrubbed

Rosemary sprigs (one for each beet)

Olive oil

Fine sea salt

Balsamic vinegar (optional)

Whole Roasted Beets

The French word for beets is *betterave* (pronounced bet-rahvuh). I believe this is useful information, because if you go up to a farmer at the market and compliment him on his *beau* beet, thinking you are praising his beautiful red root vegetable in Fran-glish, you might get quite the shocking response. This happened to a very demure friend, who thought she was complimenting a farmer on his market display. I'm pretty sure he was ready to take her home with him. That is how I found out that *bite* (pronounced "beet") is slang for male genitalia. The more you know.

The French find whole beets to be such an important everyday ingredient (mostly for salads) that you can buy cooked beets at markets, ready to take home in a vacuum-sealed bag. I roast a couple of pounds at a time. They keep in the fridge for at least a week, and make great flavor additions/colors for dips and gazpachos, as well as for salads. If using different colored beets, roast them separately because the red beets will tint the others. MAKES 6 BEETS

1. Preheat the oven to 450°F. Wrap the beets in a large sheet of parchment paper and put them in a lidded casserole or roasting dish large enough to hold them in a single layer. Don't worry if the paper isn't completely closed. Top each beet with a sprig of rosemary, a drizzle of oil, a pinch of salt, and a splash of vinegar, if using. Cover the parcel tightly with the lid.

2. Roast until the beets are tender and can be easily pierced with a skewer or thin knife, 45 minutes to 1 hour. The exact cooking time will depend on the size of the beet. Uncover and let cool. Leave the skins (they are edible) or peel the beets, it's up to you. (The beets can be stored in a covered container and refrigerated, covered or not, for up to a week.)

- *Heavy knife*
- *Kitchen scissors*
- *Aluminum foil*
- *Roasting pan, or two 9-inch cake pans*

4 large artichokes, the bigger the better

2 lemons, cut in half

Olive oil

Fine sea salt and freshly ground black pepper

2 teaspoons herbes de Provence, or 1 teaspoon dried thyme

4 garlic cloves, grated

Hollandaise (page 54),
Béarnaise (see Note page 54),
Mayonnaise (page 52), or
Your Dream Vinaigrette (page 55)
for serving

Oven-Roasted Artichokes

Earthy artichokes can lose their flavor when they are overcooking in boiling water or steam. This recipe fixes that problem by roasting in a hot oven, which applies flavor instead of taking it away. That being said, artichokes are often more about the sauce than their flesh, and the French acknowledge this with copious servings of béarnaise or hollandaise.

Don't toss the artichoke leaves! Use them for an artichoke broth (see page 49). **SERVES 4 AS A STARTER**

1. Preheat the oven to 425°F. Using a heavy knife, cut the top of each artichoke off about 1 inch from the pointed tip. Cut off the thick stem, if attached. Using kitchen scissors, snip the thorny tip from every other leaf. Rub the artichoke all over with the cut side of a lemon half.

2. Place each artichoke on a piece of aluminum foil large enough to wrap it. Opening up the leaves to accept the seasonings, drizzle a healthy glug of oil over the artichoke, season with the salt and a few cracks of pepper, sprinkle with about ½ teaspoon of the herbes de Provence, and sprinkle with the garlic. Rub the seasonings between the leaves as best as you can. Squeeze the juice from the lemon half all over the artichoke, and wrap the artichoke in the foil. Nestle the artichokes in a roasting pan.

3. Roast until the artichoke leaves are tender enough to be easily pulled off, 1¼ to 1½ hours. (Carefully open a packet—watch out for the steam—to check for doneness.) Unwrap the artichokes.

4. Serve the artichokes warm with small bowls of the sauce of your choice on the side. Provide an empty bowl to hold the scraped leaves.

FOR THE BONES AND MUSHROOMS

4 beef bones with marrow, each about 8 to 12 inches long, sawed in half lengthwise by the butcher or 8 to 12 crosscut bones

Fine sea salt

2 tablespoons vegetable or canola oil

6 ounces shiitake, stemmed, or other wild mushrooms, stemmed and thinly sliced

FOR THE HERBED VINAIGRETTE

½ cup coarsely chopped mixed fresh herbs, such as parsley, cilantro, or chives

2 shallots, finely chopped

2 tablespoons red wine vinegar or apple cider vinegar

2 garlic cloves, grated

Fine sea salt and freshly ground black pepper

4 tablespoons olive oil

Crostini (page 60) or store-bought thin toasts, for serving

Roasted Bone Marrow with Crisp Mushrooms and Herbed Vinaigrette

Bone marrow has become a common sight on American restaurant menus, finally crossing the pond after generations on the continent. I first came across it at a restaurant in Burlington, Vermont. The bone was split lengthwise, looking like a canoe, and was served with tiny spoons and crisp toasts. I was hooked. In France, beef bones filled with marrow are often considered discard items and only used for stock, so I can get them for free (or cheaply) from the neighborhood butcher. The minute I discovered this, bone marrow became a staple of my diet. I think its richness demands that it be paired with vegetables to give the dish some balance. SERVES 4

1. **MAKE THE BONES AND MUSHROOMS:** Preheat the oven to 450°F. Place the bones, cut sides up, on the half-sheet pan. Season generously with salt. Roast until the marrow is soft but not melting, about 20 minutes.

2. Meanwhile, heat the oil in a large skillet over medium-high heat. Add the mushrooms and cook, stirring very infrequently, until the liquid evaporates and the mushrooms are sizzling and golden brown with crisp edges, about 8 minutes. Using a slotted spoon, transfer to the paper towel–lined plate and let cool.

3. **MAKE THE HERB VINAIGRETTE:** Whisk the herbs, shallots, vinegar, and garlic in a medium bowl and season with salt and pepper. Gradually whisk in the oil. The sauce should not be completely emulsified, and it's fine if it is "broken." Taste and adjust the seasoning, adding more vinegar or oil if you like.

4. Arrange 2 bone halves, cut sides up, on each plate. Divide the mushrooms and vinaigrette evenly over the bones. Serve hot with the crostini and small spoons (espresso spoons work) for scooping out the marrow.

- *Very sharp chef's knife*
- *Mixing bowl*
- *Serving plates*
- *Microplane*

FOR THE SAUCE

2 large egg yolks

2 tablespoons Dijon mustard

1 shallot, minced

2 garlic cloves, grated

¼ cup drained nonpareil capers

2 tablespoons Worcestershire sauce

1 teaspoon prepared horseradish

1 teaspoon sumac

½ cup walnuts, toasted (see Note page 139) and finely chopped

1 pound ice-cold beef tenderloin

5 tablespoons finely chopped fresh chives

Potato chips, for serving

Steak Tartare

I love to order steak tartare at restaurants because I don't make it often at home for myself. When I do make it, however, I take the time to chop the beef by hand because this is the ultimate secret to great tartare. And *technically* what makes it tartare. Overhandled meat will become mushy, especially with the easy-way-out method in a food processor, and no, no one likes mushy steak tartare. So sharpen your chef's knife, give it some hand-chopped love. **SERVES 4**

1. **MAKE THE SAUCE:** Whisk the yolks and mustard together in a medium bowl. Add the shallot, garlic, capers, Worcestershire sauce, horseradish, and sumac and whisk again. Whisk in the walnuts. Set aside.

2. Using a very sharp knife, cut the tenderloin crosswise into ¼- to ½-inch-thick rounds. Now cut them into thin strips, then crosswise into ¼-inch dice. Do not hack away at the beef, but do the chopping methodically and with intent. You'll be done before you know it. Transfer the meat to a medium bowl.

3. Stir in about half the sauce, and give it a taste. Continue to stir in as much of the sauce as you like to season the beef until you reach you desired seasoning and salinity. Stir in 3 tablespoons of the chives and reserve the remainder for garnish.

4. Mound the tartare on dinner plates. Sprinkle with the reserved chives. Serve with potato chips.

1½ to 2 pounds butternut squash, seeded, peeled, and cut into 1- to 2-inch cubes

2 tablespoons olive oil

4 garlic cloves, unpeeled (optional)

3 to 5 sprigs fresh thyme, or 1 to 2 sprigs fresh rosemary, or a combination of the two

Fine sea salt

2 cups stock (page 23 or 43)

½ cup freshly grated Parmesan cheese

2 teaspoons soy sauce

⅓ cup heavy cream

Freshly ground black pepper

Herbed Butternut Squash Soup

This soup has relatively few ingredients, so there are decisions to be made to get the best flavor. I use a rich homemade poultry stock. It makes the soup more brown than I wish it were, but it is more deeply flavored than if I used a light stock. And because butternut squash is on the bland side, it is important to give it some umami with soy sauce (also dark) and Parmesan cheese. I make garlic optional because this soup is perfect without any alliums, but it is equally delicious with garlic as well.

SERVES 4 TO 6

1. Preheat the oven to 400°F.

2. Spread the squash on a half-sheet pan. Drizzle with the oil and toss to coat. Tuck in the garlic, if using, and herb sprigs. Season with salt. Roast until the squash is tender and beginning to brown, 20 to 25 minutes. Remove from the oven and set the herb sprigs aside for garnish. Transfer the squash mixture to a blender and add the stock, Parmesan, soy sauce, and peeled garlic (if using); process until smooth. Taste for seasoning; the cheese and soy sauce may make it seem a little saltier than desired, but that's necessary here, as we're about to lower the salinity with cream. Pour in cream, and blend again for 10 seconds. Transfer to a large saucepan and heat over medium heat until it is piping hot.

3. Remove the herb leaves from the reserved sprigs and discard the stems. Ladle the soup into shallow bowls, add a few cracks of pepper, and sprinkle with herb leaves. Serve hot.

4. The soup can be cooled to room temperature and refrigerated in a covered container for up to 3 days or frozen for up to 2 months.

Olive oil

1 yellow onion, sliced

1 head fennel, sliced

2 pounds baking potatoes, such as russets, cut into thin rounds, or any equivalent weight in potato scraps and peels

3 leeks, white and light green parts only, sliced and rinsed well

Fine sea salt

3 garlic cloves, grated

¼ cup dry white wine

½ teaspoon herbes de Provence or dried thyme

1 quart Chicken Broth (page 46) or canned chicken broth

1 tablespoon fresh lemon juice

Freshly ground black pepper

Chopped fennel fronds
Flaky salt

Fennel, Potato, and Leek Soup

This recipe is one of my favorites in my soup arsenal, because you can use potato peels as well as potatoes—or just use peels if you have enough. I'm all about avoiding kitchen waste where possible, and this magical soup makes a blessing of those peel scraps rather than a curse. So whenever you have potato peels, use them as a substitute for the whole potatoes. You can freeze the scraps until you have an amount that you want to use up, either alone or in tandem with whole potatoes. **SERVES 6**

1.   Heat a glug of oil in a large saucepan over medium-high heat. Add the onion and fennel and cook, stirring occasionally, until the vegetables start to color, about 5 minutes. Add the potatoes and cook, stirring occasionally, until some of them get a little crispy, about 10 minutes. Stir in the leeks and a hearty pinch of salt. Cook until they begin to soften, about 3 minutes.

2.   Add the garlic and cook until the mixture is beginning to brown. Add the wine and stir with a wooden spoon to scrape up any browned bits. Stir in the herbes de Provence, followed by the broth. Bring to a boil over high heat. Reduce the heat to low and simmer until the potatoes are tender, about 20 minutes.

3.   Purée the soup in a blender or in its cook pot with an immersion blender. Add the lemon juice, season with fine sea salt and pepper, and blend again to combine. Reheat in the saucepan. Ladle into bowls. Sprinkle with the fennel fronds and some flaky salt and grinds of pepper. Serve hot. (The soup can be cooled and refrigerated in a covered container for up to 2 days.)

MISE EN PLACE
- *Half-sheet pan*
- *Blender*
- *Large skillet or griddle (you can cook more sandwiches on a griddle)*

FOR THE SOUP

4 large ripe tomatoes

2 shallots, cut in half lengthwise

6 unpeeled garlic cloves, crushed under a knife

4 sprigs fresh rosemary or thyme or a combination of the two

Olive oil

Fine sea salt and freshly ground black pepper

1 tablespoon sherry vinegar, or as needed

FOR THE SANDWICHES

Salted butter

8 slices French bread, cut on the bias, as big as possible

½ cup mayonnaise (store-bought is fine but you can use your homemade mayonnaise from page 52)

6 ounces thinly sliced Gouda cheese

2 ounces (about 1 cup) shaved Parmesan cheese (use a vegetable peeler)

Roasted Fresh Tomato Soup with Grilled Cheese

When I attended Smith, our dining room menu featured grilled cheese and tomato soup once a month to much rejoicing. Here, I've upped the flavor of that happy comfort soup memory by roasting all the soup ingredients together. And I've developed the grilled cheese to be a little bit less messy than the traditional and to pack a more umami-rich flavor punch. **SERVES 4**

1. **MAKE THE SOUP:** Preheat the oven to 400°F. Scatter the tomatoes, shallots, garlic, and herbs on a half-sheet pan. Spread them out so they get maximum browning for the best flavor. In particular, the tomato juices need to be concentrated by roasting. Drizzle with oil and toss to coat, but don't add so much oil that it pools. Season with salt and pepper. Bake until the vegetables begin to brown, about 15 minutes. Remove from the oven, and reserve the herb sprigs.

2. Cut out and discard the tomato stems and squeeze the garlic flesh from the cloves, discarding the skins. Transfer the vegetables and any juices to a blender. Add the leaves from the herb sprigs. Blend until the soup is very smooth and creamy, about 1 minute. Add the vinegar, season with salt and pepper, and blend again. Pour into a medium saucepan and heat over very low heat to warm for serving.

3. **MAKE THE SANDWICHES:** Heat a knob of butter in a very large skillet or griddle over medium heat. Depending on the size of the sandwiches, you may have to cook them in batches and keep warm in a preheated 200°F oven until they are all cooked.

4. For each sandwich, spread about a tablespoon of mayonnaise over one side of the bread. Place in the skillet, mayonnaise side down, and top with one-quarter of each cheese, being sure the bread is completely covered. Cook, adjusting the heat as needed to find the sweet spot so the underside of the bread is browning at a steady pace without burning, until the cheese is starting to melt, about 2 minutes. Spread another slice of bread with mayonnaise, and place it on top of the cheese, mayonnaise side up. Cook until the underside is golden brown, about 2 minutes more. Flip the sandwich over, add more butter to the skillet if needed, and cook to brown the other side, another 3 to 4 minutes. Transfer the sandwiches to a chopping board and cut each in half.

5. Ladle the hot soup into bowls and serve with the sandwiches. Some people like to use the sandwich as a big spoon, and others eat their soup with a spoon. It's up to you.

MISE EN PLACE
- *Medium skillet*
- *Paper towel-lined plate*
- *Slotted spoon*
- *Immersion blender or blender*
- *Dinner plates*

4 to 6 cups of chicory (about 2 tight heads of radicchio or 2 to 3 heads of mixed loose leaf chicory)

Vegetable oil

3 tablespoons capers (preferably salt-packed, rinsed well and patted dry with paper towels)

Olive oil

4 anchovy fillets packed in oil

1 garlic clove, grated

Crème fraîche or sour cream

1 preserved lemon, peel only, coarsely chopped, or use the finely grated zest of 1 lemon and a pinch of salt

Finely chopped fresh chives

Mixed Chicories with Anchovy Cream Dressing and Fried Capers

Every autumn we plant a variety of Italian chicory seeds in the La Pitchoune garden for a long harvest over the winter. In January and February we have baby radicchio to mix into salads. In March they become tiny heads, which we add to any salad, use as a soup garnish, or as an accent to mushroom carpaccio. Come April, we have full leaves and heads for hearty salads. If our larger chicories turn too bitter, we grill them for a few minutes before making the salad. The light cooking mellows the leaves.

This salad is a hit no matter what kind of chicory you use—lettuce works, too. Try to use salt-packed capers because they are drier than the brine-packed ones, and work best for frying. One other tip—this creamy dressing is very versatile, and can be made without garlic or anchovies (but use one or the other). SERVES 4 TO 6

1. Separate the chicory heads into leaves and discard the stems. Tear the leaves in half if they are bigger than palm-size.

2. Heat enough oil to come about ⅛ inch up the sides of a skillet and heat over medium-high heat until it shimmers. Test the heat with a single caper—it should dance around in the oil but not spit at you, and should crisp in under a minute. Toss the capers in the oil, and fry until they brown and burst open, about 45 seconds. Using a slotted spoon, transfer the capers to the paper towel–lined plate to drain.

3. Pour out the used vegetable oil. Add a healthy glug of olive oil to the skillet and heat over medium heat. Add the anchovies and cook, mashing them up with a wooden spoon. In a minute or so, they will break down. Stir in the garlic and cook until fragrant, about 3 minutes. Transfer to a medium bowl.

4. Add the crème fraîche and preserved lemon and process with an immersion blender until smooth. (Or purée in a blender.) Adjust the thickness with more crème fraîche, or dilute with milk if too thick.

5. Arrange the chicories on plates and drizzle the dressing on top. Add fried capers and a sprinkle of chives. Serve immediately.

MISE EN PLACE
- Chef's knife
- Half-sheet pan

2 pounds fennel bulbs, fronds chopped and reserved for garnish (If your fennel doesn't have fronds, that's okay. You just won't have them for garnish.)

1 large grapefruit, peeled and cut into ½-inch-thick rounds (see page 34)

6 tablespoons olive oil

Sea salt

3 to 5 whole cloves, grated on a microplane

Warm Roasted Grapefruit and Fennel Salad

Here is my nomination for the world's easiest roasted salad. It's a one-pan dish, and requires just five ingredients. Six if you're feeling frisky and want to crack on some fresh ground pepper. And if that doesn't convince you? I must confess I strongly dislike strong anisette flavors. And my husband? Hates grapefruit. And yet, we both *love this salad*.

SERVES 2 TO 4

1. Preheat the oven to 425°F. Cut the fennel lengthwise into ½-inch slices. Do not worry if the pieces separate. Varying sizes means varying degrees of cooked, which means *contrast in texture, color, and end result*. And that is where the magic of this salad happens. So, trust the process. Scatter the fennel on the sheet pan.

2. Tuck about three-fourths of the grapefruit between the fennel, reserving the rest for its juices in step 3. Drizzle with the oil and season lightly with salt and the cloves. Toss to combine. Roast for 10 minutes, and then open the oven door quickly to "burp" the oven and let out excess moisture that would slow down browning. Roast another 5 to 10 minutes, or until the smaller fennel pieces are beginning
to char.

3. Transfer the fennel and grapefruit, along with the pan juices, to a platter. Coarsely chop the reserved fennel fronds, if using. Squeeze the juice from the reserved grapefruit over all and sprinkle with the fennel fronds.

- *Skillet*
- *Small plate, with ¼ cup cornstarch on it*
- *Paper towel-lined plate*

1 large bunch small radishes, about 24, each about the size of an unshelled almond, with lush, beautiful greens

2 cans sardines packed in oil

4 tablespoons cornstarch

Olive oil

Flaky salt, such as Maldon

Vegetable oil

Freshly ground black pepper

1 lemon

Burnished Radish Salad with Fried Sardines

The first guests I hosted at La Peetch were a group of food writers. I remember one guest whipped up burnished radishes from a beautiful bunch we had picked at the market. The method stuck with me, and burnished radishes now are staples in my list of side dishes. This is a great accompaniment to many main courses, but especially anything roasted.
SERVES 4

1. Cut the green tops from the radishes, leaving ¼ inch of stem attached, if desired. You should have about 24 topped radishes to a pound. Separately wash the radishes and the greens. (The greens can be sandy, so wash them well.) Spin the greens dry and transfer to a medium bowl. Do not dry the radishes.

2. Open both cans of sardines, and drain off the excess oil. Remove the sardines one at a time gingerly, avoiding breaking them up, roll in the cornstarch, and set aside.

3. Heat 2 tablespoons of the olive oil in a large skillet over medium-high heat until it shimmers. Add the radishes, cover, and cook until the skins begin to split, about 5 minutes. Season with salt and cook, uncovered, until they are just tender, about 3 minutes more. Transfer to a plate.

4. Wipe out the skillet and add about ½ inch of the vegetable oil to the skillet, and bring to a shimmer. Add the sardines to the oil. After 2 minutes or so, flip the sardines over. They should get golden brown. Remove, place on the paper towel–lined plate, and once all fried, sprinkle with a teaspoon of flaky salt and some freshly cracked pepper.

5. Grate the zest from the lemon over the greens. Cut the lemon in half and squeeze the juice from one lemon half over the greens. Drizzle with 1 tablespoon of the olive oil, and season with flaky salt. Toss gently to combine.

6. Divide the greens among individual plates, top with the radishes and fried sardines, and serve.

MISE EN PLACE
- *Small saucepan*
- *Mixing bowl*
- *Half-sheet pan*
- *Bowl for ice bath*
- *Large skillet*
- *Paper towel–lined plate*

2 pounds Brussels sprouts

Olive oil

2 garlic cloves, grated

1 teaspoon fine sea salt

½ teaspoon garlic powder

¼ cup balsamic vinegar

2 teaspoons honey

¼ pound thinly sliced pancetta

2 eggs, at room temperature (optional) (see Note)

Freshly ground black pepper

Flaky salt

Balsamic-Glazed Brussels with Sprout Chips and Pancetta

When the components of this dish come together, it is a beaut, with a trio of roasted brussels sprouts, crisp chips from their outer leaves, and meaty pancetta. Yet, it doesn't require a lot of dishes. Brussels sprouts are one of the best things about winter produce, so keep this in mind as a side dish or even as a vegetable-forward (leave out the pancetta to make it meatless) main course. SERVES 6

1.   Preheat the oven to 475°F and set a small saucepan three-quarters of the way full of water over medium-high heat.

2.   Trim the bottom stem from each sprout and discard (or save for stock). Cut each sprout in half from top to bottom. Transfer the halved sprouts and the loose leaves to a large bowl. Add a glug of oil, the grated garlic, salt, and garlic powder and toss to combine.

3.   In a small bowl, add about ½ teaspoon of piping hot water (hot as you can out of your tap). Add the vinegar and honey, and mix until a slurry forms. Pour over the sprouts and toss to coat. Spread on a half-sheet pan, separating the sprouts as much as possible so they crisp and don't steam. Roast until the sprouts are barely tender and the leaves are deeply browned and crisp, 10 to 15 minutes.

4.   While the Brussels sprouts are roasting, tackle the pancetta and the eggs, making them in your preferred style, see Note below.

5.   Place the pancetta in a large skillet and cook over medium heat, turning once, until crisp and browned. Transfer the pancetta to the prepared plate to drain. Cook the eggs, if using, as desired.

6.   Transfer the Brussels sprouts to a platter. Crumble the pancetta and sprinkle over the sprouts. Crack some pepper on top, add a scattering of flaky salt, and serve.

Note: To make this a larger meal you can top with soft-boiled, fried, or poached eggs. A runny yolk over crispy brussels sprouts and the pancetta is a dinner that even my kiddo loves.

MISE EN PLACE
- *2 small mixing bowls*
- *Half-sheet pan*
- *Serving bowl*

1 pound assorted large mushrooms, such as baby bellas and shiitakes, stems removed (reserve for stock)

¾ cup (1½ sticks) salted butter, at room temperature

1 bunch fresh parsley, finely chopped (about ½ cup)

6 garlic cloves, grated

Olive oil

Roasted Mushrooms with Escargot-Style Butter

Before leaving village life for the countryside of Grasse, I lived in Valbonne. I was lucky to live across from a restaurant where everything was cooked in a wood-fired pizza oven. The temperamental oven resulted in the most wonderful roasted . . . everything. Sadly, just about three months after I moved in, the restaurant changed owners and the wood-fired oven was replaced with an oven that, well, works. I understood the choice, but I would be lying if I didn't admit that I was bereft. During the original tenure, the restaurant made a roasted mushroom with garlic butter dish that was utterly transcendent. They were our daughter, Magnolia's, favorite food when she was eight months old. So I taught myself the closest version I could, without the need for wood fire. It's not quite the same, but it's very close. SERVES 4 TO 6

1. Preheat the oven to 475°F. Clean the mushrooms by brushing off any dirt or debris with your hands. If you must, rinse them very quickly under water and then pat dry. The mushrooms must be dry or else they will steam in the oven rather than roast.

2. In a small mixing bowl, mash the butter, parsley, and garlic together until thoroughly combined. In another small mixing bowl, toss the mushrooms with a healthy glug of oil, which will help them brown. Transfer to a half-sheet pan, with the stemmed sides facing up. Using a small spoon, scoop the garlic butter into each mushroom.

3. Place in the oven and immediately reduce the heat to 425°F. Roast until the mushrooms are browned, 10 to 15 minutes. Transfer to a serving bowl and serve immediately.

MISE EN PLACE
- *Vegetable peeler*
- *Large mixing bowl filled with cold water*
- *1 metal or cast-iron baking dish, about 9 x 13 inches, or a large skillet and a ceramic or glass baking dish*

3 pounds narrow baking potatoes, such as russet, peeled

Olive oil

Fine sea salt

5 tablespoons salted butter, divided

1 head garlic, papery outer skin removed, top cut off to expose the cloves

1 cup Rich Stock (page 43)

5 to 10 dried bay leaves

10 sprigs fresh thyme or rosemary

Freshly ground black pepper

Fondant Potatoes

This is a magical recipe. The potatoes are crisp on the outside with a sweet creaminess through its interior and additional flavor from the stock. This is about as close as I can get to french fries without a fryer. It is best to buy narrow potatoes so you don't have to whittle larger ones down. There is a bit of prepping, but it's worthwhile in the long run. And, besides, you'll have trimmings to start the Fennel, Potato, and Leek Soup on page 223. SERVES 4 TO 6

1. Our goal is cylindrical-ish potatoes at the end. They can vary in size, but need to be able to stand on their own. Working with one potato at a time, trim off the top and bottom. Next slice the potatoes into 2 ½ to 3 inch long pieces. Finally, trim off any excess "shoulders" so each potato is no wider than it is tall.

2. Preheat the oven to 400°F. Heat a good glug of oil in a metal or enameled cast-iron rectangular baking dish on medium-high heat. Or heat the oil in a large skillet.

3. Drain the potatoes well. Pat them dry with a kitchen towel, and arrange them wide side down in the pan so they have space between them. If necessary, work in batches. Sprinkle the tops of the potatoes with a hearty pinch of salt, and cook until the undersides are golden brown, about 5 minutes. Flip the potatoes and cook until the other sides are golden, about 5 minutes more.

4. Remove the pan from the heat and add 3 tablespoons of the butter, and let it melt. (If cooking in a skillet, transfer the browned potatoes to a ceramic or glass baking dish and pour the melted butter on top.) Place the garlic, cut side down, in the potatoes. Pour in the stock and tuck in the bay leaves and thyme. Bake for 15 minutes. Dot the remaining 2 tablespoons of butter to the dish.

5. Bake until the potatoes are a burnished golden brown, and most (if not all) of the stock is absorbed, about 35 minutes. Remove the thyme and bay leaves. Season with salt and pepper. Serve immediately.

- *Medium saucepan*
- *Mandoline (optional)*
- *Baking dish, 8- or 9-inch square*
- *Wire sieve*
- *4-cup glass measuring cup*

2 cups heavy cream

1 head garlic, outer skin removed, cut in half crosswise

5 bay leaves, or cinnamon leaves if you have them

3 sprigs fresh rosemary and 4 sprigs fresh thyme, or 3 tablespoons herbes de Provence

1 teaspoon pink peppercorns

2 pounds baking potatoes, peeled

About 2 tablespoons salted butter, softened, for the dish

Fine sea salt and freshly ground pepper

Urfa biber chile flakes (optional)

SWEET POTATOES DAUPHINOISE:
Substitute peeled sweet potatoes for the standard potatoes. Bring 3 cups heavy cream, the garlic, 2 shallots cut into a few pieces, a handful of cilantro stems, and 2 teaspoons cumin seeds (crushed) to a simmer and infuse. Layer and bake in the same way as the Potatoes Dauphinoise.

Potatoes Dauphinoise

Pommes Dauphinoise are a beloved everyday French dish, and they have been in recorded French history for hundreds of years, hailing from the Dauphiné region of France. A purist version does not include cheese, but you can certainly add it if you'd like (Gruyère or Comté are the usual suspects) but keep in mind that there is already ample cream. Sometimes the dish can run a little bland, so I've made my rendition full of garlic, herbs, and spices to give it some character. I think infusing them in the cream right off the bat is what makes these so delicious. With just a few alterations—a few spice shifts, and a bit more liquid—you can make Sweet Potatoes Dauphinoise, which is a wonderful holiday side dish. **SERVES 6 TO 8**

1. Heat the cream, garlic, herbs, and peppercorns in a medium saucepan over medium heat just until it begins to simmer. Remove from the heat and cover. Allow to infuse while preparing the rest of the dish.

2. Preheat the oven to 450°F. Using a knife or a mandoline, cut the potatoes into ⅛-inch slices. You shouldn't see through them, but you don't want them too thick either because they will take too long to cook. The sweet spot is about ⅛ inch, where they hold their shape and texture in the oven, but also have ample surface area to thickness to absorb all that gorgeous, infused cream.

3. Smear the inside of the casserole with the butter, but don't overdo it because too much will make the final dish too oily. Strain the infused cream through a sieve into a 4-cup glass measuring cup or other container with a spout.

4. Begin layering the potatoes into the prepared dish. Start with one row of potatoes, overlapping about one-third of the next potato over the first, like shingles. Pour a few tablespoons of the cream on top and season with salt, pepper, and a pinch of Urfa chile, if using. Once you have a first row, shingle another layer in the same manner over the first and repeat, adding the cream, salt, and pepper. (This shingle technique helps the potatoes hold together when served.) Repeat to make four or five layers, pouring any remaining cream over the last layer. Place the dish on a large baking sheet to catch any drips.

5. Bake, uncovered, until the cream is absorbed and the potatoes are tender (check with a small sharp knife) with the edges beginning to brown, 25 to 35 minutes. Let stand for a few minutes before serving. Slice (just like a rectangular cake) and serve hot.

Romanesco Romesco

This was a silly turn of phrase that rattled around my head for months. Turns out that rattling about had some purpose because red and green color contrast is stunning and it uses a number of ingredients available during the colder weather season. The roasted romanesco and the raw romesco sauce are happy playmates in all the right ways. **SERVES 4**

FOR THE ROMESCO

1 small red bell pepper, seeded and coarsely chopped

1 tomato, about the same weight as the bell pepper, coarsely chopped

½ cup coarsely chopped walnuts

1 to 2 small garlic cloves, to taste

2 tablespoons olive oil

1 teaspoon sherry vinegar

Fine sea salt

FOR THE ROMANESCO

1 head (about 1 pound) romanesco, broken into florets, thick stems sliced into ½-inch rounds, and any leaves reserved

Olive oil

Fine sea salt

Finely chopped fresh tarragon or parsley

1. Preheat the oven to 500°F.

2. **MAKE THE ROMESCO:** Purée the bell pepper, tomato, walnuts, and garlic in a blender until very smooth, about 2½ minutes. With the machine running, gradually add the oil. Season with the vinegar and salt and blend again.

3. **MAKE THE ROMANESCO:** Spread the romanesco florets and slices on a half-sheet tray and drizzle with the oil, season with salt, and toss. Roast until the romanesco tips are beginning to brown, about 5 minutes.

4. Toss the romanesco leaves in a small bowl with a drizzle of oil, just to coat them. Remove the pan with the florets and stems from the oven and sprinkle with the leaves. Return to the oven and roast until the floret tips are beginning to char, about 3 minutes.

5. Pour the sauce on a serving platter, top with the romanesco, sprinkle with the herbs, and serve.

1 cup spelt

2½ cups Rich Stock (page 43)

One 1-inch chunk of fresh ginger, peeled

2 garlic cloves, smashed and peeled

4 bay leaves

Stock-Simmered Spelt

I used to make this with quinoa. But in Provence, spelt, which is higher in protein than quinoa, is a local product. And, best of all, this simple side dish is shove-in-your-mouth delicious. When you serve it I promise people will say, "Oh my goodness! You muuuuust tell me what you did to this." This excels as a side dish. You can also mix the warm spelt with the Warm Brown Rice Salad dressing on page 191, and serve at room temperature. (Other vinaigrettes would be good, too.) The spelt will absorb the flavors of the dressing. And, you can mix and match the other way around: this recipe works well with other wheat-related grains, such as farro and quinoa. **SERVES 4**

1.   The night before, put the spelt in a medium bowl and add enough water to cover by 1 inch. Let stand overnight at room temperature. If the weather is warm, refrigerate the bowl. Alternatively, if you forget to soak the spelt or don't have time, you can add about 20 minutes to the cooking time.

2.   Drain the spelt in a wire sieve and rinse under cold running water. Put the spelt in a medium saucepan and add the stock, ginger, garlic, and bay leaves. Bring to a boil over high heat. Reduce to medium-low, cover about halfway, and cook at a strong simmer until the spelt is tender, about 1 hour.

3.   Drain in a sieve and discard the ginger and bay leaves (the garlic will have dissolved). Transfer to a serving dish and serve hot. Or dress the warm spelt with the Warm Brown Rice Salad dressing on page 191 and let cool.

SPICED SPELT: Omit the ginger, garlic, and bay leaves. Substitute ½ yellow onion or 1 whole shallot (both peeled), studded with 2 whole cloves, 2 pods of star anise, and 1 cardamom pod.

MISE EN PLACE
- *Large mixing bowl*
- *Half-sheet pan*

About 2 pounds mixed vegetables, mostly winter root produce or brassicas, such as Brussels sprouts, turnips, plain (or purple) or sweet potatoes, large radishes, carrots, and parsnips, cut into 1- to 2-inch pieces

2 whole shallots, cut in half lengthwise

6 garlic cloves, crushed under a knife and peeled

½ cup red wine vinegar

About ¼ cup olive oil

Fine sea salt and freshly ground black pepper

2 tablespoons tahini

Vinegar-Roasted Veggies

With all of the cooking at La Peetch, we collect a lot of leftover vegetables in the course of a week, and this is what I make to use them up. First, I soak the vegetables in vinegar, which makes all the difference between dull and complexly flavored veggies. You can use almost any vinegar, except dark balsamic; white balsamic is lovely. Olive is your best choice for oil. If you want to round out the roasted vegetables, look no further than the Stock-Simmered Spelt on page 242. SERVES ABOUT 4

1. Combine the vegetables, shallots, and garlic in a large bowl. Toss with the vinegar. Let stand at room temperature for at least 4 hours and up to 8, tossing occasionally.

2. Preheat the oven to 425°F.

3. Pour the vegetables and vinegar onto a sheet pan and spread evenly. Drizzle the oil on top. Season with salt.

4. Roast for 20 minutes, or until the vegetables are just tender with some browned edges. Finish with a few cracks of pepper, drizzle with the tahini, and serve.

ASIAN-SEASONED ROAST VEGETABLES: This is one of my daughter's favorites. Substitute rice vinegar, dark sesame oil, and fish sauce for the red wine vinegar, olive oil, and salt. Serve with or without the tahini drizzle.

CHAPTER 9
COOLER WEATHER BIGGER DISHES

4 chicken leg quarters, or 4 each legs and thighs

Fine sea salt

Beurre Blanc (page 58), timed to finish at the same time as the chicken

2 tablespoons finely chopped fresh tarragon, dill, or your favorite herb

Chicken Legs with Herbed Beurre Blanc

I fell in love with Provençal cuisine not in Provence, but in Boulder, Colorado, long before my feet hit Provençal soil. This was thanks to Mateo: Restaurant Provençal, where I have eaten at least a hundred times over fifteen years, and most times, I've ordered chicken frites with tarragon beurre fondue. This recipe is a home version of a restaurant dish. Although simplified, it is remarkably good in its own way. The only trick here is to prepare the beurre blanc so it is done at about the same time as the chicken. If you can, serve french fries with this, or at least crusty bread, for dipping into the sauce. **SERVES 4**

1. Season the chicken all over with the salt. Let stand at room temperature for 30 minutes to 1 hour to lose its chill.

2. Preheat the oven to its highest setting, preferably 550°F. Put a large, heavy, ovenproof skillet in the oven and let it heat for 5 to 10 minutes.

3. Place the chicken, skin side down, in the hot skillet. Reduce the oven temperature to 450°F. Roast until the undersides are browned and the chicken can be turned without tearing the skin, 7 to 10 minutes. Flip the chicken over and continue roasting until an instant-read thermometer inserted in the thickest part of the chicken reads 165°F, about 15 minutes more. Turn off the oven and let the chicken rest in the hot oven if you need time to finish the beurre blanc. Because of the dark meat, there is limited risk of it drying out. And a piping hot crispy chicken is ideal.

4. Stir the herbs into the beurre blanc. Spoon the sauce onto a serving platter. (The sauce is best under the chicken so the chicken can remain crisp.) Top with the chicken and serve immediately.

- *Medium saucepan*
- *Skillet*
- *9-inch round baking dish, at least 2-inches deep*

5 tablespoons salted butter, divided

3 tablespoons all-purpose flour, plus more for rolling out the pastry

2 cups whole milk

Olive oil

½ cup diced (¼ inch) yellow onion

Fine sea salt

¼ cup diced (¼ inch) carrot

¼ cup diced (¼ inch) peeled kohlrabi (can be omitted entirely if you struggle to find it—just replace the ¼ cup with extra carrot and celery)

¼ cup diced (¼ inch) celery

¼ cup diced (¼ inch) leek, white parts only

Glug of dry white wine

2 cups bite-size cooked chicken, preferably from Roast Chickens with Lemon and Sumac (page 166), or use store-bought rotisserie chicken

¼ cup Dijon mustard

¼ cup chopped fresh dill

Freshly ground pepper

Softened salted butter for the dish

1 disk (one-third recipe) Flaky Buttery Pastry (page 72) or store-bought puff pastry

Chicken and Root Vegetable Dilly Potpie

This recipe was an accidental discovery. I had originally planned to use mustard and tarragon in the béchamel sauce that laces the dish, but I was out of tarragon and substituted dill. When I served it to some friends, one of them remarked, "Oh my god! This tastes just like pickles!" And thus, this "pickle" potpie was born.

Béchamel sauce is a crucial recipe in French cuisine. It begins with a roux (equal parts butter and flour), with milk added and simmered to thicken into a beautiful sauce.

For more servings, double the recipe and bake it in a 9 by 13-inch ovenproof dish. SERVES 4 TO 6

1. Preheat the oven to 400°F.

2. Melt 3 tablespoons of the butter in a medium saucepan over medium heat and whisk in the flour. Let cook, whisking constantly, until the mixture turns golden and smells toasty. Whisk in the milk and bring to a simmer. Reduce the heat to very low and let the sauce cook at a bare simmer and thicken while cooking the vegetables, about 15 minutes. Whisk often to be sure the sauce isn't sticking to the bottom of the saucepan. It isn't supposed to reduce, but the flavor improves with cooking.

3. Add a glug of oil and the remaining 2 tablespoons butter to a large skillet and heat on medium heat until the butter melts. Add the onion, and cook, stirring often, until it turns golden, about 5 minutes. Season with a pinch of salt. Stir in the carrot and kohlrabi and cook until beginning to soften, about 3 minutes. Season with another pinch of salt. Stir in the celery and leek and cook until the onion is taking on some golden tinges, about 5 minutes more. Remove from the heat and stir in the chicken.

4. Return to the béchamel, remove from the heat, and stir in the mustard and dill. Season with salt and pepper.

5. Butter the baking dish with the softened butter. Pour in the chicken and veggies, and smother with the sauce.

6. On a lightly floured work surface, roll out the pastry into an 11-inch round about ⅛ inch thick to fit over the top of the dish, and stretch and press it onto the sides. Using a small sharp knife, cut four to six slits in the dough, each about 2 inches long.

7. Bake until the crust is golden brown, about 40 minutes. Serve hot.

MISE EN PLACE
- *Wide, shallow bowl*
- *2 plates, one lined with paper towels*
- *Dutch oven*
- *Shallow serving bowls*
- *Deep platter, for serving*

1 rabbit, about 3 pounds, cut into 6 to 8 serving pieces, or chicken thighs, or cabbage quarters

Fine sea salt and freshly ground pepper

½ cup all-purpose flour

Vegetable or canola oil, as needed

4 large shallots, cut into ½- to 1-inch chunks

3 tablespoons stone-ground Dijon mustard, divided

2 cups dry white wine

1 bouquet garni (see page 25), including a sprig or 2 each of rosemary, thyme, and savory, a couple of bay leaves, and 8 sage leaves

2 cups Rich Stock (page 43) or use dark store-bought stock (not pale canned broth), as needed

Homemade Semolina Pasta (page 188), or use store-bought fresh fettuccine, freshly cooked and drained

2 tablespoons crème fraîche, sour cream, or heavy cream

Fresh chives or parsley, minced

2 tablespoons nonpareil capers, chopped if using larger capers

Rabbit with Mustard-Shallot Sauce

In mid-spring, flowering wild thyme grows rampant in Provence. When the thyme becomes so abundant that you can smell it in the sweet air, I know precisely what to make: braised rabbit.

Hear me out. Rabbit does not need to be terrifying to find or to cook. In the United States, Italian butchers have rabbit, and you can often find it frozen in specialty markets. Rabbit is an especially lean meat, and so the sauce here shares the spotlight, along with the pasta, which helps "beef up" the dish. This classic French treatment for rabbit could not be more luscious, with tangy mustard and buttery cream playing off each other, accented by bits of aromatic shallot. To make it is to love it.

If you can't find rabbit, or just can't make it your thing, this is equally fantastic with chicken thighs. You can also use the same method to braise cabbage quarters for a meatless meal using vegetable stock.

SERVES 4 TO 6

1. Preheat the oven to 350°F. Generously season the rabbit with salt and pepper. Spread the flour in a wide, shallow bowl. One piece at a time, dredge the rabbit in the flour, covering completely in an even layer without any lumps and shaking off any excess flour. Transfer to a plate.

2. Heat a large glug of the oil in a large Dutch oven over medium-high heat until it is shimmering. In batches without crowding, add the rabbit, and cook, turning occasionally, until browned, 5 to 6 minutes. Transfer to prepared plate to drain.

3. Add more oil to the Dutch oven, if necessary. Add the shallots and cook, stirring occasionally, until browned, about 3 minutes. Reduce the heat to medium. Stir in 2 tablespoons of the mustard and pour in about half of the wine and bring to a boil, scraping up any browned bits in the pot with a wooden spatula. Add the bouquet garni and pour in the remaining wine.

4. Return the rabbit to the pot. Pour in enough stock to come three-fourths up the rabbit, adding water if necessary. Bring to a simmer over medium heat. Cover with the lid and bake in the oven until the meat is pulling away from the bone, about 45 minutes.

5. While the rabbit is roasting, make your pasta. If using homemade, start right away. If using store-bought, get the water on to boil so you don't forget later on.

6. Using a slotted spoon, transfer the rabbit and shallots to a deep platter and cover with a kitchen towel to keep warm. Bring the cooking liquid in the pot to a

boil over high heat and cook, stirring often, until reduced by about one-third and until the sauce coats a wooden spoon, about 10 minutes.

7.   Remove and discard the bouquet garni. Whisk in the crème fraîche and the remaining tablespoon of mustard and heat until simmering. (If using sour cream, heat through, but do not boil, or it may curdle.) Season with salt and pepper.

8.   To serve, divide the pasta among serving bowls. Add a portion of the rabbit, and top with the sauce. Sprinkle with the herbs and capers. Serve hot.

2½ pounds beef for stew, such as chuck, cut into 1½-inch chunks

Vegetable or canola oil

Kosher salt

2 large yellow onions, cut into ½-inch dice

6 celery stalks, cut into ½-inch dice

4 carrots, cut into ½-inch dice

2 cups red wine

3 medium beets, scrubbed but unpeeled, cut into ½-inch dice

1 garlic head, papery outer layer discarded, top cut off to reveal the cloves

1 bouquet garni (see page 25)

1 quart Rich Stock (page 43), or canned beef broth

1 teaspoon freshly ground black pepper

2 star anise

A Not-So-Bourguignon Boeuf Braise

It may come as no surprise that the dish people most want to learn how to make at the Courageous Cooking School is boeuf bourguignon. According to "the rules"—a bourguignon literally means "from Burgundy"—you must make this with red wine from Burgundy. Considering that there are literally *dozens* of versions of beef stews in France, our obsession with Bourguignon is a Julia holdover. So, as long as you would enjoy drinking the red wine, you can use it to braise. It doesn't have to be from Burgundy, but it should be red to create the luscious fall-apart texture we know and love.

A few tips for the perfect beef braise: First, use homemade stock. Next, beware of over-browning, which leads to overcooking the beef. And finally, low and slow is the way to go, so be patient. Serve with the Semolina Pasta on page 188 or a nice baguette. You absolutely need *something* to soak up all the sauce. SERVES 4

1. Preheat the oven to 400°F.

2. Pat all sides of your beef dry. Pour enough oil to fill the bottom of a large Dutch oven. Heat over high heat until the oil is hot but not smoking. Add a piece of the beef and be sure it sizzles immediately. If it does, add about half of the beef and cook, turning as needed, to brown on at least two sides. (That is enough to give the stew a meatier flavor.) Transfer the browned beef to a large plate or bowl and season it with salt.

3. Reduce the heat to medium-high and add the onions to the pot. Cook, stirring well to loosen any browned bits at the bottom of the pot, and until the onions are golden brown, about 5 minutes. Add the celery and carrots and cook, stirring occasionally, until they soften, about 3 minutes. Add the wine and stir well. Tuck the beets, garlic head (cut side down), and bouquet garni into the Dutch oven. Nestle the beef on the vegetables. Pour in enough stock to barely cover (you don't want the top of the meat to be exposed to air to brown). Add the pepper and star anise. Bring just to a simmer over high heat—do not let it come to a boil!

4. Cover the pot and place in the oven. Bake for 10 minutes. Reduce the heat to 325°F, and cook, without peeking, until lusciously tender, about 3 hours. Remove the star anise. Serve hot. (The beef can be cooled, covered, and refrigerated for up to 2 days. If you refrigerate, skim off some but *not all* of the fat. Reheat slowly on the stove before serving.)

½ leg of lamb, shank end (about 3 pounds)

2 garlic cloves, grated

2 teaspoons dried oregano

1 teaspoon ground coriander or well-crushed seeds

1 teaspoon ground cumin or well-crushed seeds

1½ teaspoons fine sea salt

1 pound green seedless grapes or red

8 shallots, coarsely chopped

2 tablespoons white wine
Freshly ground black pepper

FOR THE YOGURT SAUCE

1 cup plain Greek yogurt

¾ cup minced fresh herbs (a combination of parsley and mint or just tarragon or cilantro)

Fine sea salt

Roast Leg of Lamb with Roasted Grapes and Honey

Roast leg of lamb is one of the most sumptuous things you can make. This version is relatively straightforward. The grapes are a delightful addition, and the entire dish screams fall in Provence. This is a mostly hands-off main course, and I love to make this on cool evenings to share with friends. Serve it with Potatoes Dauphinoise (page 239) and burnished radishes (see page 231), or perhaps a side salad of Mixed Chicories with Anchovy Cream Dressing and Fried Capers (page 227). **SERVES 4 TO 6**

1. Preheat the oven to 500°F. Rub the lamb with the garlic. Mix the oregano, coriander, cumin, and salt together in a small bowl and rub all over the lamb. Place in a roasting pan.

2. Roast for 15 minutes. Reduce the temperature to 450°F, and roast until an instant-read thermometer inserted in the thickest part of the meat reads 135°F for medium-rare, about 40 minutes.

3. Transfer the lamb to a serving platter. Leave the oven on. Pour off all but a few teaspoons of liquid from the roasting pan. Add the grapes, shallots, and wine into the hot pan, scrape up the browned bits in the pan with a wooden spatula, and mix to coat the grapes. Return the pan to the oven and roast, stirring once or twice, until the grapes are browning and almost completely deflated, about 10 minutes. Spoon the grape mixture around the lamb on the serving platter. Finish with some freshly ground black pepper.

4. **MEANWHILE, MAKE THE SAUCE:** Mix the yogurt and herbs in a serving bowl and season with salt.

5. Thinly slice the lamb at the table and serve with the yogurt sauce passed on the side.

MISE EN PLACE
- *Large Dutch oven or heavy-bottomed saucepan*
- *Large plate for holding the browned meat*
- *Small bowl*

2 pounds osso buco/veal shanks (about 4 pieces), let stand at room temperature for 1 hour

Fine sea salt

Olive oil

1 small yellow onion, chopped

2 carrots, cut into ¼-inch rounds

2 cups rosé wine

2 teaspoons sumac

3 sprigs fresh thyme, or 1 sprig fresh rosemary

3 bay leaves

15 pink peppercorns crushed lightly, or 1 teaspoon freshly ground black pepper

2 preserved lemons, cut into quarters

½ cup pitted green olives (preferably Castelvetrano)

Fresh chives, minced

Chive blossoms or other spring edible flowers (optional, if available)

Veal Shanks with Green Olives and Rosé

Rosé is just one of the ingredients I use in this richly flavored braise to make it special, along with preserved lemon and sumac. I like rosé for the floral and mineral touches, the very qualities that make it easy to drink, although it is borderline blasphemy to cook with it in France. (But I do. *C'est la vie!*) Even more magical than the wine is the dish's easy and speedy preparation, which allows one all the more time to sip wine with friends. When choosing veal shanks, look for crosscut rounds with a good ration of meat and marrow. They should fit in your Dutch oven in a single layer.

SERVES 4

1. Preheat the oven to 325°F. Pat the veal shanks completely dry with paper towels. Do not skip this step. A dry surface will let the meat brown for a more flavorful sauce. Season the veal shanks with salt.

2. Heat a healthy glug of oil in a large Dutch oven over medium heat until very hot but not smoking. Add the veal shanks (do this in batches, if necessary, as they should not be crowded). Cook until nicely browned, 3 to 5 minutes per side. Transfer to a plate, leaving the fat in the pot.

3. Add the onion and cook, stirring occasionally, until softened, about 3 minutes. Stir in the carrots and cook until they soften, about 3 minutes. Add the wine and bring to a boil, scraping up any browned bits in the pot with a wooden spatula. Stir in the sumac, thyme, bay leaves, and peppercorns.

4. Return the shanks to the Dutch oven (the pieces will be snug at this point). Tuck the preserved lemon quarters between the osso buco. If necessary, add just enough water to come up the sides of the ingredients, not quite covering them. Bring just to a simmer on top of the stove—it should not boil—and cover.

5. Bake until the shanks are fork-tender and easily pull away from the bone, about 2 hours. Remove and reserve the preserved lemon. Transfer one preserved lemon to a chopping board and chop it, discarding the remaining lemon. In a small bowl, combine the olives and chopped preserved lemon.

6. Divide the osso buco among four dinner plates, and top with a spoonful of the vegetables and cooking liquid. Scatter the olive-lemon mixture over each. Sprinkle with the chives and blossoms, if using. Serve hot.

1 pound large (31 to 35 count) shrimp

4 celery stalks

1 large fennel bulb

Olive oil

2 shallots, sliced

1½ cups dry white wine, or rosé, divided

½ teaspoon saffron threads, or to taste

2 cups heavy cream

Zest and juice of 1 lemon

Fine sea salt and freshly ground black pepper

1 pound cod fillets

½ teaspoon sumac

12 to 18 mussels, scrubbed and debearded, if necessary

8 ounces bay scallops

Bouillia-bish

Bouillabaisse, which hails from Marseille, just two hours from La Peetch, is one of the most famous recipes of the French Riviera. Bouillabaisse was originally peasant food made from bycatch, the fish that were too small to sell; today the working-class stew is now considered high-end cuisine. This is the version we have taught for years at our cooking school's weekly Stews-Day, which is, yes, on a Tuesday. In the photo, you'll see I was lucky enough to nab langostine at my local fish market. You can sub the shrimp for another other shellfish you have on hand. Same goes for the mussels; you can swap for clams. I picked the ingredients based on what I knew you could find in your own local store. Feel free to play! SERVES 6

1. Peel and devein the shrimp, reserving the shells and flesh separately. Trim the thick bottoms and leafy tops from the celery. Reserve the trimmings and cut the celery into ½-inch dice. Trim the tops and fronds from the fennel and reserve those trimmings. Cut the fennel bulb into ½-inch dice.

2. Make a shrimp stock: Add a healthy glug of oil to a stockpot and heat over medium-high heat until very hot but not smoking. Add the shrimp shells, celery and fennel trimmings, and shallots and cook, stirring occasionally, until the vegetables are golden brown, about 5 minutes. If the vegetables are sticking or burning, add a little more oil.

3. Stir in ½ cup of the wine and scrape up any browned bits with a wooden spatula. Stir in 2 quarts of water. Bring just to a low boil over high heat and then reduce the heat to medium and cook at a strong simmer until reduced by half, 30 to 45 minutes. Strain the shrimp stock through a large sieve into a large bowl, pressing hard on the solids. Discard the solids.

4. Heat a glug of the oil in a large saucepan over medium-high heat. Add the reserved diced celery and fennel and cook, stirring infrequently, until the vegetables are golden brown, about 5 minutes. Stir in the remaining 1 cup wine and scrape up any browned bits with a wooden spatula. Bring to a boil and cook until reduced by half, about 5 minutes. Stir in the shrimp stock. Bring to a boil. Reduce the heat to medium and cook at a strong simmer until the fennel is tender, about 15 minutes.

5. Crush the saffron between your fingers over the pot and stir it in. Reduce the heat to medium-low so the stock is simmering more gently now. Stir in the cream and simmer for 5 minutes.

6. Using an immersion blender, purée the soup. (Or blend the soup in batches in a standing blender and return to the pot.) Add the juice from half of the lemon and season with salt and a few cracks of pepper.

7.   Season the cod with the sumac and salt. Let stand for 5 minutes. Return the soup base to a strong simmer. Add the cod, cover, and simmer for 4 minutes. Add the mussels, cover, and cook for 3 minutes. Stir in the scallops and shrimp. Remove from the heat. Cover and let the residual heat finish cooking the seafood, about 4 minutes. The mussels should have opened and the cod and scallops should be opaque. Return to the heat and simmer only if absolutely necessary to finish cooking the seafood. Break the cod into six portions with a spoon. Discard any unopened mussels.

8.   Divide the soup and seafood among six soup bowls. Finish with the lemon zest and serve hot.

4 ounces pancetta, cut into strips about ½ inch thick, and then into 2-inch lengths

Vegetable or canola oil

1 yellow onion, chopped

4 celery stalks, leaves reserved, stalks cut ¼ inch thick on the bias

3 garlic cloves, grated

2 cups dry white wine

20 to 24 littleneck clams, well scrubbed under cold running water

2 (14-ounce) cans white beans, 1 drained and 1 with the liquid

1 tablespoon minced fresh thyme, or 2 teaspoons dried

Finely grated zest of 1 lemon

2 scallions, white and light green parts, finely sliced on the bias

Freshly ground black pepper

Flaky salt

Crostini (page 60), for serving

Beans and Clams Chowdah-ish

In Provence, beans and clams are a common pair on menus. In this recipe, I combine them for a creamy and nourishing chowder-like soup. No longer living near Boston, I desperately miss traditional clam chowder. This "chowdah," as they say in Boston, feels American and French at the same time. Since there are no chowder crackers in France, substitute Crostini (page 60). **SERVES 4**

1. Put the pancetta and a small glug of oil in a large saucepan and heat over medium heat. Cook, stirring occasionally, until the pancetta is browned (it does not have to be crisp), about 5 minutes. Stir in the onion, celery, and garlic. Increase the heat slightly and cook, stirring occasionally, until the vegetables are browned, about 5 minutes.

2. Add the wine and increase the heat to high. Bring to a boil, scraping up the browned bits in the pot with a wooden spatula. Add the clams, cover, and cook, occasionally shaking the pot, until the clams have opened, 3 to 5 minutes.

3. Drain 1 can of beans and add to the pot. Add the second can of beans with their liquid and the thyme. Reduce the heat to medium-low and simmer for 5 minutes. Cover, remove from the heat, and let stand for 5 to 10 minutes. Discard any unopened clams.

4. Ladle the soup and clams into bowls. Garnish each with a few pulls of lemon zest, a sprinkle of scallions, a few grinds of pepper, and some flaky salt. Serve hot, with crostini.

12 sea scallops

Fine sea salt and freshly ground black pepper

Olive oil

Beurre Blanc (page 58), timed to finish just before cooking the scallops

2 preserved lemons, rind only, very finely minced

Flaky salt

Sea Scallops with Preserved Lemon Beurre Blanc

For years, I believed that scallops were restaurant-only fare. My Oma (who gave me my beloved *My Other House Is in France* pillow) would always order them when we went out to eat. When she was fading away, I cooked for her, and I was thrilled to find gorgeous sea scallops at her local market in landlocked, mid-western Missouri. I made them as often as two nights a week. This is almost the way I made it for her. I knew how to make beurre blanc, but I had not yet varied it with preserved lemons. I am sure she would have loved the change, too. SERVES 4

1. Gently pat the scallops dry with paper towels. Season the scallops with salt and pepper. Add a healthy glug of oil to a large skillet over medium-high heat until the oil is shimmering.

2. Carefully add the scallops to the skillet, one at a time. Cook until golden brown on the underside, about 5 minutes. For rare scallops, transfer them to a plate. Otherwise, flip the scallops and cook to lightly brown the other side, about 2 minutes more. The scallops should be barely opaque throughout.

3. Stir the diced preserved lemon into the beurre blanc, and spread onto a serving platter. Add the scallops, with the browned sides facing up,

4. Sprinkle on some flaky salt, and serve.

2 trout, about 1 to 1½ pounds each (any larger and it is a bit unwieldy in the pan)

Fine sea salt and freshly ground black pepper

4 tablespoons salted butter, divided

Olive oil

¼ cup chopped shallots

3 sprigs fresh thyme, rosemary, or tarragon

1 lemon (optional)

Butter-Basted Trout Meunière

Before we dive in (pun intended), **BE NOT AFRAID OF WHOLE FISH!** This recipe calls for whole, small trout. If you're scared of trout, you can use another fish. Meunière style works with any thin fish—whole or fillets. But I encourage you to do the whole fish.

One of Julia Child's first meals in France was sole meunière, a whole, thin fish (or its fillets) basted repeatedly in an herbed butter until the meat of the fish cooks to a mind-blowingly tender state. The preparation is one for the gods, in my not-so-humble opinion. I use trout instead of sole, but once you get comfortable with trout, pretty much any thin-bodied whole fish (less than 2 inches thick) will work splendidly. Another plus is that meunière can be adapted to your favorite flavors. Once I have mastered any technique, I like to play with other ingredients, so I have given you variations so you can do the same, along with a basic method with shallots and an herb of your choice. I don't use lemon because I love this for its buttery goodness, but if you want some added acidity to cut the richness, add a bit of lemon juice to the butter during cooking.
SERVES 2 TO 4, WITH 2 TROUT

1. Let the fish stand at room temperature for 15 to 30 minutes to lose its chill. Pat the skin completely dry with paper towels. If the fish seems too long to fit into the skillet, cut off the head and trim down the tail. (I try *not to do this*, as intact is better overall.)

2. Heat 2 tablespoons of the butter and a glug of oil in a large skillet over medium-high heat until the butter foams up. Add the two fish to the pan. Cook until the underside is lightly browned, about 4 minutes. Flip the fish to the other side. Add the remaining 2 tablespoons butter with the shallots and herb sprigs on one side of the skillet. Let the butter melt. Tilt the skillet so the butter collects in a pool, but keeping most of the skillet over the flame. Use a soup spoon to baste the top of the fish with the melted butter. This adds a metric ton of flavor to the fish. Cook until the fish looks opaque when pierced in the thickest part with the tip of a small knife, 2 to 3 minutes. (Or a bit less if you like your fish rare.)

3. Transfer the fish to a dinner plate. Spoon the butter (which will have browned) and seasonings on top. If you wish, top with a squeeze of lemon, or a few pulls of lemon zest, and serve hot.

MEUNIÈRE VARIATIONS

BAY LEAF: Substitute 3 to 4 fresh bay leaves for the thyme.

GARLIC AND CHIVE: Substitute 3 garlic cloves, crushed and peeled, for the shallot, and a couple tablespoons of minced fresh chives for the thyme.

WHITE ONION AND ROSEMARY: Substitute white onion for the shallot and rosemary for the thyme.

GARLIC AND SAVORY: Substitute 3 garlic cloves, crushed and peeled, for the shallot and savory for the thyme.

GRENOBLOISE: Omit the shallots and thyme. Add the juice of 1 lemon, 2 tablespoons drained nonpareil capers, and 1 tablespoon minced fresh parsley to the skillet toward the end of the cooking time.

LEEK AND TARRAGON: Substitute leek (white part only), finely chopped, for the shallot.

RED ONION WITH CILANTRO: Substitute red onion and cilantro sprigs for the shallot and thyme.

SCALLION, GREEN GARLIC, AND SAGE: Substitute about 1 tablespoon chopped green garlic and 1 whole chopped scallion for the shallot, and sage for the thyme.

- *Roasting pan or baking dish*
- *Ramekin or small ovenproof dish (such as a Pyrex custard cup)*
- *Medium skillet*
- *Tongs*

2 to 3 chard leaves, stems removed and reserved

Olive oil

½ shallot, sliced

Large pinch of green, leafy fresh herbs, such as oregano, basil, or thyme (alone or in combination)

Salted butter

1 large egg

2 tablespoons heavy cream

Fine sea salt and freshly ground black pepper

Crostini (page 60) or toast points, for serving

Hearty Greens and Cream Oeufs en Cocotte

Here is another in my *oeufs en cocotte* collection to encourage you to make this simple egg recipe for breakfast, lunch, or dinner. Make this in the cooler autumn months when hearty greens like chard and kale are thriving in the garden. **SERVES 1**

1. Preheat the oven to 350°F. Place the roasting pan in the oven and pour in enough hot water to come about halfway up the sides. Heat the filled pan for 5 minutes.

2. Finely chop the chard stems. Roll up the leaves into a cylinder and cut them crosswise into shreds (chiffonade). Heat a glug of oil in a medium skillet over medium heat. Add the shallot and chard stems and cook, stirring often, until softened, about 5 minutes. Add the chard leaves and cook, stirring often, until wilted, about 3 minutes. Stir in the herbs.

3. Lightly butter a 4-ounce ramekin. Spoon the chard mixture into a ramekin and make a nest for the egg with the back of a spoon. Add a knob of butter, then crack an egg on top, being careful not to break the yolk. Pour the cream around the exterior of the egg. Sprinkle with salt and pepper.

4. Place the ramekin into the roasting pan, and add water to the roasting pan until it reaches halfway up the sides of the ramekin. Bake until the egg whites are set, 10 to 13 minutes. Check at 10 minutes, and if they need more time, go ahead. Be careful not to overbake, as they will be hard-cooked with firm yolks after 15 minutes. Using tongs, remove the ramekin from the water. Place the ramekin on a plate and serve hot. Eat straight from the ramekin with a spoon and serve with crostini or toast.

1 head (1 to 1½ pounds) green cabbage

1 to 2 tablespoons olive oil

1 tablespoon sumac

2 teaspoons Urfa biber or other chile flakes

1 teaspoon fine sea salt, plus extra to finish

½ cup plain Greek yogurt

¼ cup finely chopped fresh mint, cilantro, or parsley, plus extra for garnish

1 lemon

1 teaspoon freshly ground black pepper

Pomegranate seeds (optional)

Roast Cabbage (or Cauliflower) with Herbed Yogurt Sauce

Oh, the humble brassica, a wildly misunderstood set of vegetables. I grew up near a cabbage farm, and I suppose it was too close to home for me to fully appreciate it. Now, I love cabbage. Mostly because I don't treat it like cabbage—I treat it like meat and give it a high-heat roast, which creates all sorts of beautiful flavor possibilities. Cabbage's cousin, cauliflower, also works well prepared this way. Sometimes I will top each serving with a spoonful of trout caviar, or substitute the Roasted Beet Hummus with Cumin (page 83) for the yogurt sauce. **SERVES 4**

1. Preheat the oven to 475°F.

2. Cut the cabbage into quarters. Make a V-shaped cut around the core and cut out, but leave enough so the leaves will hold together. Rub the cabbage all over with the oil and season with the sumac, Urfa biber, and salt. Transfer to a half-sheet pan, flat side down.

3. Roast for 10 minutes. Flip to the other side and roast until the cabbage has browned, beginning to char on the edges, and is tender when pierced with a thin knife or skewer, 10 to 15 minutes more.

4. Put the yogurt in a small bowl. Add the herbs, grate in the zest of the lemon, and stir well. Season with salt and pepper.

5. Remove the pan with the cabbage from the oven. Squeeze the juice of half the lemon over all. Plate the yogurt sauce onto a platter, add the cabbage on top, and sprinkle with the herbs and pomegranate seeds, if using. Serve immediately.

ROAST CAULIFLOWER WITH YOGURT SAUCE: Substitute 1 head cauliflower for the cabbage. Cut into quarters and keep them intact. Roast as directed.

A MOSTLY FRENCH HOLIDAY MEAL

Before I moved to France, cooking for the holidays could be fraught. I felt as if everything had to be made one way or "the way everyone on this side of the family likes it best." But now that France is my new home, and where my family and I spend Thanksgiving and Christmas, I have found peace in building new traditions and cooking during the holidays. (This is no doubt in part because we are not spending holiday weeks navigating crowded airports attempting to make quick turnaround flights.)

One Thanksgiving, just two years after moving to France, I decided to go rogue. I invited my guests to make their favorite dish in a classic way, and I would make my own rendition of these classics, off the cuff. This meant we had two potatoes, two mac and cheeses, two turkeys, two of everything. What resulted was a blend of a classic menu paired with an updated take on each of these classic dishes.

It gave all of us room at the table to enjoy our holidays the way we each wanted to. Each of us discovered new loves, new dishes, and reexperienced old favorites. Even my grandmother-in-law—a pocket-size firecracker of a human, ninety-five years young—found new things to revel in, and even some of the family liked *my mac and cheese better*. And so did she.

We so often fall into the rut of tradition for better or for worse.

I've followed the "let's see if we can find something new here" method for these recipes. I've played off the classics and added some fun twists to create something altogether familiar and different at the same time.

MENU

RAINBOW RADISH SALAD *272*

ANYTIME SPICED SANGRIA *114*

SPATCHCOCKED TURKEY
with Rich Herb Jus *274*

SAVORY VANILLA BEAN DRESSING
with Toasted Pumpkin Seeds
277

POMEGRANATE-KUMQUAT RELISH
273

CREAMY GREEN BEANS
and Mushrooms
276

BUTTERNUT SQUASH CHEESECAKE
with Gingersnap Crust
282

- *Mandoline*
- *Medium bowl*
- *Microplane*
- *Serving bowl or plates*

2 to 3 green, purple, watermelon meat radishes, and daikon, in a colorful combination

½ red onion, thinly sliced

1 to 2 tablespoons olive oil

1 lime

2 tablespoons chopped fresh cilantro

Flaky salt, for finishing

Cobanero chile flakes or other smoky chile flakes

Corn nuts, preferably Peruvian giant or Spanish quixos, coarsely crushed

Rainbow Radish Salad

As simple as this may be, it was inspired by a local Michelin-starred restaurant where they served the classic hors d'oeuvres combination of French radishes and butter (infused with lime zest). But, they included a bowl of crunchy corn nuts alongside. The combination impressed me so much that soon after I put some of the components into a salad, using Asian meat radishes (daikon). You will find large meat radishes at Asian grocers and at some farm stands. Their outsides are usually green, but inside the flesh runs from magenta to green. You can use white daikon as part of the mix. SERVES 4

1. Using a mandoline, cut the radishes into very thin rounds, almost paper-thin. You can use a knife, but a mandoline works best. Transfer to a medium bowl and add the red onion. Toss gently with enough oil to coat the vegetables.

2. Add a few pulls of the lime zest. Cut the lime in half and squeeze the juice over the vegetables. Stir in the cilantro, season with salt and chile flakes, and serve immediately.

2 pomegranates

8 ounces kumquats, cut crosswise into thin rounds, discarding any easy-to-remove seeds

⅓ cup packed cilantro leaves

2 tablespoons olive oil

Finely grated zest and juice of 2 limes

Kosher Salt

Pomegranate-Kumquat Relish

A bright-tasting relish is a must-have at holiday feasts, because it cuts through the rich food. This one gives a sour punch of sunshine, both in color and flavor thanks to the kumquats and pomegranates, both of which grow near La Peetch. I find the relish's jewel-like tones to be utterly transfixing and the flavor to be worthy of more than a once-a-year treat. Try it with the Braised Chicken in White Wine with Bacon-Radish Gremolata (page 168) as a variation of the bacon-radish gremolata, or with the Fondant Potatoes on page 236. **MAKES ABOUT 3 CUPS**

1. Fill a large bowl with water. Cut the top and bottom from a pomegranate so you can see its inside. Using a small sharp knife, score cuts where you see the membranes make natural segments. Submerge the pomegranate in the water. Pull it apart at the scored cuts. Using your fingers, patiently coax the arils (seeds) out of the membranes—the membranes will float and the arils will sink. Discard the skins. When the first pomegranate is done, tackle the second one. Skim off the membranes. Drain the pomegranates and reserve the arils.

2. Combine the pomegranate arils, kumquats, and cilantro in a medium bowl. Gently fold in the oil and lime zest and juice. Season with salt. Cover and refrigerate for at least 1 and up to 8 hours before serving. Serve chilled or at room temperature.

MISE EN PLACE
- 2 half-sheet pans
- Small bowl
- Serving platter

FOR THE TURKEY

1 small turkey (8 to 12 pounds), spatchcocked (see page 36)

1 tablespoon ground coriander

2 teaspoons fine sea salt

1 teaspoon ginger powder

½ teaspoon ground cardamom

½ teaspoon ground cinnamon

½ teaspoon freshly ground black pepper

Olive oil

2 heads fennel, cut lengthwise into 1½-inch slices

1 orange, or 3 mandarins, unpeeled, cut into ½-inch rounds

8 to 12 dried bay leaves

1 cup chicken glaze, from Jus (page 48)

1 bouquet garni (see page 25)

FOR THE GARNISH

2 oranges, skins removed and cut into rounds (see naked citrus from Citrus Prep, page 33)

1 head fennel with fronds, sliced raw and paper-thin, fronds chopped finely

½ teaspoon kosher salt

Freshly ground black pepper to taste

1 tablespoon olive oil

Flaky salt

Spatchcocked Turkey with Rich Herb Jus

Another day, another spatchcocked poultry. For big holiday meals, it just makes sense. It cooks more quickly, more evenly, *and* all of the skin, most people's favorite part, crisps, so that's a good thing.

This turkey is served with a rich jus instead of the usual gravy, which I think really elevates this familiar holiday main course and adds a lot of deep flavor. The bed of fennel and oranges makes a very cheery presentation, and adds bright flavor.

I call for a smaller bird in this recipe so that when spatchcocked it will fit on a half-sheet pan. SERVES 6 TO 8

---

1. **MAKE THE TURKEY:** Spread the spatchcocked turkey, cut side down, on a half-sheet pan. Mix the coriander, salt, ginger, cardamom, cinnamon, and pepper in a small bowl. Rub the turkey all over (the underside, too) with the spice mixture. Let stand at room temperature for 1 to 2 hours. (Or, cover loosely with plastic wrap and refrigerate overnight. Let stand at room temperature for 2 hours before roasting.)

2. Preheat the oven to 500°F. Spread a healthy glug of oil onto a second half-sheet pan. Scatter the fennel, orange, and bay leaves on the pan and season with salt. Place the turkey, cut side down, on top. (Wash and dry the first half-sheet pan so it is ready for the last step.)

3. Place in the oven and roast until nicely browned, 15 to 20 minutes. Reduce the heat to 450°F. Roast until an instant-read thermometer inserted into the thickest part of the breast reads 165°F, 30 to 45 minutes.

4. Transfer the turkey to the cleaned half-sheet pan. If you wish, cover the sheet pan with a kitchen towel to keep wandering pickers away from the thigh meat.

5. Pour the pan drippings into a glass measuring cup or bowl, skim the fat from the top, and pour the drippings back into the pan. Add the chicken glaze and bouquet garni. Bring to a boil on the stove over high heat, carefully scraping up the browned bits in the pan with a wooden spatula to avoid splashing. Simmer over very low heat, about 5 minutes. Strain the sauce through a wire sieve into a sauceboat or bowl with a ladle, and discard the bouquet garni.

6. **MAKE THE GARNISH:** Toss the orange rounds and raw fennel with fronds, add flaky salt and pepper and the olive oil, then toss together.

7. Set the broiler to high and broil the turkey to crisp the skin, 5 to 10 minutes. Transfer to a carving board and sprinkle with flaky salt and a few cracks of pepper. Serve with the sauce and orange fennel salad on the side.

MISE EN PLACE
- *Large saucepan with water*
- *Slotted spoon or colander*
- *Medium bowl of ice water*
- *Large skillet*
- *9 x 13-inch casserole dish*

2 pounds thin green beans, French-style haricots verts

2 tablespoons duck fat or bacon fat, or olive oil

1 pound hearty mixed mushrooms (such as shiitake, portobello, cremini, chanterelle), sliced various widths

½ pound shallots, thinly sliced lengthwise

Fine sea salt

2 tablespoons rosé wine or dry white

6 sprigs fresh thyme

2 sprigs fresh rosemary

1 quart heavy cream

Freshly ground black pepper

1 (6-ounce) can crispy fried onions

Creamy Green Beans and Mushrooms

This is not your grandmama's casserole. Maybe that will be thrilling to you (because you never liked canned green beans doused with Campbell's Cream of Mushroom Soup), or maybe it feels like sacrilege (because you still love that classic green bean casserole). Either way, this will remind you of green beans from yore, and elevate it to new heights with crunchy fresh beans, and a classic topping. While I am a fan of my version, I am also a human who has an old green bean casserole dish with the original recipe on it in my kitchen cabinet. I suppose you can call me Switzerland regarding which team I am on. SERVES 8 TO 10

1. Bring a large saucepan of salted water to a boil over high heat. Add the green beans and cook just until crisp-tender, about 5 minutes. Drain. Transfer to a bowl of iced water to stop the cooking and so they retain their color. Let stand for 3 to 5 minutes, then drain well.

2. Heat the fat in a large skillet over medium-high heat. Add the mushrooms and cook, stirring occasionally, until they begin to shrink, about 5 minutes. Add the shallots and season with salt; allow them to cook for 5 minutes. Stir in the wine, thyme, and rosemary and let the wine reduce by half, about 1 minute. Add the cream and bring to a boil.

3. Preheat the oven to 475°F. Spread the green beans in a 9 by 13-inch baking dish. Pour the creamed mushrooms on top. Mix lightly and season with salt and a generous amount of pepper. The casserole can be prepared up to 2 hours ahead and kept at room temperature.

4. Bake until the cream is beginning to thicken, about 10 minutes, or 15 minutes if the casserole was at room temperature. Scatter the fried onions on top and continue baking until the sauce is bubbling and the onions are browning, about 10 minutes. Serve hot.

- *Half-sheet pan, if toasting bread*
- *2 large bowls*
- *Large skillet*
- *9 x 13-inch casserole dish*

1 pound French bread, preferably a day or two old, torn into bite-size pieces

Salted butter, plus softened butter for the baking dish

Olive oil

1 large white onion, cut into ¼-inch dice

6 celery stalks (8 ounces), cut into ¼-inch dice

4 carrots (8 ounces), cut into ¼-inch dice

2 Granny Smith apples (8 ounces), cored and cut into ¼-inch dice (I like to leave the peel on, but you can remove if you prefer.)

¼ cup dry white wine or Rich (chicken) Stock (optional)

2½ cups Rich (chicken) Stock (page 43), as needed

3 large eggs, beaten lightly

2 tablespoons fresh sage, cut into thin shreds

½ teaspoon vanilla powder, or the interior of one whole vanilla bean

Fine sea salt and freshly ground black pepper

½ cup shelled pumpkin seeds (pepitas), toasted in a dry skillet until they begin to pop, for serving

Savory Vanilla Dressing with Toasted Pumpkin Seeds

My late grandfather was a sage fiend, and he never thought the dressing/stuffing at the holidays had enough sage in it. While it is not my favorite herb (I think it tastes like marijuana), I do love it in this holiday classic. The vanilla and sage blend together in a rich and savory concoction that balances the turkey jus beautifully. If you like a soft and custardy texture, add another beaten egg. Since I have started making this stuffing, there are never any leftovers, so I can't reliably tell you how good it is over the Thanksgiving weekend. **SERVES 6 TO 8**

1. Preheat the oven to 350°F. If the bread is fresh and soft, spread the torn pieces on a half-sheet pan and bake until toasty and crisp on the edges, but not browned, 10 to 15 minutes. Put the bread in a large bowl.

2. Melt two knobs of butter with a small glug of oil in a large skillet over medium-high heat. Add the onion and cook, stirring occasionally, until golden, about 5 minutes. Add the celery, carrots, and apples, and cook, stirring occasionally, until the vegetables soften, about 5 minutes. (If you like them tender, cook them 2 minutes longer.) Add the wine, if using, and scrape up the browned bits in the pan with a wooden spatula. Add to the bread in the bowl and mix.

3. Gradually stir 2 cups of stock into the bread mixture (your hands work better than a spoon here). Mix in the eggs. The stuffing should be moist, not soggy. Add the remaining stock only if the mixture seems dry. Mix in the sage and vanilla. Season with salt and pepper. Transfer to a buttered 9 by 13-inch baking dish and spread evenly.

4. Bake just until the edges are beginning to brown, 25 to 30 minutes. Sprinkle with the pumpkin seeds and serve.

CHAPTER 10

COOLER WEATHER SWEETS

- 9-inch springform pan or round cake pan
- Parchment paper if using a round cake pan
- 2 medium mixing bowls
- Electric mixer with large bowl
- Small bowl

Softened butter and flour for the pan, or nonstick baking spray with flour

FOR THE CAKE

1¾ cups all-purpose flour

1½ teaspoons baking powder

½ teaspoon ground ginger

½ teaspoon kosher salt

¼ teaspoon ground cinnamon

¼ teaspoon freshly grated nutmeg

¾ cup sour cream, at room temperature

3 tablespoons dark rum

1 teaspoon vanilla extract

1 cup granulated sugar

¾ cup (1½ sticks) salted butter, at room temperature

3 large eggs, at room temperature

FOR THE CRUMB TOPPING

½ cup all-purpose flour

⅓ cup (packed) light brown sugar

½ teaspoon ground cinnamon

¼ teaspoon kosher salt

¼ cup (½ stick) salted butter, at room temperature

2 sweet-tart baking apples, preferably Honey Crisp, peeled, cored, and thinly sliced

Not-Too-Sweet Whipped Cream (page 59), for serving

Apple Crumble Cake

Although I am not a cake person, I've always loved French apple cake and also American coffee cake. Coffee cake isn't sold in French patisseries, so I had to make my own. What I fell upon was this apple spice cake in the best American farmhouse tradition. It is made with sour cream, streusel, and cinnamon (a spice that is not popular in French baked goods). Try it for breakfast if you're into that. I know I am. SERVES 8 TO 10

1. Preheat the oven to 350°F. Butter the inside of a 9-inch springform pan. (If using a cake pan without a removable bottom, line the buttered bottom with a round of parchment paper.) Dust the inside with flour and tap out the excess. (Or spray the pan with nonstick baking spray.)

2. **MAKE THE CAKE:** Whisk the flour, baking powder, ginger, salt, cinnamon, and nutmeg together in a medium bowl. Set aside. Whisk the sour cream, rum, and vanilla together in another bowl.

3. Beat the granulated sugar and butter in a large bowl with an electric mixer at high speed, occasionally scraping down the sides of the bowl with a spatula, until light and fluffy, 2 to 3 minutes. One at a time, add the eggs, mixing thoroughly until absorbed after each addition. With the mixer on low speed, add the flour in thirds, alternating with two equal additions of the sour cream, mixing until combined, scraping down the sides of the bowl as needed. Do not overmix.

4. **MAKE THE CRUMB TOPPING:** Combine the flour, brown sugar, cinnamon, and salt in a small bowl. Add the butter and mix with your fingertips until soft crumbs form. Set aside.

5. Spread about a quarter of the batter into the bottom of the prepared pan and spread evenly. Top with an even layer of apple slices. Repeat three more times, finishing with a layer of apples. Sprinkle the crumb topping over the batter and press it lightly to adhere.

6. Bake until a toothpick inserted into the center comes out clean (a few crumbs are okay, as the apples will make the cake rather moist), 50 to 55 minutes. Do not overbake—check to be sure that any moisture on the toothpick is not apple juices. Transfer to a wire rack to cool completely. Run a small knife around the inside of the cake to loosen. For a springform pan, remove the sides. For a cake pan, place a plate over the pan, flip them over, and remove the pan and parchment paper. Place another plate on top of the cake and turn right side up. Slice and serve with the whipped cream. (The cake keeps well, covered with a moist towel or in an airtight container, refrigerated for up to a week.)

- 9-inch springform or removable bottom tart pan
- Half-sheet pan
- Food processor
- Electric mixer
- Wire cooling rack

Softened butter, for the pan

1 small butternut squash (about 2¼ pounds), halved lengthwise and seeded

2 tablespoons cornstarch or all-purpose flour

1½ cups finely crushed gingersnap cookies (about 7 ounces)

¼ cup (½ stick) salted butter, melted

2 pounds cream cheese (not "lite"), at room temperature

¾ cup packed dark brown sugar

½ cup maple syrup

4 large eggs, at room temperature

2 teaspoons vanilla extract, or 1 tablespoon dark rum

1½ teaspoons fresh ginger, grated on a Microplane

¼ teaspoon fine sea salt

¾ teaspoon ground cinnamon

⅛ teaspoon freshly grated nutmeg

Finely grated zest of ½ lemon

2 tablespoons fresh lemon juice

Not-Too-Sweet Whipped Cream (page 59), for serving

Butternut Squash Cheesecake with Gingersnap Crust

Canned pumpkin is just not a thing in France. Except during the holiday season, and even then it's sold in specialty stores reserved solely for expatriates and immigrants from Anglophone countries. It is quite costly at eight euros a can. So, I am always seeking new ways to use other ingredients. I fell into this butternut squash cheesecake quite by accident. But it's wildly delicious, and frankly . . . I like it better than canned pumpkin based recipes. It's ultimately a bit lighter and serves as a perfect finale to a mostly French holiday meal. SERVES 10 TO 12

1. Position the rack in the center of the oven and preheat the oven to 375°F. Butter the inside of a 9-inch springform pan.

2. Place the squash halves, cut sides down, on a half-sheet pan. Bake until the squash is tender and can be easily pierced with the tip of a small sharp knife, about 1 hour. Cool until easy to handle. Scoop the flesh into a food processor, discard the skins, and purée the squash. Measure 2 cups of purée. (Save the remaining purée for another use—it's great added to mashed potatoes.) Sprinkle the cornstarch over the purée and whisk until smooth. Set aside.

3. Mix the gingersnap crumbs and melted butter in a medium bowl. Press firmly into the bottom and ½ inch up the sides of the prepared pan. Bake until firm and fragrant, 8 to 10 minutes. Let cool on a wire cooking rack. Reduce the oven temperature to 325°F.

4. Beat the cream cheese and brown sugar in a large bowl with an electric mixer at medium speed until smooth, scraping down the bowl often, about 2 minutes. Beat in the maple syrup. One at a time, add the eggs, beating until smooth after each addition.

5. Add the squash mixture with the vanilla, ginger, salt, cinnamon, nutmeg, and lemon zest and juice. Pour the batter into the crust and bake until the edges of the cheesecake are puffed, about 1 hour. Turn off the oven and let stand, with the oven door closed, for 1 hour.

6. Transfer to a wire cooling rack. Run a small sharp knife around the edges of the cheesecake to loosen it (this discourages cracking as the cake cools and

contracts), and let cool until tepid, at least 1 hour. Cover and refrigerate for at least 2 hours (preferably overnight). Remove the sides of the pan. Slice and serve chilled with the whipped cream.

- *Medium saucepan*
- *Metal mixing bowl to fit over the saucepan*
- *Large glass bowl for mixing and serving*
- *Electric mixer*
- *Rubber spatula*

FOR THE CHOCOLATE MOUSSE

17.5 ounces unsweetened chocolate, coarsely chopped

15 large eggs, separated, at room temperature

¾ cup granulated sugar

TOPPINGS

Not-Too-Sweet Whipped Cream (page 59)

Chocolate shavings

Crushed cacao nibs

Whole citrus fruit, served with a zester (My favorites are orange, lemon, lime, grapefruit, and Makrut limes.)

Fresh fruit (Choose 2 or 3 from pomegranate arils, clementine segments, raspberries, quartered strawberries, sliced bananas, pineapple pieces, and sliced figs.)

Dried fruit (Goji berries and dried cranberries or cherries are options.)

Spice powders (ground cinnamon, anise, allspice, and mesquite salt)

Sauces (caramel sauce, but also fruit purées—the French call them *coulis*—such as raspberry, strawberry, and mango)

Flaky salt (At the very least, put out some unflavored, but include smoked, if you have it on hand.)

Surprises (like sumac or crushed red hot chiles)

Chocolate Mousse Social

This approach to mousse is for a *party*, a soirée if you will. And it brings me back to my childhood, where ice cream socials were the event of the year. (Did you know the first recorded ice cream social as an event in the US was in 1774?!) Now that I am in France, and ice cream socials are *not a thing*, I spread the whimsical joy of choose-your-own-adventure, seemingly limitless dessert through chocolate mousse. You make it, chill it, serve it in a massive bowl, and leave your people to pick their own serving size, and top it however they like to invoke childlike wonder and a dessert with a high-end feeling at the same time. To hearken to the days of the ice cream social you'll want ample choices of toppings. I like to pick at least six. I've given you some choices in the ingredients, but you do you!
SERVES 12 TO 16

1. Bring about 1 inch of water to a simmer in a saucepan over high heat. Reduce the heat to low so the water is steaming, but not boiling. Place the chocolate in a large metal bowl that fits over the simmering water (but make sure the bowl is not touching the water). Stirring occasionally, melt the chocolate. Remove the bowl from the heat.

2. Meanwhile, using a hand-held electric mixer, beat the yolks and sugar together in a large glass serving bowl until they are pale yellow and thickened, about 2 minutes, scraping down the sides of the bowl often with a rubber spatula.

3. Using clean beaters, whip the egg whites in a separate bowl with the mixer until stiff peaks form.

4. A few tablespoons at a time, gradually whisk the melted chocolate into the yolks. About a quarter at a time, fold the egg whites into the chocolate mixture, keeping as much loft as possible, while also creating a homogeneous consistency.

5. Cover and refrigerate until well chilled, at least 3 hours.

6. To serve, put out the bowl of mousse with a large serving spoon, dessert bowls, and dessert spoons, along with the toppings you have chosen. Spoon the mousse into the bowls, top with abandon, and eat with childlike wonder and giggles.

- Metal baking dish, about 9 x 13 inches
- Medium saucepan
- Wire sieve
- Immersion blender or whisk
- Ice cream maker
- Food processor, if needed

FOR THE ICE CREAM

1 cup whole milk

1 cup heavy cream

½ cup honey

2 pinches smoked salt

4 large egg yolks

1 cup rindless, soft, and creamy plain goat cheese, crumbled

FOR THE GRANITA

⅓ cup honey

⅓ cup hot tap water

1 rosemary sprig

1 cup balsamic vinegar (supermarket brand is fine)

Fresh thyme leaves, rosemary blossoms, or other fresh herb leaves, for garnish

Goat Cheese Ice Cream with Balsamic Granita

I wrote down the idea for this recipe in my notebook over a decade ago, and now I have finally brought it to delicious fruition. Note that the honey will give the ice cream a soft consistency, so be sure to let it freeze for a few hours before serving. SERVES 4 TO 6

1. **MAKE THE ICE CREAM:** Heat the milk, cream, honey, and smoked salt in a medium saucepan over medium heat until almost boiling. Whisk the yolks in a small bowl. Gradually whisk in about ½ cup of the hot liquid. Whisk the yolk mixture into the saucepan.

2. Cook over medium-low heat, whisking often, until the mixture is thick enough to nap a wooden spoon. If you're new to this, dip the spoon into the mixture and allow the excess to drip off. Now, run your finger over the back of the spoon. If the custard does not budge, and your finger cuts a swath, it's thick enough. If not, cook some more. Do not let the custard come to a boil.

3. Remove from the heat and add the goat cheese. Using an immersion blender for the best texture, process until the goat cheese melts smoothly into the custard. (You can also use a whisk.) Strain the custard through a wire sieve into a medium bowl and let cool to room temperature. Cover with plastic wrap and refrigerate until very cold, at least 4 hours or overnight.

4. Pour the custard into an ice cream maker and freeze according to the manufacturer's instructions. It will be somewhat soft. Transfer the ice cream to a covered container and place in the freezer until firm enough to scoop, about 4 hours. (The ice cream can be frozen for up to 2 days.)

5. **MAKE THE GRANITA:** In a metal baking dish about 9 by 13 inches, dissolve the honey in the hot water by using the rosemary sprig like a spoon. Stir in the vinegar. Leave the sprig in the dish and let cool to room temperature, about an hour. Discard the sprig.

6. Freeze the dish (be sure it is lying flat). After 30 minutes, give the mixture a stir with a fork to break up the ice crystals. Continue doing that every 30 minutes until the granita is slushy, about 2½ to 3 hours. Leave the granita in the freezer until ready to serve.

7. To serve, divide big scoops of ice cream into 4 to 6 serving bowls. Top with the granita and a sprinkle of fresh herbs. Serve immediately.

FOR THE WHOOPIE PIES

2 Fuyu (not Hachiya) persimmons, stems removed

1 cup all-purpose flour

½ teaspoon baking powder

½ teaspoon baking soda

¼ teaspoon ground cinnamon

½ teaspoon ground ginger

½ teaspoon kosher salt

½ cup (packed) light brown sugar

½ cup vegetable oil

1 large egg

1 tablespoon fresh lemon juice

1 teaspoon vanilla extract

FOR THE BUTTERCREAM

2 cups confectioners' sugar

½ cup (1 stick) salted butter, at room temperature

2 teaspoons vanilla bean paste, 1 teaspoon vanilla bean powder, or ½ teaspoon vanilla extract

½ teaspoon kosher salt

2 tablespoons whole milk or heavy cream

Winter Whoopie Pies with Cranberry or Persimmon

What's more American than whoopie pies? I'd argue—not much. It's one of the few desserts I long for regularly when in France. Before making the leap across the pond, I was a university instructor in economics and business. And making pumpkin whoopie pies was my signature "before you go on break, here's a cookie" gift to get my students through finals week. This recipe is for the way I make it now. We grow persimmons at La Peetch on a very old tree that bears fruit every November and December. When persimmons aren't available, I turn to frozen cranberries as a replacement, because they are also a high-liquid, low-sugar fruit.

MAKES 12 SANDWICHES

1. Preheat the oven to 375°F. Line two half-sheet pans with parchment paper.

2. **MAKE THE WHOOPIE PIES:** Purée the persimmons in a blender until smooth. Measure ¾ cup purée into a medium bowl and set aside.

3. Whisk together the flour, baking powder, baking soda, cinnamon, ginger, and salt in a medium bowl. Whisk the persimmon purée, brown sugar, oil, egg, lemon juice, and vanilla to combine in a large bowl. Add the dry ingredients and fold together with the whisk until smooth. Let the batter stand for 10 minutes.

4. Using an ice cream scoop or a soup spoon, drop the batter in 3½-inch mounds on the prepared pans, spacing at least 2 inches apart. (You can also transfer the batter to a 1-gallon plastic bag, snip a ½-inch opening in the corner with scissors, and pipe out the batter.) Bake until the cookies spring back when pressed in the center, 12 to 14 minutes. Let cool for 5 minutes on the pans, then transfer to a wire cooling rack to cool completely.

5. **MAKE THE BUTTERCREAM:** Beat the confectioners' sugar, butter, vanilla, and salt in a medium bowl with an electric mixer on low speed until crumbly and combined. Increase the speed to high, beat in the milk, and mix until light and fluffy, 2 to 3 minutes.

6. Pipe or spoon the buttercream onto the flat side of half the cookies. Sandwich with the remaining cookies, pressing lightly to adhere.

7. The whoopie pies can be refrigerated in an airtight container for up to 1 week. Or wrap individually in plastic wrap and freeze for up to 2 months; defrost overnight in the refrigerator before serving.

CRANBERRY WHOOPIE PIES: Substitute ¾ cup fresh cranberry purée (not canned sauce) for the persimmon. Use frozen cranberries, if you wish.

- *Candy thermometer*
- *8 x 8-inch square baking dish*
- *Parchment paper*
- *Nonstick cooking spray*
- *Heavy-bottomed saucepan*

¼ cup salted butter, plus 1 teaspoon for greasing the parchment

1 cup heavy cream

3 tablespoons culinary lavender buds (dried)

¼ teaspoon kosher salt, plus extra for sprinkling

¼ cup honey

½ teaspoon vanilla extract

1½ cups granulated sugar

¼ cup water

Note: The process described here results in soft caramels. These caramels are cooked to a temperature of 248°F (120°C), which is typically the temperature range for making soft and chewy caramels. If you want them to be more like traditional hard caramels, you would need to cook them to a higher temperature, usually around 300° to 310°F. Keep in mind that cooking caramels to a higher temperature will yield a firmer and more brittle texture, so be cautious if you decide to do so.

Lavender Salted Caramels

This is about as Provençal American as a dessert can be, and if you've ever eaten at a fine dining restaurant in France, you know that there are *always multiple dessert courses*. I know some people love that, but I must admit that it's not my thing. Yet, these little caramels make me *almost love that idea*. I like to make batches of caramel and keep them around for a post-dessert treat. If you're not a lavender fan, you can infuse the cream with almost *anything*. Earl Grey is another favorite. SERVES 8

1. Line an 8 by 8-inch baking dish with parchment paper, leaving some overhang for easy removal. Grease the parchment paper with 1 teaspoon salted butter.

2. In a small saucepan over medium heat, heat the heavy cream over medium-low heat until it's warm but not boiling. Add the dried lavender buds and salt to the warm cream and let it steep for about 15 minutes. This infuses the cream with a subtle lavender flavor. Strain through a fine-mesh sieve, and discard the lavender.

3. In a heavy-bottomed saucepan, combine the lavender-infused cream, honey, vanilla, and remaining butter. Warm this mixture over low heat until the butter has melted. Keep it warm over low heat.

4. In another saucepan, combine the sugar and water. Stir to dissolve the sugar. Avoid stirring once the mixture starts to boil, as it will disturb the mixture and make for less smooth end result.

5. Attach a candy thermometer to the saucepan with the sugar syrup. Cook the syrup over medium heat, without stirring, until it reaches 340°F (171°C), which is the hard crack stage. This should take 10 to 15 minutes. Once the mixture reaches 340°F, immediately remove from heat.

6. Slowly pour the lavender-infused cream mixture into the sugar syrup while stirring continuously. Be careful as it may bubble up.

7. Once the two are combined, return to the heat and continue cooking the mixture, stirring constantly, until it reaches 248°F on the candy thermometer. This should take 10 to 15 minutes.

8. Pour the hot caramel into the prepared baking dish. Wait 10 minutes before adding salt flakes on top.

9. Let the caramel cool at room temperature for several hours or overnight until it's completely set. Time on cooling varies on thickness of caramel.

10. Once the caramel has cooled and set, use a sharp knife to cut it into small squares or rectangles.

11. Wrap the individual caramels in wax paper or parchment paper, or serve them directly. Enjoy your homemade Lavender Salted Caramels!

Not a lavender fan? Infusing cream with all sorts of things works for these caramels! Tea is a great friend to them.

EARL GREY TEA: Earl Grey is a classic choice for infusing caramels. Its bergamot oil-infused black tea flavor adds a delightful citrusy and floral note to the caramels.

CHAI: Chai, with its warm blend of spices like cinnamon, cardamom, and cloves, can give your caramels a rich, spiced flavor profile that's perfect for the fall and winter seasons.

MATCHA TEA: Matcha-infused caramels will have a subtle earthy and slightly bitter taste, complemented by the vibrant green color of the matcha powder.

ROOIBOS TEA: Rooibos caramels have a naturally sweet and nutty flavor. The caramel and rooibos combination can be quite comforting and unique.

JASMINE TEA: Jasmine tea can lend a subtle floral aroma to your caramels, creating a sophisticated and fragrant treat.

- *Large saucepan*

2 ripe pears

3 cups water

1 cup dried hibiscus flowers

¾ cup granulated sugar

1 cinnamon stick

1 vanilla bean, or 1 teaspoon vanilla extract

Zest and juice of 1 lemon

5 whole cloves

3 star anise pods

Toasted pistachios (optional)

Not-Too-Sweet Whipped Cream (page 59) or vanilla ice cream, for serving (optional)

Hibiscus Poached Pears

Pink poached pears are not only elegant, they are *delicious*. Hibiscus is one of my favorite things to use because that neon pink is otherworldly, and the tartness is unique and floral. As someone who often skips dessert, I would never say no to one of these pears. The syrup reduction takes a bit of time, but much of the preparation is hands-off. You will have time to enjoy an after-dinner drink before you dive into dessert. SERVES 2

1. Peel the pears, leaving the stem intact, and core them from the bottom, using a melon baller or a small spoon. This will help them cook evenly and absorb the poaching liquid.

2. In a large saucepan, combine the water, hibiscus flowers, sugar, cinnamon stick, vanilla, lemon juice, cloves, and star anise. Bring the mixture to a boil, then reduce the heat to low and let it simmer for 10 to 15 minutes to infuse the flavors.

3. Carefully place the prepared pears into the poaching liquid. Ensure the pears are fully submerged. You can use a lid or a parchment paper circle with a small hole to help keep the pears submerged.

4. Simmer the pears for 8 minutes, or until they are tender (timing will depend on ripeness and density of pears. Bosc pears will take 10 to 15 minutes, a well-ripened Bartlett pear might be finished in 10.) To check for doneness, insert a knife or toothpick into the pears; it should go in easily.

5. Once the pears are tender, carefully remove them from the poaching liquid and set them aside on a serving plate. Discard the anise, cloves, and cinnamon stick.

6. Bring the poaching liquid to a boil and let it simmer for 15 to 20 minutes or until it has reduced and thickened to a syrupy consistency. If you used a vanilla bean, remove it at this stage.

7. Drizzle the hibiscus syrup over the poached pears on the serving plate. Add the lemon zest and toasted pistachios, if using, on top.

8. Feel free to add a dollop of whipped cream or a scoop of vanilla ice cream, if that's your cup of tea.

AFTERWORD

I owe Julia Child a huge debt of gratitude, as Julia was the catalyst for so much of who I am today. She is the reason I went to Smith College, and ultimately she was the instigator for me to start to fall in love with ... well ... myself. I used to say, "If Julia Child could be a television star, I can do [insert pretty much anything here]."

I love what Julia Child did for cooking, and especially for women in cooking. And I love that deeply. I adore, respect, and admire her as much as anyone can regard someone they've never met in person.

Her books are a constant reference and touchstone for me. Everything she represents shapes the way I think about food, and more broadly, the culture of the United States writ large. She blazed the path for women to be seen as experts in their fields, and her show, which debuted decades before I was even born, inspires me to think differently about myself and how I show up in the world.

It was Julia Child who first inspired me to pack up my life, leave behind my home and country, and move (sight unseen) to the South of France. The Riviera. An entire region I had never even visited before. And all for a quaint pegboard kitchen that Julia herself once occupied for a few decades.

I grew up watching reruns of *The French Chef*. Not so much for the cooking, as I then had almost no interest in cooking, but rather to watch Julia. I remember being taken aback that this bumbling, giggly, and massive woman had been given a TV show. Her own show. I tuned in between episodes of *Batman*, *Baywatch*, *Knight Rider*, and *The Adventures of Pete and Pete*.

It was her straightforward, jubilant, and her very apparent what the hell attitude that mesmerized me. I saw a gargantuanly tall person navigating the world a little more herself than perhaps I was. She instilled in me an abiding love for curiosity, passion, and embodiment of being one's true selfs

And, isn't that all we can ever ask for in our idols?

But, this cookbook is not a love letter to Julia Child. That book has been written. That movie watched.

Nor is it a treatise on how to cook or feed friends as she did. She's done an exquisite, exemplary, and exhaustively amazing job of teaching you exactly how to cook the way she and Simone Beck did. Her legacy is a library of cookbooks, ones I turn to again and again, pulling a technique from here, and a cooking strategy from there. I treat them as encyclopedias, the start of a journey. Not the complete journey in and of itself. And of course, her work on television is still wildly informative and entertaining. Because who doesn't love watching a woman, so unabashedly herself, cook from the heart and the head? Every time I watch an episode, I feel like an old friend is holding my hand to walk me through the door from culinary mishap to culinary greatness.

My first day at La Pitchoune, I received a sign: I came across her shoes—a pair of wooden clogs, ones she wore in a photo Paul Child took on the very ground near where I was standing. So, I tried them on.

Jet-lagged and overwhelmed I burst into tears. Between heaving breaths I gasped to my friends and family (who were helping to get La Peetch ready for guests arriving in six weeks' time) "I. Don't. Fit. In. Her. Shoes."

I wailed. I cried in part because Julia had smaller feet than me, despite being taller. A gift that immediately made me jealous, since I will never own a cute pair of designer shoes, with my size 13 pegs. But mostly because ... I felt as if I had already failed before I began.

But here's the thing. I hadn't failed. Those clogs weren't right for me. I am not her and never will be. At first this was a devastating blow, but then it was

liberation. An opportunity to forge my own way, my own path, to aspire to be the best version of myself, rather than attempt to embody the ghosts of the greats who came before us.

Without Julia, I might never have found my own courage to upend my life. To move to France, to teach cooking classes in what is really a small, hot kitchen in a not terribly modern house. Take to the internet. And get my own television show.

Or to cook with such courage. And with such abandon.

More than anything, I think of *Mostly French* as a love letter to the Riviera, to its history of joie de vivre. It's also an adoring portrait of a place I called home for three years, the minuscule yet majestic medieval village of Valbonne. It truly is a place where one might break into song, à la Belle in *Beauty and the Beast*. Because yes indeed, "There goes the baker with his tray like always," the same Valbonnais (the bread unique to this petit village) to sell. From an oven, under a village house, to the actual boulangeric. Precisely at 11:00 a.m., six days a week.

And, perhaps most important, this book is a missive. A billet-doux, to La Pitchoune, the "little one," the home built by a human I have admired and loved from afar. A tiny cottage that captured my attention in the *New York Times* one morning in 2015. Since then, it has held me close through my divorce, and falling in love, in my pregnancy, raising a child, and weathering a pandemic.

It has sheltered me and lent me more than a bit of courage while moving through life in a new country.

I hope you, too, will find a balm in La Pitchoune and discover nourishment and joy in the cuisine I have come to know and love. And that, just maybe, you'll stretch out of your comfort zone—order a rabbit, and make a mustardy sauce for it from scratch.

The fruits are worth the labor. I can attest to this without a hint of diffidence.

From my kitchen(s) to yours. Bon appétit.

ACKNOWLEDGMENTS

I have so many people to thank for this intense labor of love. It's never easy to decide to take on such a huge project, and it's not done by one person. Even if it's *my* name on the cover.

First and foremost, I have to say "holy moly thank you to the moon and back" to my agent, Janis Donnaud, and my editor, Doris Cooper. They found me during the darkest night of my soul, in the middle of a near bankruptcy and COVID, with a flailing feeling of *What now?* When the world felt like it was falling apart at the seams, their belief in me was a light for which I'll be forever grateful.

To the crew at Simon Element. Thank you to Richard Rhorer for seeing the gold in a first time author's proposal when it hit your desk. Thank you, too, to Jessica Preeg and Nan Rittenhouse for your publicity ingenuity; to Elizabeth Breeden and Alyssa DiPierro in marketing; and to Jen Wang, Laura Jarrett, Katie McClimon, and Maria Espinosa, who helped bring this book to fruition. Finally, thank you to Jenny Davis for her beautiful book design and terrific suggestions along the way.

To my husband, Chris. For your unwavering commitment and support every step of the way. From being my best friend, to my husband, to a co-owner of a business, to a coparent. Your love and belief in me have been my buoy for more than ten years, and there aren't enough words to say thank you, but I'll do my best always.

HeatherAsh Amara has held my hand through the literal fires of life for over ten years. She is the human who said, "Go write." So I did. Thank you for your steadfast friendship.

To the late Beth Kirby, if it wasn't for you, I wouldn't be half of who I am. I miss you terribly, and your absence is a daily thorn.

To my photography and styling team: Emma, Indiana, and Kitty Coales. Your gorgeous work is what makes my words shine. I am so grateful to have found you and that you were able to bring the magic of Provence alive in a way few books have done. I appreciate your eye for light, food, and community. Thank you for shining a lens into my world so exquisitely.

To my chef partner, daughter-sister-wife—Kendall Lane—for diving headlong into the ether of entrepreneurship and saying "Why the hell not?" to *all the things*. From firewalk trainings, to recipe development, to teaching without recipes, to TV shows, to food styling, to opening a restaurant.

To Ross Lane, thank you for sharing Kendall so graciously and being our catchall on the ground.

Without the team past/present/future at Okay, Perfect and RecipeKick, I wouldn't have been able to write this darn book (or any others). Their willingness to take the vision I have and make it real while I am head down writing will never be forgotten: Anna Barab, Mary-Alice Duff, Ruby Peel, Anne Stuart Folkes, Shane O'Sullivan, Traci Tooman, and Mai-ya Mersereau. All of you were instrumental in making this *happen*.

To my recipe testers: Danie Armstrong, Olivia Clulow, and Zonya Dawson. Thank you for your thorough notes, and your enthusiasm! Without y'all, this would just be a mishmash of my brain and not half as good of a cookbook.

To my baking recipe developers who helped take the ideas from my head and execute them: Alexander Roman and Katie Rosenhouse.

To all the food folk who have inspired me, mentored me, and been islands in stormy seas. So many of you are the reason why I long to reach for the stars and believe in the impossible but most specifically to: Renée Erickson, Aran Goyoaga, Bobby Stuckey, Lachlan Patterson, and Ellen Marie Bennett.

INDEX

SIMON
ELEMENT

An Imprint of Simon & Schuster, LLC
1230 Avenue of the Americas
New York, NY 10020

Copyright © 2025 by Makenna Held Nylund

All rights reserved, including the right to reproduce this book or portions thereof in
any form whatsoever. For information, address Simon Element Subsidiary Rights Department,
1230 Avenue of the Americas, New York, NY 10020.

First Simon Element hardcover edition April 2025

SIMON ELEMENT is a trademark of Simon & Schuster, LLC

For information about special discounts for bulk purchases, please contact Simon & Schuster
Special Sales at 1-866-506-1949 or business@simonandschuster.com.

The Simon & Schuster Speakers Bureau can bring authors to your live event. For more information
or to book an event, contact the Simon & Schuster Speakers Bureau at 1-866-248-3049
or visit our website at www.simonspeakers.com.

Cover and interior design by Jenny Davis

Manufactured in China

1 3 5 7 9 10 8 6 4 2

Library of Congress Cataloging-in-Publication Data has been applied for.

ISBN 978-1-9821-9956-2
ISBN 978-1-9821-9957-9 (ebook)